Coercive Concern

D1594078

Anthropology of Policy

Cris Shore and Susan Wright, editors

Coercive Concern

Nationalism, Liberalism, and the Schooling of Muslim Youth

Reva Jaffe-Walter

Stanford University Press
Stanford, California

Stanford University Press

Stanford, California

Printed in the United States of America on acid-free, archival-quality paper

Library of Congress Cataloging-in-Publication Data

Jaffe-Walter, Reva, author.

  Coercive concern : nationalism, liberalism, and the schooling of Muslim youth / Reva Jaffe-Walter.

     pages cm — (Anthropology of policy)

  Includes bibliographical references and index.

  ISBN 978-0-8047-9621-7 (cloth : alk. paper) — ISBN 978-0-8047-9842-6 (pbk. : alk. paper) — ISBN 978-0-8047-9860-0 (electronic)

  1. Muslim youth—Education—Denmark. 2. Immigrant youth—Education—Denmark. 3. Children of immigrants—Education—Denmark. 4. Muslims—Cultural assimilation—Denmark. 5. Nationalism—Denmark. 6. Liberalism—Denmark. I. Title. II. Series: Anthropology of policy (Stanford, Calif.)

  LC3736.D4J34 2016

  371.829088'29709489—dc23

                    2015030663

Typeset by Bruce Lundquist in 10.25/15 Brill

This book is for my teachers. As a young person on the move growing up across communities and schools (a total of ten in my K–12 years), I was fortunate to be supported by teachers whose vision of concern changed my life. To Steve Jenkins, my high school teacher who created a space of inquiry that grounded me, where we sat talking for hours about Plato and Zen and the Art of Motorcycle Maintenance. *Then to the important teachers that followed: Ayala Gabriel, Stacey Lee, and Michelle Fine, strong women scholars who kindled a commitment to social justice and ethnography, in ways that brought me more fully into the world, with all of its complexity, heartbreak, and beauty.*

And for my husband, Gideon, for this beautiful life we share.

Contents

Acknowledgments

I BEGIN by extending my gratitude to the young people who invited me into their lives, in particular three students, who, like all my participants must remain anonymous, but whom I call Dhalia, Aliyah, and Sara, who shared their experiences across continents and stages of life—without our conversations and work together, this book would not have come to pass. Also, to the teachers and administrators who opened their classrooms, engaged in difficult conversations, and helped me understand the world of Danish schools. I would also like to acknowledge the important contributions of my mentors Stacey Lee and Michelle Fine, who were central in supporting me throughout the research and writing of this book as well as Robert Smith, Wendy Luttrell, Susan Opotow, and Ofelia García from the CUNY Graduate Center, who also provided critical feedback and support along the way. I am also indebted to Cris Shore and Susan Wright for inviting me to contribute to this series and for their support in the development of this book. To my Danish colleagues: Anne Holman, who gave me a home at the Danish Pedagogical University's Department of Educational Anthropology and who provided critical support in the early stages of research; Christian Horst, who provided generous and ongoing support related to understanding the Danish policy context; and Laura Gilliam, Sally Anderson, Eva Gulløv, Iram Khawaja, and Gritt Nielsen for their research and friendship. Also to Richard Jenkins for his incisive reading and comments on the final manuscript. I am particularly indebted to Thea Abu El-Haj for her research, which has been an inspiration, and for her careful reading of multiple drafts of this book. To my sisters in scholarship who supported me through the long process of writing this book: Anna Rios-Rojas, Dafney Dabach, Beth Rubin, Cheri Fancsali, Jamie Lew, Nadia Nadir, Isabella Smith and Christina Baker Kline. I am also grateful for the deep well of love and support from my husband, Gideon, and my children, Hannah and Jacob.

This book has benefitted from the valuable feedback and intellectual support from my colleagues from the CUNY Graduate Center Mayida Zaal, Michelle Billies, Maddy Fox, Carolina Muñoz Proto, and Edwin Mayorga. I would also like to thank the Department of Educational Theory, Policy and Administration at Rutgers University and the Public Science Project at the CUNY Graduate Center for providing affiliation while I was writing the book. Special thanks to Janet Keller, who provided coaching and editorial support and to Richard Gunde, the copy editor, for his excellent contributions. To the Danish painter Tal R for permission to use his beautiful painting for my book cover. To the anonymous reviewers for their generous suggestions, Michelle Lipinski for her interest and ongoing support for this book, Nora Spiegel and Anne Fuzellier Jain of Stanford University Press.

Coercive Concern

Introduction
Ethnographic Journeys through Concern

ALIYAH,[1] a fifteen-year-old student who was born in Denmark and identifies as a Somali from Ethiopia, mimics the voice of a newscaster and shakes her head, seemingly tired of the discursive figure of the oppressed immigrant girl that swirls around her:

In Denmark, when you watch television and the news, every day they have something new about what the immigrants are doing. They say immigrant girls don't get to decide who they get married to. 'Immigrant girls have to have an operation to make sure their parents don't find out if they have had sex.' Immigrant girls are always in the news. If we weren't here, who would they talk about?

At the end of a long focus-group discussion, Aliyah explains, "The problem is not with the teachers, it's up here [she outlined a circle with her index finger in the air]—it's everywhere, in the newspapers and on the streets."

Following the circle that Aliyah traces, I examine here how young people experience the contradictory discourses surrounding Muslim immigration in schools in Western liberal democracies. Like Aliyah, Muslim youth are increasingly growing up on the front lines of globalization and nationalism, negotiating their identities in the midst of contentious nationalist politics and rising anti-Muslim discourses. They intimately know what it feels like, in the words of Dubois, "to be a problem"; they are both overlooked and subjected to continual surveillance (Bhabha 2005; Sirin and Fine 2008).

In this book I explore the mechanisms through which the multiple discursive narratives and stereotypes of Muslim immigrants in Western liberal societies flow into the public schools, insinuating themselves into everyday interactions, informing how Muslim youth are perceived by teachers and peers. Beyond identifying the presence of racialized discourses in schools, I examine the work that they do—illuminating Muslim bodies as a site of cultural and national intervention.

Much has been written about the global spread of neo-racist discourses and policies that seek to protect democratic societies from the perceived threat of Islam by invoking a "clash of civilizations" between "enlightened" Western societies and "barbaric" Muslim societies, perpetuating the racialized stereotypes of "oppressed" Muslim women and "terrorist" men (Balibar 1991; Said 1993; Razack 2008). However, adequate attention has not been paid to how Muslim youth experience these narratives in putatively liberal democratic schools. Examining the blind spots of liberal educational discourses, I explore how nationalist and liberal politics become blurred in the schooling of Muslim immigrant students. Drawing on fieldwork in a Danish high school and comparative insights from elsewhere in Europe as well as the United States, I examine how everyday practices of coercive assimilation are cloaked in benevolent discourses of care and concern.

Analyzing Immigration across Sites

In 2007–2008, I moved with my family from the United States to Copenhagen, Denmark, where I was a visiting scholar at the Department of Educational Anthropology at the Danish Pedagogical University. At the time, I was finishing my analyses and writing up a study on recently arrived immigrant youth in schools in New York City and I was interested in learning more about the dynamics surrounding immigration and schooling. I observed several schools with significant populations of immigrant students. In Denmark, the public municipal school, or *folkeskole*, is a comprehensive school that educates students from preschool through the ninth grade. About 87 percent of school-age children in Denmark attend public *folkeskole*, and the remaining 13 percent attend publicly supported private schools (Danish Ministry of Education n.d.). In 2009 there were sixty-four schools in Denmark with a population of more than 40 percent immigrant students, all located near urban areas where housing was built for immigrant guest workers. At Engby School,[2] one such school where I ultimately did fieldwork for *Coercive Concern*, the student body numbered three hundred, of which 45 percent were predominantly Muslim first- and second-generation immigrants from countries such as Turkey, Somalia, Croatia, Palestine, Iraq, and Lebanon. At Engby School, there were frequent discussions among teachers, students, and the outside community about the school's image as a "ghetto school" because of its high percentage of immigrant students.

Through a series of breakdown moments (Agar 1986) or classroom interactions that I had trouble understanding because of my lack of knowledge at the time of the narratives surrounding Muslim immigration in Denmark, my initial observations in the Danish schools led me to the research that constitutes the foundations for this book. In one of my first observations in a Danish English class, a teacher asked a Palestinian student about her choice of marriage partner. I watched as a student-centered discussion subtly shifted into a personal critique. The teacher repeatedly questioned the student, who grew more and more uncomfortable. This moment catalyzed my ethnographic journey, which extended beyond the classroom and the school as I sought to understand the social processes in Denmark related to the integration of immigrants and how broader discourses shaped moments like these.

The Muslim youth in my study described how they were regularly confronted with social stereotypes or figured identities of Muslim immigrants. After my first few months of fieldwork in Engby School, I began to hear these narratives repeated. On my morning commute to the school, I bicycled past a public housing project that was being demolished as a result of de-ghettoization policies intended to foster the integration of Muslim immigrants and their children. I read the newspaper headlines on the growing problems of criminal Muslim boys, immigrant ghettos, and Muslim girls forced into marriage. As I analyzed data from multiple sources—media representations, educational policies, interviews with policymakers, and ethnographic data on everyday interactions within the school—I heard the repetition of narratives of "concern" for immigrants that reflected desires to support the integration of immigrants into Danish society as well as anxieties about the impact of Muslim immigration on Danish society.

Public Policies and the Figuring of Identities

Following Holland, Lachicotte, Skinner, and Cain's (1998) conceptualization of "figured worlds," my work considers how stereotypes of Muslim identities that are prefigured in policies and discourses are enacted in the day-to-day life of schools. Figured identities are abstracted and distilled notions of identity—cultural stereotypes—that carry with them a set of specific narratives, expectations of behavior, and charters for action. A "figured world" is defined as "a socially and culturally constructed realm of interpretation in which particular characters and actors are recognized, significance is assigned to certain acts, and particular outcomes are valued above others" (Holland et al. 1998: 52). A tension arises between socially scripted identities, captured in local discourses, and individuals' agentive acts of self-authoring within figured worlds. It is at the heart of this tension that my research is centered.

Policies are instruments that classify and govern subjects, in the case of Danish immigration producing specific notions of "citizens," "immigrants," and "the nation" that make up a figured world (Chavez 2013). My work examines how Muslim identities are figured in policies, produced as emblems of broader social problems that require immediate public attention and action. The teachers, administrators, and students in my study participated in a figured world where the narratives, discourses, and figured identities surrounding Muslim immigration informed understandings of how schools should shape and change Muslim youth and where these youth fit into the social hierarchy. In my fieldwork, I observed how figured identities of Muslims were taken up in classroom interactions, in which Muslim students were recognized in terms of the abstract figure, rather than in terms of the fullness of their identities and experiences. However, I also witnessed encounters in which the figure seemed to evaporate and Muslim students had more flexibility to define themselves. Figured identities are not simply downloaded into minds; they are actively negotiated and changed by individual actors who produce their own visions of the world within the social categories set forth by discourse (Bakhtin 1981). While all students must negotiate processes of stereotyping, some identities can be more easily adopted or rejected while others are more encapsulating and rigid.

Figured identities reflect the local figured worlds in which they are reproduced as well as broader social categories of racial, ethnic, and religious difference and durable historical narratives. Notions of "barbaric" Muslims and "enlightened" Western liberals have deep historical significance, drawing on orientalist and postcolonial discourses (Said 1993). They gain additional resonance at particular historical moments, for example, following the events of 9/11 and following other attacks by extremist groups when images of Muslim terrorists dominated the public imagination (Rana 2011).

Although figured identities become ossified over time, they also remain flexible as they stretch to encompass new groups. For example, immediately following 9/11, there was an increase in violence in the West not only against Muslims but also against individuals considered racially ambiguous, including Sikhs, Hindus, and even Latinos or others who appeared in the perceptions of some to be "Muslim-like" (Rana 2011). In 2012 in New York City, an Indian immigrant was pushed onto the subway tracks and was struck and killed by an oncoming train. A 31-year-old woman confessed to the crime, expressing hatred of Muslims following the events of 9/11. The victim was not Muslim but was targeted in this hate crime as a dark-skinned foreigner. The Southern Poverty Law Center reported a 50 percent increase in hate crimes against Muslims in 2012 (Southern Poverty Law Center 2012). The report attributes this to a rise in anti-Muslim propaganda and policy campaigns, thus connecting the ways these campaigns figure Muslim identities in ways that echo through communities, unleashing violence toward Muslims. Even though the Muslims in my study were from diverse ethnic, linguistic, and national backgrounds, they all reported that these differences were routinely homogenized by individuals who understood them in light of the figure of the Muslim "Other."

The Anthropology of Policy: A Window into Coercive Policies

There is currently a global proliferation of policies and antiterrorism measures addressing the perceived threat posed to Western nations by Muslim and immigrant communities (Maira 2009; Nussbaum 2012; Rana 2011). Shore and Wright's (1997) framework of the anthropology of policy provides a window into how these forms of governmental regulation operate, how policies simultaneously produce notions of the perceived social problems produced by Muslim immigration while calling for idealized policy solutions. As Shore and Wright explain, "A policy finds expression through a sequence of events; it creates new social and semantic spaces, new sets of relations, new political subjects and new webs of meaning" (2011: 1). Ethnography is well suited for exploring the complex ways that figured identities and policy technologies are "appropriated" in everyday life, that is, how they are taken up, resisted, and adapted by various actors in public schools (see also Sutton and Levinson 2001).

Drawing on Foucault's (1977) and on Ball's (2006) framing of policy technologies, I examine here the normalizing work of policies targeted at disciplining Muslim immigrants and liberalizing their putative intolerant ideologies and oppressive gender roles (Abu El-Haj 2010; Melamed 2006). Ball argues that "within each of the policy technologies of reform there are embedded and required new identities, new forms of interaction, and new values [as figured worlds]. What it means to teach and what it means to be a teacher are subtly but decisively changed in the process of reform" (2006: 216).

Policies work through public institutions like schools, producing ideas about the kinds of identities schools should foster and the role of teachers in encouraging the development of those identities (Ball 2006; Shore and Wright 1997). This book contributes to the anthropology of policy by tracing how nationalist discourses and policies that reflect the contested place of immigrants in Western liberal societies are enacted in the everyday practices of public schools. My analysis reveals how Muslim immigration challenges deep emotional attachments to and nostalgia for an imagined national community that once was; it also reveals how anxiety inspires the figuring of Muslim identities in policies and in schools. The problems of Muslim immigration are publicly broadcast through "figured identities" that call for processes of coercive assimilation cloaked in and discursively justified through tropes of liberalism.

I theorize that we are witnessing a proliferation of "technologies of concern" for and about immigrant communities—that is, policies and practices directed at transforming immigrants into disciplined subjects of the nation-state (Ong 1996; Foucault 1977; Behrent 2013). Unlike overt forms of state power, technologies of concern conceal their own operations within the language of science or universal values. As Foucault asserts, they are "anonymous, multiple, pale, colorless" (2008: 22). These technologies are "productive," normalizing bodies through subtle manipulations of behavior while also inspiring individuals to reform themselves in light of the norms imposed on them. While technologies are localized through policies and practices in institutions like schools, they also echo broader discourses and regimes of truth. As Dreyfus and Rabinow explain, normalizing technologies "operate by establishing a common definition of goals and procedures, which take the form of manifestos, and even more forceful, agreed-upon examples of how a well-ordered society should be organized" (1982: 198). Schools are institutions of state power that engage these technologies to produce particular types of citizens.

I explore *concern* primarily because it encompasses the multiple dimensions and emotions of the relationships between the nation and the immigrant, those who are concerned and those who are the object of this concern. *Concern* connotes interest and advocacy in its most common usage and, less often, fear, anxiety, and dread on the part of those who are concerned. Technologies of concern emerge in the context of public consensus that "something must be done" about the contemporary "problems" of Muslim immigration. They mark particular bodies as objects of state power that require particular kinds of intervention (Puwar 2004). I draw attention to the ways technologies of concern conceal their own operations through the use of universalized ideas of what is right and good, cloaking national processes of normalization within neoliberal discourses of freedom, democracy, and equality (Rose 1999). Building on Rose's (1999) analysis of how freedom acts as an instrument of government control, my analyses of technologies of concern reveal how practices of coercive assimilation are enacted in the benevolent language of concern, especially, the language of "helping" oppressed Muslim girls to enjoy the benefits of freedom and equality. Finally, I address technologies of concern as they produce particular kinds of knowledge about who Muslim immigrants are and what they require. They simultaneously co-construct notions of Muslims as unassimilable Others and regard notions of liberal societies as enlightened; both figured constructions are deployed to justify increased coercion and intervention (Abu El-Haj 2010; Brown 2006).

Through the thick description of ethnography in this book, I focus on the ways technologies of concern are enacted in schools: how Muslim students' cultural and religious differences become amplified in classrooms, invoking an extra glance or a stare inspired by an array of emotions, including desire, anger, and nostalgia (Benei 2008). Concern is mapped onto the bodies and experiences of young people, influencing their processes of identification and social incorporation. As Comaroff argues, overt state power is less instrumental "than it is 'capillary,' which is to say that it stretches, autonomously and unseen, into the very construction of its subject" (1998: 193). I argue, however, that it is critical to consider as well the complex ways Muslim youth construct their own identities, drawing on their hybrid experiences in homelands, hostlands, and digital territories. While I examine how Muslim youth lay claim to transnational forms of identity that allow them to mobilize various rights and resources (Ong 1996), I also argue that it is critical to consider the material and psychological consequences when young people are forced up against the rigid cultural borders of national belonging. Moving beyond a romanticization of young people's hybrid identities, this book reveals the psychic and material costs of living in the shadow of social scrutiny as well as the ways technologies of concern can distance young people from the resources they require for social mobility in host societies.

The Study

The primary site for my fieldwork is Engby School, mentioned above, outside of Copenhagen, with a large population of Muslim immigrant students, where I conducted a yearlong ethnographic study. [3] My analysis is also informed by the insights I have gained as a former teacher and as a researcher of immigrant education in the United States. Through these experiences, I have witnessed the various ways immigrant youth are positioned in the figured worlds of schools and how cultural difference is understood and treated by youth and adults in these spaces. Though this book is primarily based on research at Engby School, it also includes a comparative discussion of schools in New York City that serve immigrant students and other more briefly introduced comparative examples. While it is important to attend to the specificities within particular contexts and the figured worlds in which schools in different contexts are nested, cross-national ethnographic comparisons provide valuable insights into the mechanisms of inclusion and exclusion of immigrant students.

As an American and an outsider working in Denmark, I was able to critically examine aspects of schooling and processes of everyday nationalism (Billig 1995) so tightly woven into the fabric of Danish society that they are often difficult for Danish insiders to discern. My status as an outsider helped me to establish trust and rapport with a group of first- and second-generation Muslim students from Turkey, Somalia, Croatia, Palestine, Iraq, and Lebanon. Drawing on ethnographic observations, interviews, and extended relationships with a cohort of focal participants, I explored how diverse narratives about immigrants were negotiated in the space of the school. These contradictory narratives were reflected within the school, some projected on banners hanging in the front entrance, while others were silently carried in classrooms or whispered in hallways, and still others were amplified and justified through practice and tradition. One dominant discourse involved teachers who understood their work in terms of bringing "democracy and freedom" to Muslim girls by encouraging them to embrace Danish values. However, another discourse, one more often hidden within school repertoires, was that of cultural recognition. This discourse emerged in the reflections and actions of teachers and youth who challenged racialized conceptions of Muslim immigrants.

Observations

For a period of seven months, I conducted participant observations three days a week in student lounge areas, the teacher workroom, and English classes. Because of my limited Danish-language skills, participant observations primarily took place in eighth- and ninth-grade English foreign language classes, where instruction was in English. As the English curriculum in Danish schools focuses both on learning the language and on developing intercultural understandings, these classes provided a window into the treatment of cultural, linguistic, and religious differences. In the first few weeks of observation, I sat in the back of the classrooms and only answered questions that were directed to me by students or the teacher. Over time, I became more involved in the life of the classes and even acted as a substitute teacher on several occasions when the teachers were absent.

Interviews

Following observations, I invited all members of observed classes to participate in my study and identified a sample of twenty first- and second-generation students (12 girls and 8 boys) and twelve ethnic Danish students (7 girls and 5 boys). I also interviewed fourteen teachers who worked at Engby School, twelve of whom were ethnic Danish and two of whom were born in Denmark but identified as Turkish, as well as the school principal, assistant principal, and guidance counselor. I conducted interviews with teachers in English, as all of the teachers were fluent in English. The majority of interviews with students also were in English; however, a participating student acted as translator to assist me in interviews with students who were not fluent in English.

Positionality

The principal of Engby School introduced me to the teachers as an American researcher who was interested in learning more about Danish schools. When asked by individual teachers, I explained that my work concentrated on schools serving immigrant youth in the United States and I expressed interest in the child-centered, project-based approach of Danish schools. As I spoke to teachers, I was surprised by their willingness to allow me into their classrooms and to take time out of their busy schedules to answer my questions. It was clear to me that teachers saw me as an ally, a similar kind of person. As a white woman in my late thirties who frequently wore chunky Danish sweaters, jeans, and rain boots and traveled to the school on a bicycle, I was perceived to be like many of the female teachers in the school. I worked to establish common ground by engaging in conversations about the problems with the American government under George Bush and the proliferation of standardized testing in American schools, topics that Danish teachers seemed eager to discuss.

Scholars of qualitative research point out that researcher identity influences the type of data that one is able to access. Gunaratnam (2003: 53) finds that there is a "race-of-interviewer" effect. For example, black Americans have been found to be more willing to be interviewed by black, than white, researchers and to be more forthcoming with black researchers. In my relationships with teachers within the school, I intentionally mobilized an identity that would facilitate the building of rapport with my informants. I emphasized different aspects of my identity depending on to whom I was speaking. For example, I did not openly talk about my Jewish identity with Danish teachers, not wanting to mark myself as different. However, one day I was questioned by Helle, a Danish teacher who stopped in the course of a conversation and asked me, "Jaffe, Jaffe, Jaffe, what kind of name is that?" After an exceptionally long pause, I said, "It's a Jewish name." Helle said, "Oh, yes" smiling. In conversations with Aysa, a teacher and second-generation Turkish immigrant, I discussed my Jewish identity, and described how my children negotiated their Jewish identities in the context of Danish schools. When working with my focal participants, I revealed many aspects of my personal life but did not reveal my Jewish identity. Having heard them talk about the Jews who hated Muslims, I worried that it would complicate my ability to maintain the rapport that I had established.

While I sought to build on perceived similarities with Danish teachers, at times I was uncomfortable with what teachers revealed, as they assumed that I shared their beliefs. The following is from my field notes:

Today, a sunny November Monday morning, a group of teachers were catching up about the events of the weekend, huddled together on couches drinking coffee and eating homemade cake. One by one, teachers left the seating area to make copies or to gather their things for their first class. When Birgitte, the English teacher, remained alone on the couch, I asked if we could talk for a few minutes about the students in the eighth-grade class. After a discussion of immigrant students who were struggling in her class, I asked if she could give me an example of a successful immigrant student. She replied, "It would be Bashir." I asked her to explain why he is successful and she replied, "It's because of his family, especially like his mother and sister." As she spoke, she pointed to her own face with her right index finger and began tracing the form of a circle around her face as she spoke. "Bashir's family is more open than the rest of them; his mother and sister speak Danish at home." She continued to draw the invisible outline of the circle around her face and I paused and she whispered, "They don't wear the scarf." At first I was confused by the gesture and the whispering, but I realized that Aysa, a Turkish teacher who wears *hijab*, sat grading papers at the table across from the couch where we were seated and that Birgitte was whispering and gesturing so that Aysa would not hear the conversation. In this scene, I felt that Birgitte made assumptions about who I was, that I shared her values and understanding of what it would mean to be "open."—Field notes, Engby School, 11/8/2007.

I found that there were frequently moments like this during interviews, when I felt the blood rise in my shoulders and became uncomfortable with teachers' representations of immigrant students. They were moments of dislocation, when conversations that felt easy and flowing became halting as I wondered which way to go next with my questions. In retrospect, as I look at the data from my interviews with some Danish teachers, I can see these uncomfortable moments within transcripts, the point at which the interview became stilted, where discussion was no longer natural because I felt that I had crossed a line but remained smiling and nodding, trying not to reveal myself. I worked to mobilize teachers' assumptions that I was like them, to build bridges, but I felt that at times, in service of the project, I had to allow their assumptions about our sameness to breach uncomfortable territory. Still, while there were these difficult moments, there were also times that I felt strong connections with the teachers I worked with, especially when it came to conversations around neoliberal shifts in education policy. As a former educator who worked with immigrant students, I am at times uneasy with my own representations of teachers because of my own awareness that teachers find themselves under siege amid current education reforms, a problem especially true for those who work with immigrant students. [4]

Focal Participants

I experienced less tension in my work with students. And in addition to interviewing a sample of eighth and ninth graders, I developed close relationships with three ninth-grade female Muslim students who became focal participants. Dhalia, Aliyah, and Sara seemed eager to share their experiences in the school and the community to help me make sense of the positioning of Muslim immigrants in Danish society. Aliyah was born in the Somali Ogaden region in Ethiopia and came to Denmark as a baby. Dhalia was born in Denmark but identifies as a Palestinian with strong connections to Lebanon. Sara was born in the Bourj el-Barajneh refugee camp in Lebanon, identifies as Palestinian, and arrived in Denmark at the age of three. As of the spring of 2015, I was still in contact with these informants via e-mail and Skype and continue to talk to them about their educational experiences, the messages they receive about their identities within their schools and communities, and their aspirations.

Analysis of Media and Policy Documents

To provide insight into the dominant discourse related to immigration in Denmark, I analyzed newspaper articles and policy documents. Following Henry and Tator's (2002) methods of critical discourse analysis, I engaged in a content analysis of newspaper articles dealing with issues related to immigration. As themes emerged within my interviews (e.g., discussions of cousin marriage, of gender equality), I conducted newspaper searches on these issues in order to understand the relationship between the understandings of actors within schools and broader discursive narratives. I also collected and analyzed Danish policy documents, including publications of the Danish Ministry of Education, the Ministry of Social Affairs and Integration, and the Ministry of Refugees, Immigration, and Integration. At the school, I collected sections of textbooks and acquired samples of national exams. In my analysis of policy documents, I used official English translations and when those were not available my work was supported by a Danish research assistant, a graduate student in policy studies. I also drew on the research of Danish academics who specialize in integration policy.

On Terms

In this book I use the terms *Muslim youth* and *immigrant youth* to describe a diverse sample of first- and second-generation Muslim immigrants. In my research on immigrant youth and schools (Jaffe-Walter 2008; Jaffe-Walter and Lee 2011), I have been critical of analyses that homogenize the experiences of youth from any one ethnic, religious, or linguistic group, suggesting that there are essential differences distinguishing the outcomes and abilities of these young people (Ogbu 1987). However, over the course of my research, I found that these youth shared common experiences of racialization in their schools and communities that revealed important insights into the inclusion and exclusion of Muslim students in Western liberal schools.

The term *integration*, as defined by social psychologists, involves a model of social incorporation in which minority groups are encouraged to retain their identities as they become a part of a larger multicultural society that values cultural and religious differences. In contrast, the term *assimilation* involves an expectation that immigrants will shed their traditions and take up those of their host society. Politicians in the United States in the early twentieth century, like Theodore Roosevelt, were explicit about their desires to assimilate immigrants to one language and one culture in order to create true Americans, rather than what Roosevelt described as "dwellers in a polyglot boarding house." European countries like Denmark talk about promoting *integration* although enact policies that are instead intended to enforce *assimilation*. In Chapter 2, I explore how "integration" policies are created in response to the perceived threats immigration poses to Danish social cohesion. Denmark was the first nation in Europe to create a separate government office focused on integration. The first leader of that office, Anders Rasmussen, was clear that Denmark should not be considered a multicultural society, that integration policies should respond to perceived threats to cultural solidarity and enforce assimilation. This usage of the term *integration* is what Frederick Erickson calls a "hypocritical liberal obfuscation," in that it appears to be one thing when it is actually another, in this case enforcing monoculturalism while projecting an image of the nation as benevolent and inclusive toward its immigrants.

What Do We Learn from the Danish Case?

Denmark prides itself on its commitment to humanitarian aid, openness to refugees, and egalitarianism. In this context, it would be logical to expect it to provide a best-case scenario for the reception of immigrants—a model of positive integration for other nations to follow. Yet, as Denmark negotiates the transition from an ethnically homogenous country to one with a significant immigrant population, it has experienced a proliferation of nationalist discourses that position immigrants as racialized outsiders (Appadurai 2006; Balibar 1991). The conflicts and violence surrounding the Mohammad cartoons controversy and the shootings following the Hebdo incident in Paris are flashpoints that reveal the tensions in Danish society between the Muslim minority and ethnic Danes.[5] With a growing number of immigrant youth moving into new communities and host nations across the globe, deeper understanding of how schools enable either the civic engagement or the social alienation of these young people is critical. Danish schools are well resourced, do not group students by ability, and are committed to practices of experiential and child-centered education associated with achievement for immigrant students. The failures of this best-case scenario shed light on the complex social mechanisms related to inclusion and exclusion of Muslim students in Western liberal schools. Further, in *Coercive Concern* I use ethnography to reveal how Muslim youth negotiate everyday processes of racialization and exclusion in putatively liberal progressive schools. In this process, I offer portable lessons on how more equitable modes of schooling for immigrant and Muslim youth in other national contexts might be advanced. Finally, I consider the global proliferation of technologies of concern in calling for a more critical examination of the blind spots in the narratives of liberal progressive integration.

Chapter 1

Imagining the Nation

Danish Citizens and Muslim Others

Their religion has attacked our system. Back in the fifties, during my childhood, there was only one way to consider the world and how life should be lived, but now there are many aspects to be considered [*laughs sarcastically*], many cultural riches. Many immigrants have come in the sixties and seventies, and they have made their footprint in our culture and society.

—Holger, German teacher, Engby School

FOLLOWING THE HEBDO INCIDENT in Paris and the violence in Copenhagen in early 2015, there has been an upsurge in talk about the "integration" crisis in Europe and the threats to the values of freedom and democracy. These events reveal that fears of extremist violence and the recruitment of youth into organizations like ISIS are not unfounded. However, what seems to be missing from this conversation in the dominant discourse is a critical analysis of what is really meant by the term *integration*. Listening to media stories, we hear of the shock of a community when Muslim girls—described as "good students, modern, well-integrated, well-adjusted kids"—from a British private school are recruited to Syria (Shapiro 2015). European notions of integration change shape depending on the speaker and context but seem to rest with an understanding that well-integrated Muslims and immigrants do not display high levels of religiosity or emphasize their ties to their native countries. In addition, they should feel comfortable making public proclamations about feeling "British, Danish or French." In an article responding to the events in Copenhagen, a *New York Times* reporter wrote, "As in many other European countries, Muslims in Denmark may coexist with their non-Muslim neighbors, but they often cling to the values and conspiracy-driven mind-set of their home countries" (Higgins 2015). Echoing through such media and dominant discourses is an age-old story about enlightened Western Europeans and barbaric Muslims, a history that I briefly trace in this chapter.

Thus, the "integration" crisis is presented as the problem of Muslim immigrants and citizens who insist on holding on to their culture, language, and attachments to home countries, stubbornly refusing to embrace European values. As Lena, a teacher in my study, explains about the immigrant girls in her class, "They have to be part of the jobs and the education system, to be open minded to what is . . . where I can no longer live in my little safe world where I did what my mother did, and she did what her mother did. The more we can try to open them up the better it will be for their integration as a whole." There is an implicit idea that Muslim youth set themselves apart from society, residing in immigrant enclaves, refusing to take up the offerings of their generous hosts.

Absent from the conversation about the integration crisis is a historical and critical analysis of the terms of social incorporation of immigrants in Europe. Muslim citizens and migrants face a general climate of xenophobia and Islamophobia in European countries and citizenship is tied to racial and ethnic conceptions of belonging. Polls reveal that in most European countries, over half of the citizens hold negative views about the presence of immigrants, believing that immigration should be limited and that immigrants should be subjected to stricter integration requirements (Pew 2014: 26). While it is clear that Europe's Muslim citizens and migrants are positioned as outsiders within the national discourse, there is still an expectation that they should work to better their condition, to make themselves more acceptable subjects of the nation. In an interview, filmmaker Hassan Preisler, whose father immigrated to Denmark from Pakistan, explains, "Someone like me does not choose if I am a Dane. . . . I was baptized in a Protestant church, I eat pork and play football, just like every other Dane—but still I am not a Dane." He describes being set apart because of his name and skin color and challenges the discourse on integration: "Integration is an illusion. I am a living, walking, talking proof that it is an illusion. Everybody knows that it is not what we say it is about. You say it is about my cultural background, but I do not have any other background other than Danish" (Buskbjerg and Jackson 2009). In this book, I explore the contradictions that Preisler lays out, to consider the terms upon which immigrants and their children are positioned in Western liberal societies and the ways that the idea of integration is an illusion that is not as it seems and not accessible for most.

· · ·

How are we to make sense of the seemingly contradictory responses of Western liberal nations toward immigrant Others? How do immigrants provoke public sympathy and anger, desires to rescue and to control? Current discourses on immigration are produced at the intersection of the forces of globalization and nationalism. Some theorists of globalization have argued that the growth of cross-border flows of trade and people, along with the proliferation of trans-national networks, has led to the decreasing relevance of national borders. Others describe how globalization informs a renewed focus on national borders and on protecting the national imaginaries of nation-states (Sassen 2006; Castells 2004; Appadurai 1996; Anderson 2006). Increasing globalization strains national sovereignty, leading to the fear that immigrants pose an internal threat and hence new forms of exclusionary nationalism are needed. As Appadurai argues, "given the systemic compromise of national economic sovereignty that is built into the logic of globalization, and given the increasing strain this puts on states to behave as trustees of the interests of a territorially defined and confined 'people,' minorities are the major site for displacing the anxieties of many states about their own minority or marginality (real or imagined)" (2006: 43). Thus, globalization drives a need to defend the "imagined community" of the nation, what Hedetoft (2006: 406) describes as a "right peopling" of the state. We hear this in the words of politicians across Europe and the United States who propagate fears of immigrant takeover and design policies that seek to control the flow of immigrants (Chavez 2013).

In the wake of 9/11 and the "war on terror," anti-Muslim discourses and policies have gained traction as right-wing leaders in Europe and the United States have publicized and exploited fears about the possibility of a Muslim takeover (Nussbaum 2012; Bunzl 2005). Leaders promise to take control of national and cultural borders, protecting nations and Western civilization from the threat of Islam. They warn of the creation of parallel societies, of the possibility of majorities suddenly becoming minorities in their own land. The Gatestone Institute, a right-wing think tank in the United States, warns of the possibility of Muslim takeovers of European cities in which Muslim groups will establish autonomous enclaves ruled by Islamic law (Sharia), and of a "cycle of Islamic honor killings, sexual assaults, beatings, and murder spiraling out of control" (Kern 2011). Following the Hebdo incident in Paris in January 2015, Fox News spoke with terrorist expert Steve Cameron, who reported that in some cities in England, the United States and France there are entirely Muslim neighborhoods, "no-go zones" for non-Muslims. He also added that in these areas "there are actually Muslim religious police that actually wound seriously anyone who doesn't dress according to religious Muslim attire" (Holehouse 2015). Fox News eventually apologized after the report was discredited, but this kind of reporting often goes unchallenged.

Stirring up dystopic images of the loss of all that is familiar, these nationalist agendas produce images of what Holland, Lachicotte, Skinner, and Cane refer to as "counter-worlds" in public consciousness. These are figured worlds that show "what should not be, what threatens us, and they [these figured worlds] position the persons presumed to inhabit them as relationally inferior and perhaps beyond the pale of any imagined community we would ever want to join" (1998: 250). Counter-worlds provide stock images or figures easily taken up in the national imaginary, used by individuals to explain the everyday changes they see around them. Further, they are a powerful tool in political discourse, unleashing anxieties that in turn justify more restrictive and coercive policies.

Imagining the Nation

The national imaginaries of Western countries are continually being reproduced in relation to immigrant Others. As Holger expresses in the epigraph to this chapter, "*Their* religion has attacked *our* system"; their footprint is in "our" culture and society. Holger wistfully looks to the past, the '50s, as a time when life was simpler, before the arrival of Muslim guest workers and their families. His tone and facial expression as he talks with me reveal he is upset about immigrant challenges to "the one way to consider the world and how life should be lived." In countries like Denmark with a deep internal sense of cultural solidarity and a taken-for-granted sense of shared norms and values, immigration and globalization introduce a disruption. One can no longer assume that citizens share a time-honored set of values and norms. Such conceptions of shared values are socially constructed and produced (Anderson 2006; Gellner 2008); they are felt and experienced in the hearts of citizens. Before moving more deeply into the roots of this "disruption" I examine how conceptions of the nation are imagined and produced within the minds and hearts of individuals like Holger and within political discourse and policy.

While the discourses on nationalism and immigration in European countries are remarkably similar in recent days, with an emphasis on border control and preserving the distinctive aspects of national cultures (Sassen 1999; Chavez

2013), European nations have each had their own unique ways of defining their criteria for admission into the nation. For example, historically, German conceptions of the nation were based on the principle of *jus sanguinis*, or a nation that is formed by those with common blood. This translated into citizenship laws that allowed Germans residing abroad in the early twentieth century to maintain their German citizenship while it excluded Turkish guest workers who were born in Germany from being considered citizens. Even though the German economy required immigrant labor to fuel its industrial growth, it did not conceive of itself as an immigration nation and made it very difficult for migrants to acquire German citizenship. Thus the nation is constructed in terms of *ethnos*—a shared biological connection stemming from the past and a reference point for the nation's existence and coherence—rather than *demos*, the peoples of a nation-state.

France has taken an alternative approach, with membership in the nation defined in terms of shared universal political values rather than blood or descent. The French Republic was founded on the ideals of equality, secularism, and unity—a country where all citizens are equal regardless of their racial, ethnic, and religious backgrounds and where all are united around a common history, language, and culture (Pelvey 2000). The French model reflects a confidence in the power of French schools, government, and the military to assimilate all members of society into this common culture. While Germany sought to clearly define immigrants who resided in the nation as semi-permanent guests, France conceived of itself as an immigration nation based on the ideal of *demos* and encouraged immigration with the ideal of "let them come and make them all French" (Sassen 1999).

In comparison to European countries, the United States has been touted as more inclusive, as a nation of immigrants. However, historical analysis reveals that the United States has deployed exclusionary practices to maintain a white national imaginary. At the same time that the colonial image of the melting pot represented American racial blending and harmony, the government declared Chinese laborers in the U.S. West "aliens ineligible for citizenship," continued to dispossess Native Americans, and colonized Mexicans in annexed territories. Critical race scholar Eduardo Bonilla-Silva explains: "The idea of the melting pot has a long history in the American tradition, but it really was a notion that was extended exclusively to white immigrants. That pot never included people of color: Blacks, Chinese, Puerto Ricans . . . could not melt into the pot. They could be used as wood to produce the fire for the pot, but they could not be used as material to be melted into the pot" (Adelman 2003). Thus, while U.S. civic nationalism perpetuates the idea that the United States is a joining of diverse peoples around common principles of equality and freedom and scholars use this as a counterexample to countries like Germany and Japan, where national identity is based on ethnic nationalism, a closer analysis reveals how racialized hierarchies are central to U.S. constructions of nationhood.

Interrogating the distinction between ethnic and civic nationalisms to explore the myths and assumptions that underlie each provides a useful foundation for further understanding the assimilative nature of Western citizenship and education. Michael Ignatieff sets out the distinction:

Civic nationalism [or *demos*], maintains that the nation should be composed of all those—regardless of race, color, creed, gender, language, or ethnicity—who subscribe to the nation's political creed.... It envisages the nation as a community of equal, rights-bearing citizens, united in patriotic attachment to a shared set of political practices and values.... Ethnic nationalism claims ... that an individual's deepest attachments are inherited, not chosen. It is the national community which defines the individual, not the individuals who define the national community. (1995: 3–5)

The distinction between civic and ethnic nationalism serves to distinguish civic or "good" inclusive nationalism from "ethnocentric" visions of nationalism. Civic nationalism sets out a more palatable vision of a nation for many democratic citizens, one that channels national feelings and emotions into a liberal political order allowing for individual rights and diversity. Yet as Bernard Yack explains, "I am skeptical about this familiar contrast between civic and ethnic nationalism. It all seems a little too good to be true, a little too close to what we would like to believe about the world. The civic/ethnic dichotomy parallels a series of other contrasts that should set off alarm bells: not only Western/Eastern, but rational/emotive, voluntary/inherited, good/bad, *ours/theirs!*" (Yack 1996: 105, emphasis in original).

The appeal of liberal "civic" nationalism is that it creates an illusion of unity and a sense of the nation as tolerant of difference. But the truth is nationalisms are not inherently pluralistic as they seek to perpetuate particular cultures and agendas (Lichtenberg 1999). Is the "civic" identity of the French citizen less rooted in an inherited notion of peoplehood and culture than the "ethnic" identity of the German citizen? Although liberal nationalists make great claims about their commitment to individual rights and tolerance, these values are de-livered through a political system that has produced an imaginary that draws on specific cultural practices, ways of being, and historical traditions. To believe in the liberal idea of civic nationalism one must ignore a whole series of particular social practices, the cultural specifics of what it means to be French or German, Danish or American.

What does the distinction between ethnic and civic nationalism reveal about the stories Western liberal nations tell themselves regarding national identity and belonging? How does this tension between wanting to "feel at home" in national culture and wanting to believe in one's own goodness and openness translate into everyday nationalisms that inform how immigrants are positioned within Western liberal nations? National culture provides its citizens with a sense of feeling at home in the world, familiar sounds and smells of particular geographies and a coherence in which things seem in their place. This introduces one of the great contradictions of liberal nationalisms. Bhikhu Parekh speaks to this limitation: "However liberal she might be, a nationalist remains more or less antipathetic to strong forms of cultural diversity. Since she cherishes and feels at ease only in a homogenous cultural environment, the nationalist is profoundly disoriented by difference, which she finds threatening, and [to which she] lacks the psychological resources to respond positively" (1999: 318). Inevitably, this disorientation or disturbance leads to desires to preserve a sense of life as it once was or is imagined to have been, to reduce the complexity introduced by immigration. Duyvendak describes how the increasing diversity in Europe is largely responsible for national nostalgia based on a vision of a nation of the past and a "renewed popularity of the nation-as-home ideal" (2011: 2). He concludes: "many of those who see the reaffirmation of national identity as a solution to the current malaise dig deeper and deeper into the national past, feeling nostalgia for a time when populations were—supposedly—still homogenous. Nostalgic nations feel a loss of unity, of collective identity; even the most progressive among them look backwards to find a way out of their national crises" (2011: 3).

Defining "Our" People

The most prominent twentieth-century scholars of nationalism reject the claim that nations actually reflect true preexisting ethnicities (Calhoun 1993). Nations do not naturally have an ethnic basis for their existence, instead they center on notions of peoplehood produced by cultural elites who mold a vision of the nation based on preferred notions of ethnicity and sameness (Balibar 1991). As Calhoun argues, "nationalism is not simply a claim of ethnic similarity, but a claim that certain similarities should count as *the* definition of political community" (1993: 229, emphasis in the original). National imaginaries are produced around constructed notions of the people, what Balibar refers to as a "fictive ethnicity" that typically takes the form of characteristics imagined to be inherently derived from forefathers and descendants. Parekh describes how the image of the nation is typically produced in terms of a particular racial vision: "in such countries as Australia, Canada and the United States it includes only the white immigrants and never the original inhabitants, who are confined to the prehistory of these countries and to whom no familiar bonds are established" (1999: 297). Those who existed within the geographical boundaries of the nation before its imagined inception, such as Native Americans, Hawaiians, and Puerto Ricans (within the realm of the United States), are subjected to state technologies that seek to retroactively bring them into the community of the nation. Early citizenship laws in the United States ruled that Native Americans were "domestic foreigners" because they did not share the white European values of the early republic.[1] As Tuck and Yang argue, "the racializations of Indigenous people and Black people in the US settler colonial nation-state are geared to ensure the ascendancy of white settlers as the true and rightful owners and occupiers of the land" (2012: 12). This myth of rightful ownership was deployed to justify state technologies focused on coercive assimilation and de-culturalization of indigenous communities in the name of building democracy and defending liberal values (Spring 1990). As Kymlicka points out, "civic nationalism in the United States has historically justified the conquering and colonizing of national minorities and the coercive imposition of English-language schools" (1995: 135). So for nations that project the image of themselves as centering on particular liberal and political principles, there is always a cultural and imaginary racial basis for national identity. Nations, be they characterized as ethnic or civic, develop around a conception of a common people with a shared history, language, and culture.

Despite the commitment of Western liberal nations to ensuring equality and democracy for all, immigrants unsettle national imaginaries. Invoking Mary Douglas's well-used expression that dirt is really "matter out of place" (2013: 165), immigrants are typically understood by receiving countries of the West to be out of place, threatening the purity of nation-states. While European countries and the United States have craved the labor of migrants to build their economies and to compensate for declining fertility rates, these nations are profoundly ambivalent about the cultural and racial challenges brought on by immigration. Goldberg argues "states will open or stem the flow of the racially figured labor supply in response to the needs of capital, but delimited also by political demands and worries" (2002: 111). Immigrant labor is treated like a natural resource, managed and used to serve economic goals. In times of economic need, nations welcome immigrant labor but with profound ambivalence about the identity threats these laborers introduce.

John Bowen's research in contemporary France describes how Muslim signs and symbols are interpreted as a threat to public order. "The headscarf and the mosque are not objectively more visible than the nun's habit and the cathedral, but they are, or were, subjectively shocking because they were new, foreign— or perhaps, [served] as reminders of a bloody colonial past" (2007: 20). This is evidenced in the current bans on *hijab* in France, national policies that claim to encourage the liberation and self-actualization of Muslim women. In 2003, the French parliament enacted a law that forbids the wearing of the Muslim veil or *hijab* in schools on the grounds that it violates the ideals of French secularism. It contended that the veil represents a conspicuous religious symbol that prevents students from learning and embracing the republican values of secularism and individualism. Proponents of the law argued that the veil attacked the dignity and equal status of women, that women are pressured by men to wear the veil, and that the veil encourages violence against women in their communities (Bowen 2007). Further, the law contends that it is critical that young people and especially girls not be hampered by religious symbols in schools; they should be free to become individuals and to embrace the values of French society.

French criticisms of Muslim communities are that they are insular and constrain Muslims from being emancipated (Bowen 2007). Thus, the law insists on assimilation to French norms in the name of protecting Muslim girls to realize their potential as liberal subjects. Restrictions on *hijab* have intensified in France with the passage of a 2010 ban on *niqab*, the full-face veil, in public spaces. In 2011, those who wore the veil in public were subjected to a fine of up to 150 euros. Annie Sugier, leader of the International League for Women's Rights, argued that the ban encouraged women's liberation because the *niqab* "constitutes a true deletion of the woman as an individual in public" and that it is "totally incompatible with the idea of equality" (BBC News 2013). The French case provides a window into how anti-Muslim nationalist discourses are cloaked in the liberal tropes of individualism and secularism. As Asad argues, French secularism, or *laïcité*, is not imagined to encourage assimilation to one way of being but rather to encourage individual development. "The flowering of individuality that *laïcité* encourages, however, is founded on positivism and [Western] humanism. It is only a *particular* kind of individuality that is sought" (2006: 519).

The bans on *hijab* and *niqab* in France emerged in the context of post-9/11 reactions to the violent youth protests in the suburbs of Paris. Politicians drew on the visibility of these events and public anxieties about the increasing outward displays of Muslim signs in French society aimed at gaining political capital. The media whipped up collective anxieties about the risk of immigrant suburbs ruled by Islamists, the threats of Islam to Western civilization, and the dangers Islam posed to women. This nationalist fervor ultimately led to a public belief that something should be done, that there needed to be stricter immigration laws to bring young immigrants under control. These campaigns drew public support from both right-wing anti-immigrant groups and left-leaning feminist groups that linked the veil to the worldwide oppression of women. Rather than addressing the historical policy failures of the French government in dealing with the isolation and lack of access to employment of Muslims living in immigrant housing projects, the policies defined Muslim women's bodies as an appropriate field of intervention, *the* way to encourage the integration of Muslims in France and to preserve the integrity of the French Republic. Thus the figure of the oppressed Muslim woman was amplified and used to stir up public anxieties that politicians then exploited to gain political traction.

Appadurai explains that minorities can unleash national anxiety and rage because they "are reminders of the failures of various state projects. They are marks of failure and coercion. They are embarrassments to any state-sponsored image of national purity and state fairness" (2006: 42). Immigration is profoundly unsettling in that the flows of people, practices, and ideas disrupt the cultural coherence of the national landscape and challenge liberal notions of national benevolence, i.e., Western nations' ability to believe in their own inherent goodness.

"New" and "Old" Racisms:
Defining Western Selves and Muslim Others

Nations are continually imagined and reimagined. Western nations are consolidated around conceptions of Western civilization and progress that rely on the discursive figure of the heathen Other. As Stuart Hall argues, "'The Other' was the dark side—forgotten, repressed, and denied; the reverse image of enlightenment and modernity" (2001: 314). In the history of immigration in Europe one sees how national boundaries were first defined in relation to one foil, the Jew, who was viewed as the stateless Other. Notions of national belonging and even supranational or European belonging are constructed in relation to ethnicized Others, Jews and Muslims whose cultures and transnational affiliations are held to pose a fundamental threat. Balibar explores this relationship between anti-Semitism and European nationalisms: "The racial-cultural identity of 'true nationals' remains invisible, but it can be inferred (and is ensured) *a contrario* by the alleged, quasi-hallucinatory visibility of the 'false nationals': the Jews, 'wogs', immigrants, 'Pakis', natives, Blacks" (Balibar 1991: 60). I connect this history in what follows to a deeper discussion of Islam as it has been implicated in global racial formations.

Racialization is understood as the process by which different aspects of personhood, including ethnicity, religion, and physical attributes, are attributed specific meanings (Omi and Winant 1994; Silverstein 2005). Omi and Winant describe how concepts of race are mobilized to do particular "work," and how representations of race are a part of national and global racial formations that "reorganize and redistribute resources along particular racial lines" (Omi and Winant 1994: 56). In this book, I draw on Balibar's notion of race as a "transnational phenomenon" that considers race beyond categories of phenotype. He draws on Taguieff to theorize a differentialist racism:

Ideologically, current racism, in which France centers upon the immigration complex, fits into our framework of 'racism without races' which is already widely developed in other countries, particularly the Anglo-Saxon ones. It is a racism whose dominant theme is not biological or heredity but the insurmountability of cultural differences, a racism which, at first sight does not postulate the superiority of certain groups or people and relations to others but only the harmfulness of abolishing frontiers, the incompatibility of lifestyles and traditions; in short, it is what Taguieff has rightly called differentialist racism. (Balibar 1991: 21)

Notions of racial difference are heterogeneous, change over time, and may be referenced through categories of nation, religion, cultural, ethnicity, or language. Race is not a static category and extends well beyond skin color as is revealed in the historical experiences of the Irish, the Jews, Muslims, the Roma, and Asians.

Racial boundaries are constantly being drawn and redrawn in relation to liberal nation-states as different racial categories are positioned in different ways in particular historical moments. For example, while it is currently acceptable to publicize policies that seek to stem the flow of Muslim immigration in Europe, because of the legacy of World War II it has become taboo to publicly speak in parallel ways about Jews.

In the opening of her book on Muslim labor migrants, Junaid Rana asks, "How did 'Muslim' become a category of race?" She traces the complex historical shifts in the category of race in Europe and concludes that Muslims are implicated in "concepts of race and racism through histories that span European and American forms of orientalism and the formation and maintenance of empire through war and conquest" (2011: 28). Current Western discursive constructions of the figure of the Muslim draw on historical antecedents that conflate religious, cultural, ethnic, and biological differences. Rana explains:

The process of reframing Islam from a religious category to a racial category in the contemporary United States speaks to a wider historical discourse that emanates not only from racism and the maintenance of white Christian supremacy, but also from the historical pre-eminence of imperialism and the maintenance of empire. Specifically, the process of racializing Islam through social identifications takes place through a kind of translation of the body and its comportment via a combination of identifiers such as dress, behavior, and phenotypic expression. (Rana 2011: 27)

The expansion of European capitalism and imperialism required the internal "othering" and ethnic cleansing of Jews, Turks, and Moors. During the Reconquista in Spain religious conversion of Muslims and Jews did not render them able to be incorporated into the national body. Even after conversion to Christianity, Moors were subjected to surveillance and suspicion that they were "passing" and engaging in religious practices in secret. European constructions of Muslim otherness congealed around notions of Muslims as barbaric, depraved, and sexually deviant. These representations of the Other were exported to the New World where they were used to justify the domination and repression of Native Americans and African slaves, who were understood to be the recipients of benevolent Western intervention and incapable of self-governance and reason. Notions of sexual deviance further justified the subordination of Moors, Native Americans, and African slaves. As Matar concludes: "Nothing was more convenient to the *conquistadores* than to see the pervert as the Moor or the Indian. In America the [culturally sanctioned] homosexuality of [individual] natives conveniently rendered the [larger group] immoral in the eyes of the conquerors, thereby legitimizing destruction, conversion, or domination—whichever best served the conquerors" (1999: 109). Popular images of Muslim sexual deviance, child marriage, rape, and cousin marriage reflect time-honored narratives that have traveled across nations and populations to justify coercive practices and exclusion. While this is an oversimplification, it shows how "new" racisms reflect older durable narratives about the position of Others including Muslims in enlightened Western liberal nations. This history reveals that liberal enlightenment discourses and global racialization have been historically intertwined as anti-Muslim racism has been imbricated with the development of modern liberal nation-states.

While Rana stresses the historical roots of the figure of the Muslim, others like Silverstein (2005) and Balibar (1991) find that the current historical moment is characterized by a "neo-racist" discourse that focuses on the threat Muslims pose to Western liberal nation-states and that homogenizes ethnically and nationally diverse groups of immigrants into a wider category that presumes that all Muslim immigrants (and even some non-Muslim individuals who fall within the category of Muslim-like) share a common culture and set of beliefs (Balibar 1991; Silverstein 2005; Bunzl 2005). Tariq Modood (1997: 4) offers the following definition of "Islamophobia."

It is more a form of racism than a form of religious intolerance, though it may perhaps be best described as a form of cultural racism, in recognition of the fact that the target group, the Muslims, are identified in terms of their non-European descent, in terms of their not being white, and in terms of their perceived culture, and that the prejudice against each of these aspects interacts with and reinforces the prejudice against all the others.

Whether current forms of anti-Muslim racism and Islamophobia are inherently "new" or "old" is a topic for continued debate; nonetheless, it is clear that Muslim immigrants experience racialization in Europe and the United States. The events surrounding 9/11 created what a number of scholars refer to as a "moral panic" (Maira 2009: 172; Razack 2008; Rana 2011; Abu El-Haj, 2015), which in turn has led to the sudden growth of anti-Muslim racism and an intensification of the surveillance of Muslim communities. This new wave of racialization has connected diverse groups of Muslims and immigrants imagined to possess related characteristics associating them with illegality, criminality, and deviance, qualities that call for new forms of policing and social control. Laws that restrict the wearing of *hijab* are gaining momentum in Europe; France, Belgium, and Italy have passed legislation that prohibits women from wearing *hijab* in public spaces. In Switzerland a prohibition against the building of minarets (prayer towers) was recently made a part of the constitution, and in Spain new regulations prohibit the construction of mosques (Amnesty International 2012). Politicians warn of a Muslim takeover and have passed laws banning Sharia law and prohibiting the construction of mosques in the United States. On August 25, 2013, North Carolina became the seventh state to prohibit judges from considering Islamic law. The Anti-Defamation League finds that perceptions of Sharia law infiltrating the American court system are among "the most pernicious conspiracy theories to gain traction in our country in recent years" (Anti-Defamation League 2014).

These policies simultaneously position Muslims as unassimilable Others while they propose new ways of "helping" them reap the benefits of "superior" Western liberal societies. Furthermore, they authorize "concerned" citizens to take action, unleashing new forms of everyday intervention and violence. The narratives of Muslim youth that are presented in Chapters 3 through 5 of this book reveal the complex ways that young people experience nationalist concern in their everyday lives—the ways that their negotiations of identity are constrained by the figured narratives and stereotypes about Muslims that linger in the air.

While these contemporary enactments of racialization reflect older durable narratives about Islam, they also take up a newer post-racial epistemology that is characterized by a denial of the relevance of race (Gilroy 1998; Balibar 1991; Bonilla-Silva 2003). The current "racial present" (Winant 2006) encourages commonplace assumptions that race is a less salient category than it once was. Jodi Melamed describes this sea change in racial epistemology in which nations take up "official anti-racisms" that involve a "liberal symbolic framework for race reform centered in abstract equality, market individualism, and inclusive civic nationalism" (2006: 2). As explicitly racist language has become increasingly taboo, nationalist politics have adopted new forms of liberal multicultural speech that evade charges of racism. In 2010, Angela Merkel proclaimed that Germany's attempts to establish a multicultural nation had "utterly failed" and then in 2015, she advocated for Muslim minorities marching at a rally to protest the anti-Islamic movement Pegida and declared in a speech "Islam is part of Germany" (Huggler, 2015).[2] This shift in language mirrors political discourses across Europe. Even the French far-right National Front is trying to clean up its image, moving away from racist discourse while continuing to pursue increasing restrictions on immigrants and xenophobic nationalist policies.

At times nations make claims about inclusiveness, projecting images of themselves as "better" with their immigrant and racial minorities populations than other countries. Europeans pride themselves on not having the kinds of race problems or ghettos evident in the United States, while U.S. leaders point to America's history as an immigrant nation as a reason it is more inclusive. At a White House Press conference with Prime Minister David Cameron, President Obama explained, "Our biggest advantage is that our Muslim populations, they feel themselves to be Americans. . . . There are parts of Europe in which that's not the case. And that's probably the greatest danger that Europe faces. . . . It's important for Europe not to simply respond with a hammer and law enforcement and military approaches to these problems" (Francis 2015). These discourses of national exceptionalism move attention away from the material ways Muslim communities experience racialization (Abu El-Haj 2015).

Analyzing the contemporary discourses surrounding the restrictions on *hijab* in France reveals how the coercive assimilation of Muslims may be couched in the language of antiracism. According to this logic, by wearing *hijab*, Muslim women provoke discriminatory responses within co-ethnic communities and the broader society. By limiting this, politicians are therefore protecting these women from violence and racist responses. Although new forms of racialization are characterized by official discourses of antiracism that take up the liberal tropes of equality, individualism, and secularism (Augoustinos and Every 2007), a tacit racism continues to operate in the differential allocation of resources and in forms of surveillance and social control. These new forms of liberal racism serve to reproduce a vision of the Western nation as inclusive and democratic, and reflect the illusion of inclusive forms of civic nationalism. Thus, new forms of liberal racism and nationalism are imbricated, serving to protect the need to believe in one's own national goodness as well to ensure the future of a racialized national imaginary.

Imagining the Danish Nation

When I began this work, I was startled by what seemed to me to be a great contradiction in Danish society. Denmark is a nation that has prided itself on its commitment to humanitarian aid, openness to refugees, and social equality.

Images of Danish fishermen in the Second World War smuggling Jewish residents to safety across the waters of the Oresund are imprinted in the national imagination as a symbol of Denmark's generosity to outsiders, as "a shining beacon to the rest of the world" (Jenkins 2011: 220). Yet, there are two very different discourses in relation to the presence of refugees and immigrants in Denmark: on the one hand, stated commitments to social equality and humanitarian concern toward immigrants and, on the other, the propagation of nationalist discourses that position immigrants as racialized outsiders who threaten the national community (Appadurai 2006; Balibar 1991). While at first it seemed that the two discourses were contradictory, I began to see that they are historically intertwined. Western liberal national imaginaries are produced against the notion of the immigrant Other. Through the figuring of the Other there is a clear establishment of the boundaries of what "we" are and what "they" are not.

Historically, Denmark's relative cultural homogeneity and strong sense of civic solidarity have been understood by political historians to be central to its survival among more powerful European nations. This solidarity centers on a set of shared assumptions, values, and beliefs at the heart of notions of Danish citizenship. Danish nationalism developed around perceived external and internal threats to the national community. For mid-nineteenth-century Denmark, the threat was largely from neighboring powers with significant armed forces. More recently the perceived threat is from mass immigration that began in the 1960s and has been ongoing into the present. Denmark suffered significant territorial losses in the nineteenth century. In 1814, it lost all of Norway, and in 1864 it lost vast territories along the borders with Germany as a result of German expansionism. Danish political leaders were confronted with the fundamental question of how Denmark would maintain itself amid world powers with large militaries. In response, they developed a strategy of "culture as defense" by establishing policies that sought "to build a strong internal defense primarily through social, educational, and cultural politics" (Korsgaard 2006: 150). In short, Danish leaders sought to unify the nation around a common language, culture, and ethnicity. According to Peter Munch, the foreign minister from 1929 to 1940, Denmark's lack of military might required the construction of a national project that all Danes could identify with and be proud of:

The means for this end is to enlarge our culture and to create solidarity in the Danish people by developing such states in the society that all layers of people have reason to embrace our country and its people with warm affection. Often is this sentence mocked:

It is by culture and not by weapons that we shall defend ourselves. This mockery comes from people who are not capable of understanding the meaning of the sentence. The intention is of course not that the weapons shall fall from the hands of enemies in respect for culture. . . . But a free and self-reliant culture that permeates all layers of the people can, however, create safeguarding for the subsistence of the people's national life, even if the misfortune should come upon us, and the state, by brutal laws of war and conquest, succumbed to the will of foreign violators. (In Korsgaard 2006: 334)

In this historical context, maintaining ethnic and cultural homogeneity was considered not only important but a matter of national security. The national community was developed to defend itself against an imagined "foreign violator."

Immigration in Denmark

Currently, immigrants and their descendants make up 11.6 percent of the total Danish population (657,471 people) and immigrants and descendants from "Non-Western" countries represent 7.5 percent of the population (424,558 people) (Statistics Denmark 2015a). [3] Before 1960, Denmark had little immigration, with emigrants significantly outnumbering immigrants (only 15,000–35,000 people, or less than 1 percent of the population, could be categorized as immigrants before 1960) (Coleman and Wadensjö 1999: 149). Moreover, the immigrants who did arrive in Denmark were predominantly white and Christian.

It was not until the late 1960s that Denmark became more heterogeneous, as growth within the Danish economy increased demand for immigrant workers. Like other European countries, Denmark recruited significant numbers of migrants, mostly men from Turkey, Pakistan, Yugoslavia, and Morocco, in the late 1960s and early 1970s as temporary workers. Under the terms of the Danish Aliens Act of 1952, guest workers were able to enter the country if they could demonstrate that they had funds to provide for themselves and to pay for their trip home. The number of immigrant workers grew steadily from the late 1960s until 1973. In 1965–1966, fewer than 500 immigrant workers entered the country, but by 1972 the number immigrating in that year alone had risen to over 10,000.

The numbers of immigrants in the late 1960s and early 1970s continued to rise because family members, including children, spouses, and parents, entered Denmark under the family unification law. After the rapidly rising price of oil led to long-term recession and an increase in unemployment in 1973 (Coleman and Wadensjö 1999), the Danish government banned all immigration. Even so, the number of immigrants in Denmark continued to rise because workers were not sent home and were gradually granted residence permits and were joined by families from home countries. Workers who had lived in the country for at least seven years were legally allowed to apply for citizenship.

In the 1980s there was a large influx of refugees due to the Iran-Iraq War and conditions in the Palestinian territories. Subsequently, in the mid-1990s, the civil war in former Yugoslavia sent more refugees into Denmark. The Danish government introduced a liberal refugee policy in the Aliens Act of 1983, which provided protection and rights to residence permits for those who entered Denmark. Pederson explains that the Alien Act conformed to Denmark's self-image as a haven for refugees. "Internationally, the 1983 Act drew considerable attention due to its liberal approach to the question of refugees, and with the passing of this new legislation Denmark acquired a reputation for leading the way in providing a humanitarian approach to refugees." After the passage of this act, the number of asylum seekers rose from 332 in 1983 to 8,698 in 1985 (Coleman and Wadensjö 1999: 165). Overwhelmed by the relatively large influx of refugees, the Danish government introduced amendments to the act in 1985 and 1986 that led to a reduction in asylum seekers in subsequent years.

Rise of Anti-Immigrant Sentiment:
Neo-Nationalism in Denmark in the 1990s

Although guest workers were welcomed to Denmark in the 1960s and 1970s, in the 1990s there were significant political and media responses to the burgeoning communities of Muslim immigrants. This led to the emergence of an anti-immigrant neo-nationalistic discourse of "unbridgeable differences." Hervik explains that the neo-nationalist movement emerging in the 1990s positioned immigrants as unwanted guests:

One of the key features of the neo-racist wave is the construction of a rigid dichotomy between 'we' the Danes, and 'they'—the out-group of foreigners—to the point that it [the dichotomy] is unbridgeable. However, as we shall see, the social construction of foreigners is [as] an "outwardly defined population" that uses pseudo-biological ascription but mainly focuses on cultural criteria as well, i.e. clothes, food and language. (2004: 253)

Immigrants were perceived to shake the foundations of Danish society, threatening Danish institutions and the stability of the welfare state. Hedetoft argues that in the 1990s there was a shift in Danish immigration discourse and policymaking from humanitarianism to nationalism. He finds that the following questions emerged within policymaking and immigration discourses of the 1990s:

Of national interest and utility: "What's the benefit for us? How many can we take?"; of identity scares: "Can Danishness survive the religious and civilizational challenge?"; of social cohesions: "How can we deal with criminal immigrants and ethnic ghettoes? How can we make them integrate?"; And of welfare-state policies and political participation: "Can the universalist welfare model survive? Can we afford to pay the benefits?" (2006: 410)

What triggered this anti-immigrant discourse? While the Danish economy required the labor of guest workers from the 1960s on, the Danes always assumed that guest workers would eventually return to their home countries and so they were not perceived to be a direct threat to national culture. When, in the late 1980s, most chose to apply for permanent residence in Denmark rather than to return home, references to the "immigrant problem" multiplied within the media and the public at large. The simultaneous arrival of new groups of refugees in the late 1980s spurred additional anti-immigrant sentiment. Newspapers discussed the challenges posed by immigrants in Danish society and spoke of the "Muslim invasion," drawing on broader European discourses that emphasize the incompatibility of Islam with the values of Western society (Huntington 1996). Tracing Danish immigration discourses since the 1960s, one witnesses a movement between the ideals of Danish society that led to opening its borders to outsiders and those in need followed by restrictionist reactions after Danish political parties responded to the perceived demographic and cultural challenges introduced by Muslim immigration.

Schooling the Nation

Nationalism expresses itself not only in political agendas that enact ever more restrictive immigration laws and new integration regulations, but also in quieter ways, in a banal nationalism reflected in the everyday practices of schools that determine who does and doesn't belong to the national community (Billig 1995; Abu El-Haj 2010). The work of pruning the unruly branches of the national tree and managing the identity threats such as those posed by immigrants is expressed through immigration and integration policies that seek to enforce national values. Public schools are deeply implicated in such national projects, charged with the task of transforming "outsiders" into citizens by instilling normative ideas of behavior and identity (Sutton and Levinson 2001; Abu El-Haj 2010; Ong 1996). But, like national projects, national schools are often deeply ambivalent about the idea that they are forcing their own ways on newcomers. Embracing the democratic agendas and myths of civic nationalism, Western modes of public schooling aspire to universalist principles of inclusion and equality while they enact distinctly national practices.

Baumann describes this as a "paradox of universalism and exclusiveness" in how schools in the Netherlands, Britain, Germany, and France negotiate the changing demographics of schools.

It stands to reason that the propagation at school of an outspokenly nationalist national imaginary would spell an exclusion of non-nationals, followed by marginalisation or confrontation. While the established national imaginaries were reasonably successful in projecting cohesive nation-state 'communities' from the 1870s to the 1950s, they have now reached their sell-by dates within European integration and the settlement of more migrants from outside the European Union. The time-honoured imaginaries did not drop out of school practice altogether, as we shall show in our analysis of schoolbooks and curricular guidelines; yet they were transformed into more sophisticated, less offensive, at least superficially inclusivist forms. (Baumann 2004: 10–11)

While I am sure that there are modes of Western liberal schooling that have fundamentally transformed in ways that recognize the plurality of the societies in which they exist (see Jaffe-Walter and Lee 2011; and Bartlett and García 2011, for examples), many schools in the West have continued to enforce the cultural and religious imaginaries of nation-states. Today they engage in what educational scholars describe as "color-blind liberalism," which obscures an analysis of how race operates within schools. Within the sociocultural contexts of schools, teachers see students through particular cultural and national lenses that inform ideas about how the various pupils in a class are positioned and how teachers come to understand which of them deserve continued sponsorship and which are less deserving. The contexts of schools foster a system of meanings through which pupils and teachers reproduce conceptions of social boundaries that inform the distribution of resources. Yet, in schools where color-blind discourses prevail, there is an insistence that "we see everyone the same" and "we treat everyone the same," as if saying this would somehow ensure equity. Color-blind liberalism fails to account for the implicit ways race and

racial hierarchies continue to influence how young people are positioned in relation to resources in schools and the ways notions of "ideal" and "problematic"
students continue to be defined along national and racial lines (Lewis 2003).

The Paradox of Danish Schooling:
On Being Child-Centered and Nation-Centered

The Danish government today requires that all students receive ten years of
education extending from preschool through the ninth grade.[4] The vast majority of students attend the *folkeskole*, comprehensive schools encompassing both
primary and lower secondary school from preschool through the ninth grade.[5]

Inspired by the philosophies of Grundtvig, an influential figure in Danish
history, the *folkeskole* is a model of public schooling that brought the common
people of Denmark together in schools to learn principles of democracy through
the foundations of Danishness—namely, Danish history, music, literature, and
shared celebrations. The *folkeskole* was created in opposition to early models
of schooling in Denmark that educated only the children of the elite and sym-
bolized academic hierarchy, corporal punishment, and the rote transmission of
knowledge. In contrast, the *folkeskole* is committed to the cultivation of students'
desire for learning and respect for their individual development and needs (Anderson 1996). Its core mission is to support students in becoming Danes, developing students' capacity to be active citizens of the national community.

In postwar Denmark, the Social Democratic Party argued that the *folkeskole*
would ultimately be a source of social equality (Korsgaard 2006: 154). The de-
mocratization of education in Denmark involved two principles: first, making
education accessible to all, and second, instilling the principles of Danish democracy in young students. During this period, the primary goals of Danish
education were supporting social equality rather than economic growth. It was
believed that schools should develop independent of market forces. Korsgaard
writes: "Schools should train students in tolerance and cooperation in spite of
differences in social situations and skills" (2006: 154).

To reduce class and regional distinctions, in 1903 Danish schools ultimately
moved to a *klasse* system, which involves placing students in groups when they
enter primary schools and maintaining these groups for the entire nine years of
pupils' compulsory education. Students are placed in each *klasse* randomly and
are not divided by skill level. Structured to promote equality and a lack of hierarchy, the *folkeskole* is committed to education without tracking to ensure that all

students receive the same level of education, with the exception of those who attend special education classes. Gilliam explains that Danish schools are "seen as more liberal, socially inclusive and child friendly ways to organize school. The Scandinavian schools and their embrace of all social groups, avoidance of streaming, minimal usage of tests and non-authoritarian relation between teachers and pupils are thus often looked at for inspiration by educationalists visioning more inclusive and 'less-failure-producing' ways to school children" (2007: 3). Students in Danish schools are socialized and educated within the *klasse*, which is structured to resemble a family system. It is designed to be a closely associated group of students and teachers supported by a parent group. Ideally, students remain in the same *klasse* for all nine years, with the same class teacher (*klasselaerer*). The Folkeskole Act of 1975 states that it is critical not to merge *klassen*. Anderson writes: "It is considered traumatic for students and teachers to be with people whom they do not know well, who have different work habits, threatening the Klasse as a group" (1996: 45). Between 1903 and 1993, the number of years that students stay in the same class grew from two years to ten. Keeping the *klasse* together is thought to promote a feeling of *tryghed*, or social comfort, which is believed to be a necessary prerequisite for learning. The *klasse* system is a critical structure for encouraging social unity in Denmark, designed to be an enclave or a social community more than a group of students gathered together to learn a specific set of skills (Anderson 1996).

In the postwar period, schools played a critical role in gathering regional and class-based identities into a common national identity (Korsgaard 2006; Jenkins 2011). Gitz-Johansen describes how the *folkeskole* "has played a vital part in the creation of a common linguistic and cultural base for the population, or, at least, the creation of some commonly recognized criteria of legitimate cultural and linguistic practices" (2011: 3). Thus, there is a parallel focus on teaching youth to become "proper persons" so that they may lead a fulfilling life in Danish society as well as ensuring a high degree of social solidarity within the national community. According to Jenkins, the *folkeskole* is both "child-centered" and "nation-centered" (Jenkins 2011), bringing radical education philosophies of the mid-twentieth century together with the goals of Danish nationalism. This is similar to the goals of the French education system in which schools are understood to be a site to close regional and class divisions. The work of producing liberal equity has long been associated with practices that encourage cultural homogeneity. A Danish Ministry of Education publication emphasizes the parallel collective and individual focus of instruction in Danish schools: "The teaching is organized in such a way that it both strengthens and develops the individual students' interests, qualifications and needs so that it [an education] contains common experiences and situations providing them with experience which prepares them for cooperation in the performance of tasks" (Danish Ministry of Education 2008). Danish schools have emphasized that learning should unfold naturally according to the individual pace of the child, who should not be pushed—there is an understanding that the school is a safe space designed to facilitate learning and positive relations among students.

Engby School: A Liberal Inclusive Space

In the main entrance of Engby School is a display consisting of three large decorative steamer trunks meant to represent shipments of aid to developing countries and a large banner hanging across the front hallway that reads UNICEF SCHOOL. Bulletin boards in the entrance display articles about the school's collaboration with schools in Africa and South America. In describing the culture and mission of Engby School, Per, the school's principal, explained that while the school is first a Danish school, it also promotes tolerance and cooperation between different groups:

It is very important to me that we are a Danish public school, we have Danish values but we also have tolerance, respect for individuals, and [we] work for cooperation between peoples. And I am happy that now a lot of strong Danish parents are choosing this school. Of course you show your respect for people of Turkey or Arab countries, it is not unnatural to do it.

Per describes how Engby School's humanitarian mission is expressed through partnerships and projects with schools "in poorer parts of the world" such as Africa and Brazil. Per explained the importance of this work, "given our tremendous wealth." Students and teachers engaged in collaborative projects in English classes that involved letter-writing campaigns and collecting supplies that were sent to the schools in South America and Africa. He said, "We can help them by communicating because they have to learn English, too, but we can also send them gifts such as paper and colored pencils. It is very little money for us but it is an enormous gift for them."

Per is a gentle and soft-spoken man. As I walked the hallways of Engby School with him, students would frequently stop him to chat, or grab him by the arm to get his attention. The sound of "Per," "Per," "Per" would ring out behind us as we walked the halls. As we stood in the school cantina, he described the challenges of having warm relationships with students and also being a disciplinarian while three fourth-grade students, a Somali girl and two Danish boys, ran in circles around him singing. Students and teachers described a major turn-around in the culture and climate of the school since Per had taken the position of school leader. He adopted policies that were not typical for a Danish school such as the recruitment and hiring of several ethnic minority teachers and counselors. Per also condemned the changes in recent education policies, most notably the lack of funding for mother-tongue instruction and the xenophobia he perceived in the recent changes of nationalist policies. In an interview he explained:

A minority in the parliament really don't want foreigners in Denmark. Before this law [the Folkeskole Act of 2002], we gave all bilingual children instruction in their mother tongue and it was just thrown away. But what is quite interesting is that the European Union (EU) has a rule that says that mother-tongue teaching is important and when Europeans are living in another country, they must have instruction in their own language, for free. But it is not important to Turkish people, Arab people, Asian people? The Danish government would say that the French and the Spanish should have mother-tongue instruction, but not people like the Turkish and the Indians.

Per highlights the inherent discrimination of policies that only support native language instruction for European students.

My first impression of Engby School was that it was very different from the public schools I had worked in and visited in the United States. Its physical spaces appeared bright, open and airy, and the smells of paste, paint, and fresh-cooked food wafted through the air. Children's art was displayed on the walls of the hallway leading into the school office, where small tea-light candles burned on the front desk. As the secretary explained, "We do our best to make the school cozy in the fall and winter." Unlike New York City lunchrooms, which are typically in windowless basements and feel institutional, Engby School's lunchroom is a large open room with floor-to-ceiling windows on one side that look out onto the school garden. Children eat freshly prepared organic lunches on maple tables covered with batik-print table clothes and mid-twentieth-century-designed light fixtures hang from the cathedral ceilings.

The physical spaces of the school reflect Danish commitments to hands-on learning and cooperative education. Students engage in projects together

that encourage the development of the community of the *klasse*. Directly outside the lunchroom was a series of outdoor teaching spaces including a bar-
beque area with a brick oven where the first- and second-grade children had
recently made bread. A coop full of chickens stood at one end of the outdoor
classroom area and the remains of a deer carcass hung on a rack, having been
recently dissected by a seventh-grade science class. Per explained that "the
hunter brought it right from the forest, it was still warm." Sitting at a picnic
table, Per said that the work of the school is built on Danish traditions of farming and cooperation:

In 1864, we created a cooperative movement in Denmark where everybody worked together to cooperate in making a better life through farming, cooking, and other kinds
of work. In this movement, everybody has one world; it was not depending on how rich
someone was, but that everybody was a human being.

Per helped me to make sense of the world of the Danish school—the beautiful
interior spaces, the centrality of human relationships, social units that resemble
families, and experiential learning. From the perspective of history, he situated
the work of the school within the cooperative peasant farming movement that
prospered in the 1870s—pointing to the importance of norms of cooperation
and social unity that are at the heart of Danishness (Østergård 2006). These
ideals of "community" and "being together" (*samvaer og faellesskab*) reflect late-
nineteenth-century visions of the nation as culturally and linguistically homo-
geneous (Jenkins 2011). This vision of social unity is centered on emphasizing
"common" experiences and the avoidance of discussions of class or racial inequalities, which are understood to be polarizing and threatening to the collective spirit of a class (Anderson 1996; Gilliam 2007).

Accomodating Difference at Engby School

Per, when describing his efforts to make the culture of the school more responsive to the traditions of Muslim students, explained that there had recently
been a significant debate between Danish and Muslim parents about the foods
served in the school's cantina:

Some of the Muslim parents have asked us to buy halal meat and we said no, because
you cannot buy organic halal food and we are a school that wants the children to be
healthy and not religious. Half of our children have a background where pork meat is
similar to what rat meat would be for us. I met with the parents and said that I am head-

master and I told the parents that we have to respect that pork is disgusting for some of our children and they have to respect that we are not buying religious meat.

Despite disapproval from Danish parents who objected to the removal of pork from the cantina menu, citing the significance of pork as an important part of Danish culture, Per stopped serving pork. While this change shows a respect for and accommodation to Muslim students, he emphasizes that the school intends to support students to be "healthy and not religious." He positions students' religious faith as something to be tolerated and not embraced and fosters a hope that students will choose a secular "organic" life over a religious one. Despite his displays of tolerance, Per positions Muslim students' religious beliefs as requiring careful management.

In another instance of cultural negotiation, a group of female Muslim students asked Per for a space within the school building to pray during the school day. In this instance, he decided not to accommodate the request, explaining that it violated the secular nature of Danish schools.

To me it is more important that if you show your respect to other people, you also must know what the limits of this respect are. Therefore, I have been fighting against religious fundamentalism in the school and in the thinking. For example, some of the Muslim girls came and asked for a room for praying. I said no, we are a public school and we are not religious at all, so you cannot not have a prayer room. Because I knew that they would use it to make a press to the other Muslim girls to be a real Muslims. Of course we cannot have this; in Denmark religion is not a part of the school.

Per's explanation reveals concern about the presence of Islam within the school on the grounds that it violates the secular nature of Danish schools. While Per seeks to accommodate the cultural differences of Muslim students, he points to the "limits of this respect," that is, the boundaries of Danish tolerance. Like the statement about being "healthy and not religious," Per reveals his feelings that students' affiliations with Islam should be discouraged. Further, he conflates students' observance of prayer rituals with religious "fundamentalism," reflecting a school discourse that positions Muslim students as representing a potential threat within the liberal and putatively secular space of the school.

Despite Per's insistence that the school is a secular space characterized by "openness" toward the ethnic, racial, and linguistic differences of Muslim students, observations and interviews revealed that the school is a Danish and Christian space. Observance of Islam is associated with radicalization and with students who are considered "potential terrorists" (Abu El-Haj 2010), while religious observance of Christianity is understood to be central to the work of the school and to the national culture. The Danish Church plays an important role in mediating between the nation and its citizens and this is part of the implicit background of Danish life.

For example, the school held seventh-grade confirmation activities during the school day in which a local priest either came to the school or received the class at a local church and directed them in religious study. In addition, the class participated in "Church-week," a week when students visited a local church to experience Christian rituals. Furthermore, in religion class, students studied passages from the Bible in preparation for the national exam in Christianity. While the topic of Islam was part of the curriculum in religion class, classroom discussions frequently focused on the ways Islam was contested in Danish society rather than on the beliefs and traditions of Islam. One test question on the national exam in Christian studies asked students to discuss whether members of the Danish parliament should be permitted to wear *hijab*. When I questioned the principal about what seemed to me to be a fundamental contradiction around Christian rituals and study within putatively secular schools, Per paused, and explained that these practices were not intended to teach Christian beliefs to students but were rather just a part of culture.

This emphasis on Christianity as implicit culture produces symbolic boundaries between Christian ethnic Danish students and Muslim students (Jenkins 2011). When asked if they could ever imagine a day when Danish schools would not celebrate Christmas, most teachers I interviewed answered no. They explained that celebrating Christmas together is an important time-honored tradition in Danish schools. When I asked teachers in interviews if they could imagine a time when the school would celebrate the festival of Eid at the end of Ramadan, given that forty percent of the schools' students were Muslim, most teachers replied that they could not. In one instance, Dorte, a teacher of German said, "Well [*pauses*], we would like to think that we would support that, but actually, no, we wouldn't ever celebrate it in our school. This is Denmark and this is a Danish school." Dorte's pause was telling. While there is a desire in Danish schools to be inclusive and to be open to the differences of Muslim students, these differences are also understood to present a challenge to Danish values.[6]

As Brown reminds us, "liberal discourses hide their imbrications with Christianity and bourgeois culture" (2006: 152). In the chapters that follow, I explore the ways liberal discourses operate in schools. How do they conceal the particular and national use of tropes of humanitarianism and liberalism and how do they produce notions of the Other who requires careful management and tolerance? Even though the dominant culture of Engby School reflected Danish and Christian culture, teachers conceived of that culture as "open" and as offering equal opportunity for all. Per and the teachers conceived of themselves as supporting the academic and emotional growth of all students and frequently spoke specifically of their desire to help the immigrant students. Yet, there was a lack of awareness that Muslim students were being positioned as outsiders in the Danish and Christian space of the school.

The Narcissism of Concern

In this book I examine national myths of civic inclusiveness. What are the various liberal epistemologies that nations engage to talk about their immigrant populations? What are the new narratives about "us" and "them" that emerge in political discourse? Across Europe one hears national leaders echoing UK prime minister David Cameron who announced the "failure of multiculturalism." There is a parallel movement toward policies that control and discipline immigrant populations, as evidenced by Cameron's call for "a much more active, new muscular liberalism" (BBC News 2011). European leaders continue to reach toward the protective balm of liberalism, to ensure that the nation continues to project an image of itself as compassionate, tolerant, and equitable. Like a fair-minded but stern parent, the nation is merely responding to the challenge of Muslim immigration in a clearly justifiable manner. Cameron argues that the old forms of passive tolerance are no longer adequate: "A passively tolerant society says to its citizens: as long as you obey the law, we will leave you alone. It stands neutral between different values. A genuinely liberal country does much more" (BBC News 2011). How are liberal politics refigured to take up more and more conservative and repressive positions? Other scholars, such as Hedetoft (2006), note this shift from Rawlsian rights-based notions of liberalism to more repressive or "muscular" forms of liberalism.

In addition to tracking the various liberal assumptions about who Muslim immigrants are and the interventions they require to be successful members of Western liberal nation-states, I offer an analysis of the insidious forms of state violence that target Muslim immigrants in the name of care and concern. How do liberal policies and discourses seek to imagine the realization of particular racialized imaginaries? Within Europe the violence of some becomes invisible or collectively repressed while others' becomes amplified. Muslims are ideologically constructed as not belonging within a "civilized" and secular Europe; their barbaric and violent tendencies are seen as a threat to European-ness, as reflected in political arguments against the inclusion of Turkey in the European Union. Yet, as Asad points out, European violence against European states is suppressed from collective memory: "Clearly neither the genocide practiced by the Nazi state nor its attempt to overwhelm Europe have led to feelings in Western Europe that would cast doubts on where Germany belongs" (2003:160). Asad argues that far from diluting Germany's European-ness, state violence ultimately strengthens European solidarity. Violence is ultimately intimately bound with the liberal project and as such certain forms of state violence and repression are understood to be necessary in order to realize a liberal future. We can trace the roots of policies of coercive liberalism to the "civilizing missions" of Western imperial and colonial regimes and to recent U.S. foreign policy in Iraq and Iran, which positions certain groups as incapable of self-governance and reason (Razack 2008).

Asad describes liberal violence (as opposed to the putative violence of illiberal regimes) as translucent: "It is the violence of universalizing reason itself. For to make an enlightened space, the liberal must continually attack the darkness of the outside world that threatens to overwhelm that space. Not only must that outside be conquered, but in the garden itself there are always weeds to be destroyed and unruly branches to be cut" (2003: 60). Thus racism and racial violence are part and parcel of liberalism (Sheth 2009). Within current narratives on Muslims in Europe, there is an understanding that nations must actively manage and control Muslim populations through policies that limit the flow of outsiders from without and that enforce liberal values within. Politicians argue that former policies of cultural recognition and acceptance have brought Western liberal nations to the brink of crisis and so it is now time for more "active, muscular" approaches, as Cameron suggests.

This book explores the contradictory ways policies claiming to encourage integration enact exclusion and isolation. For example, while claiming to encourage the integration of Muslim women into French society, the ban on *hijab* limits women's expressive participation in schools, the labor market, and public spaces (Amnesty International 2012). As a result of such bans, Muslim (and Sikh) students have been expelled from French schools, and among these a number have opted for long-distance learning within their homes while others have transferred to private Muslim schools (Amnesty International 2012: 44). A 2012 report by Amnesty International finds that following the passage of legislation banning the wearing of head coverings, there has been an escalation in incidences of violence against Muslim women (Amnesty International 2012: 5). The French bans direct collective anxieties and fears about the erosion of national values onto women's bodies, even providing a justification for everyday citizens to engage in public acts of violence and surveillance in the name of supporting integration. Thus, it becomes apparent that policies championing the benevolent goals of increasing the participation of Muslims in French society and discouraging discrimination in practice slide into the acts of everyday violence and coercion I explore here. The liberal nationalisms on which such developments are founded simultaneously seek to preserve and police particular racialized imaginaries and, as Holger describes in the opening of this chapter, they attempt to preserve the "one way to consider the world and how life should be lived."

In the chapters that follow I examine the narcissisms of Western liberal notions of individualism and secularism, and how they conceal their own imbrication with nationalism and Christianity. What is the liberal epistemology of nationalism that claims to be agnostic to any particular way of life asserting the universal values of equality, freedom, and tolerance? I document new grammars for conceptualizing and regulating immigrant Others and how Muslims in Western liberal societies are asked to shed traditions and practices that they hold central to their identities in order to be considered for inclusion in the nation. I also reveal the resistance, critical agency, and self-authoring of Muslim subjects who navigate everyday processes of coercive assimilation. In the end I address alternatives that might move Western liberal schooling toward more inclusive modes of education.

Chapter 2

Integration and Immigration

Creating Ideal Liberal Subjects

> On this cold drizzly Danish winter morning, passing the site of the Engby houses
> was particularly eerie. I stopped at the fence to watch construction workers
> shovel piles of sheetrock and steel into nearby dumpsters. One second-floor
> apartment still had three walls intact but the front wall was demolished, leaving
> its living room open to passers-by. The remnants of a family's life remained
> within the three walls—a sagging couch and an upturned table. I stared at these
> objects, as if to ask for an explanation of the scene, the lives of the people that sat
> at the table each night. I knew soon the site would be cleared, the bulldozers'
> work complete, and the area cleaned. I stopped into a local grocery next to the
> site, bought a small bag of almonds, and asked the Lebanese shop owner for his
> thoughts on the demolition. He said, "They say it's about improving this area but I
> think it's about something else, you know, the government's problems with the
> immigrants." When I asked where the residents of the demolished apartments
> had moved, he shrugged. "Those that have the money, could rent apartments here
> in Engby but those who didn't were forced to move to other parts of Denmark."
> Walking away from the site, along the chain-link fence toward the school, I
> wondered about those who were rebuilding lives in new communities, and new
> schools, in exile from all that is familiar.
>
> —Field notes, Engby, 12/6/2008

THIS SCENE reflects the contested place of Muslim immigration in liberal democratic societies. The Engby houses are home to 1,700 residents, 70 percent of
whom are first- and second-generation immigrants. The houses were built in the
1970s to provide public housing for workers who arrived to support the economic
boom of that era. Today, the houses are the target of integration reforms and
the subject of a racialized discourse about the problems of immigrant "ghettos" in Denmark. Drawing on Burchell, I conceive of liberal governance "not as
a theory, an ideology, a juridical philosophy of individual freedom" but rather
"as a particular way in which the activity of government has been made both
thinkable and practicable as an art" (1993: 269). How is it that government strat-

egies for policing immigrant communities become accepted by the public as necessary and warranted? In this chapter I explore how political strategies for managing Muslim immigrants in Danish society are inscribed in the landscape of the local communities and analyze how the *problems* of immigrant ghettos are (re)produced in Danish integration/assimilation strategies so as to justify the disciplining of Muslim immigrants. I ask: How do policies produce a series of stories and scripts about who immigrants are and what they require? What are the multiple ways that these policies exert their disciplinary power to cultivate ideal liberal subjects and how do they empower immigrants to liberalize themselves (Cruikshank 1993)? The reforms, technologies, and ways of seeing that are produced through policies are not bounded or isolated in individual sites; they are constantly being reproduced and remade by actors in various sites and institutions (Shore and Wright 1997). In this chapter, I walk the reader along the same chain-link fence in Engby that I traveled, from "official" acts promoted by integration policies to the particular technologies, figured identities, and perspectives on Muslim immigrants that are taken up in everyday interactions in schools.

Danish "Integration" Reforms

In analyzing how Muslim identities are figured in policies, communities, and schools, this study does not claim to portray the views of the Danish public as a whole; as in all ethnographies, the picture it presents is ultimately a "partial truth" (Clifford 1988), tracing the dominant discourses within the figured world of Danish immigration and how they are taken up by different actors. While I actively sought out incongruent voices and actors who resisted the dominant discourses, inevitably many voices are missing here. At times, I am uncomfortable offering up accounts that portray individuals in a less than flattering light. Nonetheless, I do so because it is critical to present stories that are different from the saturating anti-Muslim discourses that dominate our historical present and to show the material ways that young people experience these discourses. It is important to hold these examples of inclusion and exclusion up to the light, in order to discern how we might create more responsive policies and modes of schooling.

Denmark was the first country to create a government office dedicated to "integration." Between 2001 and 2012 the Ministry of Refugees, Immigration, and Integration Affairs implemented "integration" policies designed to restrict and control immigration. These policies were centered not on creating a society in which cultures mingled but rather on promoting assimilation to Danish norms and values. In an interview in 2001, Haarder, the first head of the ministry, presented his views on integration: "All that talk about cultural equality and that we must have ethnic equality. No we shall not. . . . In Denmark the Danish shall have preference. Of course. Anything else would be to disregard the culture. If you want a culturally based policy then it cannot be founded on equality between the Danish and the foreign. It must necessarily be a policy that favors the Danish" (*Kristeligt Dagblad*, July 12, 2001). Haarder's statement emphasizes that state policies must protect Danish culture even at the cost of "equality between the Danish and the foreign."

Beginning in 1999, the topic of Muslim immigration became salient in media and political discourses positioning immigrants as threatening the fundamental values of Danish society. Notions of immigrant Others who violate the basic values of Danish society circulate within the Danish media and discourse and are felt in everyday interactions within Danish society. They reflect what Peter Hervik (2004: 249) describes as a discourse of "unbridgeable differences" that produces a rigid dichotomy between "us" the Danes and "them" the immigrant Others. Much of this discourse focuses on immigrants' racial and cultural differences in such areas as clothing, food, and language and the challenges that these differences pose to Danish society. In Hervik's interviews, he found that participants identified racial and ethnic differences as a problem. One 27-year-old male participant argued that there is a limit to how many immigrants Denmark can absorb based on "When you reach a level where 'it' [cultural difference] becomes more visible" (2004: 259). Another argued, "When you are in another country, you should follow the rules and customs of that country, so that you won't upset anyone. I do get offended when I see a group of girls on their way to school. Their headscarves, I think, are always nicely ironed with beautiful lace and look very clean in the mornings, but I must say it annoys me" (2004: 259). Other participants spoke of the need for immigrants "to learn Danish," "to eat pork and drink beer," and "to blend in as best they can, so that they don't appear so provocative" (2004: 260).

The visible differences introduced by immigrants are widely perceived as disruptions of the social fabric. On a trip to Louisiana, a public art space north of Copenhagen, as I walked alongside two teenage participants wearing *hijab*, I noted that a number of visitors to the local museum were startled as they passed us through a narrow hallway. A tall blonde women who looked up just as she

Figure 2.1. Advertisement for the Danish People's Party Youth Group. "Danske Folkeparti 2001 Dit Danmark?" *Dansk Folkeblad*: 11.

passed seemed surprised and an older gentleman quickly stepped to the side to distance himself from us. It seemed clear that the presence of girls wearing *hijab* was unexpected and jarring to some in this space. Similarly the Danish Muslim participants of Iram Khawaja's research report they routinely experience a hyper-visibility in Danish society. Nesrin, a 27-year-old social worker, describes her frustration with co-workers and strangers who repeatedly comment on her *hijab.*

I get noticed, yes. I'm constantly being separated from the crowd . . . and all eyes are on me, and all the time I have to—no, I have to defend the veil all the time, defend Islam all the time, and it's not very pleasant to be the center of attention all the time. Sometimes, I just think, "Can't you just leave me in peace and accept me as I am?" (2014: 4; also Zaal et al. 2007)

As Hervik and others argue, in Denmark, there is a collective understanding of Danish peoplehood that is fundamentally challenged by immigration. Danish discourses emphasize how immigration threatens national identity and security, as well as the financial burden immigrants impose on the welfare state.

In 2000, the far-right anti-immigrant Dansk Folkeparti (Danish People's Party) launched a media campaign that portrayed Muslim men as criminals who threatened Danish equality as well as the basic safety of Danish citizens (see the poster in Figure 2.1).

YOUR DENMARK?

A multiethnic society with:

Mass rapes

Crude violence

Insecurity, Forced Marriage

Suppression of women

Gang Crime

IS THIS WHAT YOU WANT?

Do something—be a member of

THE DANISH PEOPLE'S PARTY'S YOUTH ORGANIZATION

A Danish future

This advertisement echoes the broader discourse on perceived threats to Danish values of gender equality and freedom. The Dansk Folkeparti advertisement implies that Denmark, as a "multiethnic society," is vulnerable to the constant threat of insecurity, violence, and oppression perpetrated by (an imagined) Muslim male oppressor. The Danish public and Danish leadership assume that ensuring a "Danish future" requires state intervention through polices that limit the influx of immigrants into Denmark and restrict the rights and mobility of immigrants who already live there. Deploying dystopic images of societal decline or "counter-worlds" replete with mass rape and crime, the advertisement appeals for political support and tries to justify restrictive policies that discipline Muslim communities in order to restore a "Danish future." While Danish political discourses have shifted away from this kind of explicit racism in recent years as the government has sought to distance itself from charges of racism, most restrictions on immigration and integration policies have remained in place (Mouritsen and Jensen 2014).[1]

A publication of the Ministry of Social Affairs and Integration entitled *Integration in Denmark* (Ministry of Social Affairs and Integration 2013) provides a historical perspective on how the dominant Danish political discourse views "problems" of immigration.

Danish society was characterized by some fundamental problems, including the fact that *social cohesion has been challenged by the lack of integration of migrants*. One reason for this was a lack of information and formal measures of integration in the 1960s and 1970s. At that time Denmark attracted a lot of migrants from countries such as Turkey and Yugoslavia who received working permits. The idea was that the migrants would reside in Denmark temporarily. However, eventually, the major part of the migrants stayed in Denmark—many of whom with a rather limited knowledge of the surrounding society. . . . Furthermore, integration problems increased further since the flow of newcomers in the 1980s and 1990s was not properly controlled and managed. By the end of the 1990s many urban communities reported massive *integration problems*. These issues were a deciding factor when the act of integration was launched in 1998. (2013: 5, emphasis mine)

Denmark's current social problems, according to this document, are a result of the failure of earlier generations of Danish politicians to properly control immigration and implement integration requirements and residency restrictions for guest workers in the 1960s and 1970s. There is an understanding that unless immigrants are "properly controlled and managed" they will violate the terms of their stay, overstaying their welcome (as they did in the 1960s and 1970s). According to this logic, it is migrants' refusal to adapt to the surrounding society that has created the "massive integration problems" that exist today. In the same way that policies invoke the future in the form of dystopic visions of an immigrant takeover, they also invoke history to justify action. As Wallerstein suggests, "Pastness is a tool that persons use against each other. Pastness is a central element in the socialization of individuals, in the maintenance of group solidarity, in the establishment of or challenges to social legitimization" (1991: 78). In order to justify more coercive policies, nationalist parties emphasize the previous government's failure to protect the nation from the threat of immigration.

Danish integration policies rely on the figured world of "us" and "them," on a romanticized notion of an ethnically homogenous "little Denmark" that is a paragon of universal equity and democracy that risks being overrun by barbaric immigrants who take advantage of the proffered good will and generosity of the Danish state and its public (Hervik 2004). As Stephen J. Ball argues, "policies are, pre-eminently, statements about practice—the way things could be or should be—which rest upon, and derive from, statements about the world—about the way things are. They are intended to bring about idealized solutions to diagnosed problems" (2006: 27). Policies shape citizens' understanding of the cultural worlds in which they live; they choreograph various actors' relationships to the state and to one another. They capitalize on and whip up public emotions in times of social change, creating feelings of unsettledness and anxiety in order to justify particular courses of action that promise to quell those anxieties. State polices increasingly draw on national anxieties by emphasizing the multiple external and internal challenges to nation-states:

These are some key areas of change and debate in contemporary society around which anxieties cluster, where traditional modes of regulation appear to have fragmented or collapsed; danger-points where a sort of collective anxiety begins to cluster, where a collective cry goes up that "something must be done." As such, they give us a set of symptomatic clues as to what seem to be the flashpoints, the unsettled issues, the underlying tensions, the traumas of the collective unconscious in late-modern societies. (Hall 1997: 231)

In Denmark those anxieties tend to cluster on some bodies more than others: immigrant women and children, who are obvious targets because their identities provide visible reminders of the changing nation.

Danish politicians within the Liberal Conservative government capitalized on public fears in the wake of the War on Terror to strengthen their own position in the government and to provide further justification for repressive interventions into immigrant communities in Denmark. Thus, current Danish integration policies are the result not only of the ambitions and efforts of a few key actors, but also of the nationwide post–9/11 politics of fear and national nostalgia for a return to Denmark before immigration. Similarly, politicians used the shootings in Copenhagen in 2015 to garner support for nationalist policies and integration reforms. Despite public pleas for unity between ethnic Danes and the immigrant community, leaders strategically deployed the events to call for more restrictions on immigration. A poll following the events found that in Denmark at that time, the far-right Danish People's Party was positioned to overtake the largest mainstream parties in Denmark. In France, if Marie Le Pen, from the far-right National Front, had run for president at that moment, she would have finished ahead of all of the other candidates, including Nicolas Sarkozy, the conservative former president of France, and François Hollande, the current Socialist president (Dominus 2015).

In recent years the Danish government has enacted policies in the name of helping immigrants and encouraging integration, but these polices actually achieve the opposite. For instance, in 2001 the government established so-called Starthelp benefits,[2] welfare provisions that in effect lowered the rate of social benefits for refugees in the first seven years of residency supposedly in order to increase their motivation to work. Beginning in 2002, the government tightened the requirements for obtaining residency and citizenship by, among other things, increasing the minimum age of potential immigrants eligible for family reunification from 18 to 24 in the government's "24-year rule." The government claimed this was intended to limit the flow of migrants to Denmark and to protect Muslim women from forced marriages. The law stipulates that in order to be granted a residence permit in Denmark when one or both individuals are from outside Denmark, the Nordic countries, or the European Union, the couple must have a greater affiliation with Denmark than any other country and both parties must be at least 24 years of age (MRII 2006). This law has been heavily criticized by the Danish Institute for Human Rights because of the lack of evidence that the practice of forced marriage is widespread in Denmark.

In 2006 the government introduced an integration contract and an integration exam in 2007. The language and culture portions of the integration exam are so difficult that they effectively bar citizenship to all but the most highly literate and resourced immigrants. From 2001 to 2010, there were thirteen changes along these lines to integration policies and a tightening of the citizenship requirements, a process described by a researcher at the Danish Institute of Human Rights as "a ladder with a new step added every time you reach the top" (Jensen et al. 2010: 61). The number of residency permits granted around this time shows that the new integration policies dramatically reduced the possibilities of residency for new immigrants. In 2003, 11,636 immigrants applied for residency in Denmark, and 9,360 were granted residency, a 19.6 percent refusal rate. By 2011, only 4,512 individuals applied for residency and only 2,726 were granted residency, representing an increase in the refusal rate to 39.6 percent (Ersbøll and Graveson 2010: 33). During the period from 2009 to 2014, the Danish government increasingly restricted access to residency and citizenship for immigrants, yet at the same time policy discourses shifted away from explicitly antiracist politics (Hedetoft, personal communication 2014).

Yet despite the Danish government's emphasis on democracy and equality, its policies enact technologies of concern that target immigrant communities. Several integration policies focus on the immigrants who are special objects of public anxiety and concern, that is, "non-Western" immigrants and particularly those from predominantly Muslim countries. For example, citizens of Australia, Canada, Israel, Japan, New Zealand, Switzerland, South Korea, and the United States are specifically exempted from signing the Danish integration contract and taking the integration test. [3]

The Danish integration regime involves a series of disciplinary technologies that seek to liberalize Muslim immigrants, "helping" them to transform themselves into acceptable national subjects. The 2005 action plan, *Employment, Participation and Equal Opportunities for Everyone*, of the Ministry of Gender Equality proposes "opinion adaptation" among immigrant youth, with the goal of educating Muslim immigrants about legal rights, education, forced marriage, violence, ideas of male and female roles in immigrant families, and the rights of women in Denmark (Jensen et al. 2010: 11).

Beginning in 2006, Danish integration policies intensified the emphasis on "active" citizenship. The integration contract of 2006 required migrants to sign a loyalty oath: "I will work actively for the integration of myself and my family into Danish society. . . . I understand and accept that the Danish language and knowledge of the Danish society is the key to an active life in Denmark. I will therefore do my best to learn Danish and acquire knowledge about Danish society as soon as possible" (Ministry of Social Affairs and Integration 2006: 1). This kind of active citizenship places the responsibility on immigrants to "integrate" themselves into Danish society and establishes a series of disciplinary measures for those who do not do so quickly enough.

Hedetoft documents the shift in Danish policies from a rights-based notion of liberalism to a duty-based regime:

The new, liberalist modality demands that ethnic minorities prove their economic self-reliance through educational performance, snappy acquisition of linguistic skills, and proactive integration into the labour-market . . . thus ridding themselves of dependence on government aid. Failing that, they have to carry the penalty in the form of reduced payments (or none at all) and additional demands, incentives or pressures to return "home," diminished hopes for permanent residence (let alone citizenship), . . . [creating as the only option] a life lived permanently on the margins of society. (2006: 414)

The state justifies its differential treatment of immigrants and its two-tiered social benefits scheme in terms of a liberal concern for immigrants that encourages them to take advantage of what Danish leaders see as the full benefits of Danish society. Mustafa, a recently arrived refugee who was a participant in a qualitative study of Starthelp, explains:

When I came to know that newly arrived persons like me are entitled to lower benefits than others I became very angry and sad. I felt that I was not trusted as if they believed that I would not look for a job if I got the same amount of money as the Danes. Instead of feeling grateful for having asylum in Denmark, I feel offended at not being appreciated by others. (Ghosh and Juul 2008: 97)

Aware of his positioning within Danish integration regimes and a racialized hierarchy, Mustafa criticizes his treatment as a problematic resident who requires state encouragement to engage with society productively.

Within current "integration" regimes, social benefits are not presented as a right, but rather an incentive to encourage immigrants to acquire Danish cultural values and practices. Nikolas Rose describes how advanced liberal societies exercise social control that emphasizes individual "choice" and encourages individuals to be active agents in furthering their own interests and those of their families. He concludes: "The powers of the state thus [must] be directed to empowering the entrepreneurial subjects of choice in their quest for self-realization" (Rose 1999: 142). The Danish government's June 2003 white paper, *Visions and Strategies for Better Integration*, a comprehensive report setting out the government's understanding and rationale for Danish integration policies, contends that:

Something for something must be the guiding principle of the coming years' integration policy. If a foreigner displays special initiatives to become integrated, he or she must be rewarded. The same applies to local councils, enterprises and citizens who contribute in a positive way to the integration process. Successful integration is in fact our common responsibility. If, on the other hand, a person refuses an assigned job, the cash box will be slammed shut. (MRII 2003)

Although the white paper frames successful integration as "our common responsibility," it makes it clear that individual immigrants are ultimately responsible for their own integration. The government promises to reward those who successfully integrate themselves with Danish society while disciplining those who refuse. It is important to point out that while the integration policies produce clear ideas about immigrant "culture" and the ways immigrants violate Danish norms (e.g., through the wearing of *hijab*), they do not explicitly define Danish values and Danish culture. Instead, Danish values are nebulously represented by the universalized liberal tropes of freedom, equality, and democracy. As Jensen and colleagues explain, "the benchmark of successful integration seems to be 'cultural transformation' although the actual content of this transformation remains open. Integration is thus paradoxical; the 'goal' is unknown yet essential in order to be included (e.g., by permanent residence permit or citizenship). Furthermore, [the substantive goal] can and will be changed continuously both symbolically and in practice; for example by numerous changes in the immigration and integration policies" (Jensen et al. 2010: 61). Within these technologies of concern, resisting the state's project has serious implications: failure to meet the terms of integration means that one is deemed unworthy of citizenship. And those who fail to meet these expectations are understood to be responsible for their own exclusion, existing outside the bounds of state concern.

Figuring Others and Justifying Intervention: Producing Citizens through Policy

Policies produce not only "problems" and "solutions," but also abstracted and distilled notions of identities. These static stereotypes, or "figured identities," carry with them specific expectations of behavior, social positioning, and charters for action. In this section I examine how Muslim identities are figured in policies, produced as emblems of broader social problems that require immediate public attention and action. Figured identities reflect the local figured worlds in which they are reproduced as well as broader social categories of racial, ethnic, and religious difference and durable historical narratives.

Liberal societies, including Denmark, produce notions of the Other through processes of essentialism and racialization that are both flexible and fixed (Silverstein 2005). They are flexible enough to be projected onto individuals from a wide diversity of class, ethnic, and national backgrounds, but they retain their shape in terms of attributing particular essentialized characteristics and tendencies to individuals who fall into the category of immigrant (Maira 2009). In Denmark, the category of "immigrant" is not ascribed to all individuals who may legally be included by having been born outside of Denmark. Rather, the category implicitly references Muslim immigrants and their children. Vanessa, a student in my study who was Christian from Romania, described her relationship to the category of immigrant: "My classmates see me as a Danish girl. They don't treat me like they would treat, say some other girls from Turkey. They wouldn't say 'like you're an immigrant.'" When describing the problems in the schools with immigrant students, Vanessa included herself in the category of "we" the Danish students. It is clear to Vanessa and to the other girls in her class that the category of immigrant does not refer to her.

Processes of figuring involve *talking and not talking* about constructions of racial difference. Danish integration policies make no direct reference to "Muslim" immigrants or to the practices of "Islam," but instead resort to implicit references. As mentioned earlier, an integral part of Denmark's self-image centers on being a benevolent and enlightened nation where racism has no place. As such, policies reference "immigrants," "foreigners," "ethnic minority families," and "Third World nationals" to describe Muslim refugees and immigrants and specific references to Muslim traditions, like the wearing of *hijab*, are cloaked, in this case, in the generalized language of "choice of clothing." But it is clear that integration policies target Muslim immigrants and refugees rather than those from the EU countries or the United States (Mouritsen and Jensen 2014).

European monitoring organizations like the Office of the United Nations High Commissioner for Refugees (UNHCR) and the UN Committee on the Elimination of Racial Discrimination (CERD) have publically raised concerns about the discriminatory nature of Danish integration policies, and in response there has been a shift toward generalizing specific concerns about Muslim communities in the neutral language of policy. In addition, as I argue elsewhere (Jaffe-Walter 2013), technologies of concern deploy liberal values in ways that are racializing, simultaneously constructing notions of Western superiority and Muslim barbarism through the shorthand of well-known tropes that do not require an explicit stating of the particulars. They engage in what Mamdani calls a "culturalization" of political conflict, claiming that culture is "the dividing line between those in favor of a peaceful, civic existence and those inclined to terror" (Mamdani 2005: 18). Wendy Brown argues that "the culturalization of conflict and of difference discursively depoliticizes both, while also organizing the players in a particular fashion, one that makes possible that odd but familiar move within liberalism: though 'culture' is what nonliberal peoples are imagined to be ruled by and ordered by, liberal peoples are considered to *have* culture or cultures" (2006: 150, emphasis in the original). The general feeling in Denmark is "we Danes" have culture while culture has "them" or while "they are a culture." This is reflected in government policies, such as the integration policy known as A New Chance for Everyone, that position immigrant women as "isolated—often in segregated residential areas too far from the remainder of society" (MRII 2005: 1). This society, is understood to be *Danish* society. Yet, such policies fail to recognize the rich network of social ties and cultural capital within immigrant communities. As Pia Kjærsgaard, the former head of the nationalist Dansk Folkeparti, stated: "It has been said that September 11 was the beginning of a struggle between civilizations. I disagree, because a struggle between civilizations would imply that there are two civilizations, and this is not the case. There is only one civilization, and it's ours" (Stanners 2012). [4]

Figuring Muslim Men

In setting out directives about how societies "should be," policies conjure notions of subjects who challenge these imagined ideals and hence require control and regulation. In setting out expectations for new citizens, Danish integration policies implicitly portray the Muslim male as oppressive and patriarchal and the Muslim female as "oppressed." For example, in order to apply for residency, all "Third World" immigrants must sign a pledge stating that "I understand and accept that it is punishable in Denmark to commit actual violence against or threaten one's spouse and others, including children.... I understand and accept that Danish society strongly condemns acts of terrorism ... [and] I understand

and accept that circumcision of girls and the use of force to contract marriage are punishable in Denmark." The pledge is designed with the expectation that an illiberal male subject who has a tendency toward violence, oppression, and sexual deviancy is the principle applicant.

Similarly, a guide for new immigrants in Denmark, *Citizen in Denmark: A Manual for New Members of Danish Society*, views immigrant men as prone to violations of Danish sexual boundaries and rape. The description on "the body and sex" begins as an explanation of the norms surrounding nudity and pornography in Danish society:

Whether or not you approve, you will often come across sex and nudity in Danish society. Newspapers write articles about sex and sex life, and adverts and commercials visually exploit the human body. This reflects a general social trend towards a more liberal view of sexual life. With this freedom, however, comes responsibility. This means there are limits on what you can and cannot do, and no one is allowed to force others to do things against their will. The assumption is that we respect each other's personal and sexual boundaries. *Semi-naked sunbathers in the park and on the beach or scantily clad or naked bathers, for example, should not be seen as an open invitation to sex*. In the same way, neither a person's body language nor provocative fashion should be interpreted as an open invitation to sex. Sexual assault must be reported to the police so that the offender(s) can be prosecuted. (MRII 2002: 126, emphasis mine)

This document appears to be a guide to Danish openness for the non-liberal subject. There is an assumption that "our" freedom and "openness" are vulnerable to "their" illiberal tendencies and inherently violent nature. The image of the sexually deviant Other has a long history in liberal enlightenment thinking. It is as if without the liberalizing work of the state to produce responsible subjects who are able to negotiate the "freedoms" of Danish society, Danish women would be victimized by immigrants (as we see in the Danish People Party's advertisement earlier in this chapter). Technologies of concern seek both to subdue the imputed violence of male immigrants and to liberate female Muslims, who are understood to be their captives.

Figuring Muslim Women and Justifying Intervention

Integration policies figure notions of immigrant families as segregated from the broader society and dominated by Muslim values; such families live in parallel societies, which threaten national values. In the 2003 the government white paper *Visions and Strategies for a Better Integration*, the Ministry of Refugees, Immigration, and Integration Affairs contends that

> many ethnic minority families adhere to the traditional role patterns, according to which women and girls are not considered equals of men and boys. This means that many minority women live an isolated life in their homes, and the young girls in particular face powerful control from their families. *It is crucial to break this isolation and give women the same, really equal opportunities as men.* In this connection it is essential that the women and young girls who opt to break out are offered help and support to make sure that this *cultural isolation* is not merely replaced by fear, loneliness and social isolation. (MRII 2003: 7, emphasis mine)

According to the white paper, immigrant women are subjected to "powerful control from their families" and are culture bound, forced to adhere to traditional gender roles within their families, yet, also fundamentally alone and culturally isolated, deprived of the "superior" culture of Danish society. According to Sherene Razack, European integration discourses produce a divide between the values of collectivist Muslim families and liberal societies: "The divide is between those who live as autonomous individuals and who make decisions without the influence of kin and community and those who live their lives within communities, the two sides serving to illustrate not only the unbridgeable cultural divide between the West and non-West but the non-West as a place of danger for women" (Razack 2008: 116). Within integration discourse and policies the frame is tightly focused on Muslim families and communities as requiring Western intervention and specifically on Muslim women who require saving.

The state's efforts are intended to transform immigrants into acceptable liberal subjects. The 2003 white paper explains: "Diversity can be a strength. But it may also involve the emergence of norm-based problems when, for obvious reasons, many people of foreign origin have other perceptions of right and wrong than those generally prevailing in Denmark" (MRII 2003: 4). The white paper continues by setting out a principle of integration: "We should not use culture as an excuse for oppressive family patterns" (MRII 2003: 5). In other words, it is critical to move beyond multicultural approaches that see "culture" as relative; it is time to act. The paper then moves from the problems of culture into a justification for action: "Respect for the private sphere and respect for individual freedom and personal integrity—concerning both adults and children—often clash in matters concerning family life and upbringing. *It is necessary for society to contribute more to a solution of the problem by defining a limit"* (MRII 2003: 7, emphasis mine).

In discussing limits, the document explains that governmental involvement with families is antithetical to a free and open society. It continues: "There are narrow limits as to how much society can and should be involved in [family affairs such as] parents' upbringing methods. But there *are* [emphasis in original] limits, as also children and young people are entitled to equality and respect for their personal integrity" (MRII 2003: 7). The document then cites the problems of forced marriage and female genital mutilation as a justification for state action and intervention. These practices provide a license for the state to move more deeply into the lives of immigrants to encourage the adoption of more "enlightened" Danish values.

I commonly heard a similar kind of vacillation in my interviews with teachers who moved between a desire to respect students' cultures and a desire to enforce a common culture. As a Danish literature teacher explained, "I really should respect their culture and values, I shouldn't tell them how to live but this is Denmark, and they should learn how to live here." I also heard school leaders and teachers invoke "the limits of our respect," echoing the language of policy. As mentioned, in a conversation with the principal about student's requests for a prayer space within the school, Per, the principal said, "To me it is more important that if you show your respect to other people, you also must know what the limits of this respect are." Throughout integration policies, political speeches, and in everyday discourses, individual actors invoke the need for a clear threshold, a cultural line that must be enforced. But in each case that threshold is defined in a different way—from Per, the principal who drew the line at providing space for prayer within the school to education officials who drew the line at having a population of more than 30 percent immigrant students in a *folkeskole*, to policy makers who insisted on the inculcation of Danish values. In each case there is an assumption that without this threshold that must be maintained, Western liberal values risk being submerged by a tide of Muslim immigrants.

Integration policies invoke the practices of forced marriage and female genital mutilation to provoke public attention and emotion and to project an image of the benevolent state protecting its residents from barbaric practices. Part of this "protection" is through encouraging assimilation to Danish norms. Clearly, the practices of female genital mutilation and forced marriage should not be condoned and young women who are victims of these practices deserve support and protection. However, it is critical to consider how policies blindly "figure" entire populations, projecting the stories of a few onto diverse communities. Even though forced marriage is strictly outlawed within Islam and there is no evidence that forced marriage is widespread in Denmark, the topics of forced marriage and violence against immigrant women dominate the Danish media and have come to represent immigrant "culture" (Andreassen 2012). This is very different from how the media and public discourse treat acts of violence by ethnic Danish men. Instead of being treated as reflecting the true nature of Danish people beholden to their culture, violence by ethnic Danes is dismissed as isolated incidents committed by lone individuals. While domestic violence is seen as a distinctly "Muslim" phenomenon in Denmark, during the decade of 2000 to 2010 it is estimated that between 28,000 to 42,000 ethnic Danish women were the victims of domestic violence—and yet the media remain silent on this issue (Andreassen 2012: 146).

Discursive images of barbaric Muslim women and men are easily taken up within the national imagination of Western nations struggling with the increased complexity of growing diversity and the perceived cultural threats related to globalization. These images reinforce notions of national superiority, the idea that "we" represent gender equity and enlightenment while "they" represent a backward culture that deserves to be scrutinized. In Denmark there is an implicit assumption that the country is a paragon of gender equality. However, Danish notions of equality warrant a footnote. An international study of women's participation in senior management of business finds that Denmark ranks thirty-seventh out of forty countries, with women making up only 15 percent of the leadership of Danish companies. In comparison, Turkey ranks eighth, with women making up 31 percent of the leadership of Turkish companies (Grant Thornton 2012: 5). Danish media and public discourse wield the topic of "gender equity" to reinforce the notion of emancipated Danish women as superior to immigrant Others; conversations about Danish women's struggles for equity are not as readily engaged.

How Figuring Silences Structural Exclusion

Focusing the lens on immigrant families as a site of intervention, Danish integration policies obscure other factors that might complicate the participation of immigrants in Danish society, such as discrimination in institutions and the labor market or the contracting economy. In integration policies, discrimination is located *within* immigrant communities, presented in terms of the "gender barriers" faced by immigrant women at the hands of Muslim men. There is very little reference in integration policies to other forms of structural discrimination against immigrant communities. The 2005 document *Employment, Participation and Equal Opportunities for Everyone* states its goals of addressing "gender barriers," or the challenges facing women in Muslim communities: "Tradition, culture, family patterns and a lack of Danish skills . . . result in the fact that many immigrants, and especially immigrant women, only to a limited extent have been in contact with the labor market" (Ministry of Gender Equality 2005: 25; translation in Jensen et al. 2010: 10). The document makes frequent mention of "gender barriers" facing immigrant women created by the putatively oppressive gender roles of immigrant families rather than addressing the structural problems that complicate women's access to jobs.

A specific cultural marker of Muslim women's subordinate status is the *hijab*. The 2005 Danish policy document *A New Chance for Everyone*, discusses the problem of access to jobs for women who wear *hijab*, pointing out that "clothes are a factor that can influence women's possibilities for employment" (MRII 2005: 10). However, the document does not suggest that this should be addressed through antidiscrimination campaigns directed at employers nor does it make specific suggestions to women who wear *hijab*. Instead the statement about clothes and employment is followed by a section on "how to break down specific prejudices and sexual role patterns within families." The document thus frames the "problem" as the patriarchal practices of Muslim traditions, not the discrimination against some Muslim men and women in the Danish labor market.

There is an implicit suggestion here that in their refusal to downplay their cultural markers, women wearing *hijab* are soliciting anti-immigrant responses. As I was wandering through a mall with my three focal Muslim participants in 2008, Aliyah and Sara looked wistfully into a clothing shop and Sara said, "Dhalia is so lucky that she can work and earn money because she doesn't wear *hijab*; we could never get hired in a Danish store." In 2013, this barrier became more pronounced for Sara, who could not finish her secretarial degree because she could not find an internship that would accept a woman wearing *hijab*.

Similarly, the *New Chance for Everyone* mentions Danish employers' discrimination against Muslim men. It explains that employers often perceived immigrant men to be aggressive or sexist. However, it does not suggest that these stereotypes are in any way unfounded, as in fact they are. It proceeds to cite a

Swedish study that finds that immigrant men have difficulty accepting direction from female superiors and doing jobs considered to be "women's" work (Jensen et. al 2010: 11). The discussion of workplace discrimination against immigrant men reproduces figured identities of Muslim men and implicitly suggests that the discrimination they experience is somehow justified. By emphasizing the problems with Muslim men, the document fails to account for the structural discrimination that hampers access to jobs, most importantly Danish employers' biases in hiring, as is evident in, for example, evaluating résumés based on the applicant's surname (and rejecting applicants with Arabic-sounding names) or on characteristics assumed to be correlated with a particular ethnicity (Hjarnø and Jensen 1997: 1).

Policy Solutions for Cultural Problems

Policies construct figured identities that rally public support for their goals in order to produce public understandings that "something must be done." In Razack's words, "The body of the Muslim woman, a body fixed in the Western imaginary as confined, mutilated, and sometimes murdered in the name of culture, serves to reinforce the threat that the Muslim man is said to pose to the West and is used to justify the extraordinary measures of violence and surveillance required to discipline him and Muslim communities" (2008: 130). Technologies of concern slide seamlessly from the figuring of identities to practices of coercive assimilation that have significant material consequences for immigrant communities. Policies create a world where the destruction of homes and the assimilation of young people's identities are seen as a natural solution to a pressing problem.

Within the language of Danish integration policies, disciplining is cloaked in the liberal tropes of democracy and equality, as assimilative technologies are justified in the name of reducing discrimination and eliminating "gender barriers." Integration policies deploy technologies to decrease immigrants' exposure to the values of their families and communities while increasing their exposure to Danish traditions and culture within Danish public institutions. As the 2003 white paper explains: "School is an essential element in the lives of all children. In addition to learning the subjects taught, pupils become acquainted at school with society's unwritten norms, values, and rules. It is at school *that they learn to create their own non-familial relations*" (MRII 2003: 8, emphasis mine). By moving young immigrants away from their families and into state institutions, policies promise to provide opportunities for students to enjoy increased gender equality and freedom. In the same way, integration policies seek to bring immigrant children into the Danish educational system at younger and younger ages. In 2004, eligibility for Danish language reception programs was changed from four to three years of age. And in order to further "encourage" immigrant parents to put their children into preschool, legislation passed in 2011 declared that parents living in "ghetto" areas who are unemployed would lose public benefits if they did not enroll their children in language-stimulation programs (Ministry of Children, Equality, Integration and Social Affairs 2015). In addition, immigrant children were encouraged to attend Danish boarding schools and to become more involved in Danish sporting associations. Policies stated that these steps were critical in ensuring proper integration in school programs.

Such integration comes at a cost, however. As we have mentioned, integration legislation enacts measures that limit immigrant youths' exposure to their families' cultures, traditions, and homelands. The Aliens Act (2013) threatened to revoke the residency permits of families that sent their children on trips to their native countries. It framed visits to native countries as "re-education journeys or other stays abroad with negative influence on schooling and integration" (Ministry of Justice 2013: chapters 3 through 17). Under the guise of concern, policies such as this position home visits as potentially damaging to young peoples' development, social relations, and integration within Denmark. In contrast, ethnic Danish students' absences from school for ski vacations and other holidays are tolerated and commonplace. In Chapter 4 I explore how immigrant students' transnational attachments to home countries are deeply grounding and help them negotiate experiences of discrimination in Denmark. Yet restrictions on immigrant home visits are part of a broader constellation of policies that restrict immigrant families' ability to transmit their cultural heritage. [5]

Technologies of concern rely on public institutions to transform immigrants into enlightened liberal subjects who can be seamlessly incorporated into the nation. As Rose explains: "In advanced liberal societies, one family of control practices operates by affiliating subjects into a whole variety of practices in which the modulation of conduct according to certain norms is, as it were, designed in. These are the practices that Deleuze referred to in his thesis that we now lived in 'societies of control'" (Rose 1999: 325). Denmark's integration project positions institutions and associations as being capable of breaking the bonds of immigrants' perceived cultural isolation (Hedetoft 2006). Danish educational institutions have always played an important role in the national project as sites of civic enculturation, taking on the civilizing duties of families and socializing Danish youth in Danish norms and values (Gilliam and Gulløv 2014; Jenkins 2011). In Danish schools, there is a parallel focus on teaching youth to become "proper persons" so that they may lead a fulfilling life in Danish society as well as on ensuring a high degree of social solidarity within the national community. There has been an assumption that the time-honored practices of Danish schooling are universally effective in attending to children's needs and producing social equity (Gilliam 2007). As such, it is natural that the state would look to Danish schools to solve the perceived social problems related to immigration. There is no doubt that getting young people more engaged in schools and community activities promotes their social incorporation in the larger society, and this is especially so for young people from low-income backgrounds. However, what is problematic is when policy technologies promote affiliation only within national spaces and erode young peoples' connections to their cultural and religious values and transnational attachments.

Encouraging Intimacy with Danish Values: Nationalist Education Reforms

Since the mid-nineteenth century, Danish schooling has tried to convey national values implicitly through everyday interactions, what Billig (1995) describes as banal nationalism. However, the challenge of Muslim immigrants has been understood to require a clearer and more explicit focus on Danish values, what Jenkins (2011: 61) calls a "systemization of Danishness" or "Danification" that makes explicit what was previously implicit. Along with this increased attention to Danish culture have come policies that aim to reduce support for any programs that recognize the culture or languages of immigrant students. In the 1990s, the Ministry of Education required municipalities to provide native-language classes for immigrant students from all countries and backgrounds and provided the necessary funding. In 2002, as part of the broader integration regime, the ministry changed this policy to provide state-funded native-language instruction only for students who are citizens of other EU member states, European Economic Area states, and Greenland and the Faroe Islands. For most Muslim immigrant students from Turkey, Lebanon, and Somalia (considered Third World countries), there is no requirement to provide native-language classes.

In 2006, the Committee on the Elimination of Racial Discrimination of the United Nations issued a critique of Denmark's language instruction policies:

The Committee, while welcoming the municipalities' obligation to offer mother tongue teaching to bilingual students coming from or originating from the European Union and European Economic Area countries, as well as from the Faroe Islands and Greenland, regrets that in 2002, the municipalities' obligation to do so for bilingual students from other countries was repealed and that municipalities no longer receive financial support for such purpose. The Committee recommends that the State party review its policy, taking into consideration its obligation under the convention not to discriminate against persons on the basis of their national or ethnic origin nor against any particular nationality. *The committee recalls that differential treatment based on nationality or ethnic origin constitutes discrimination.* (CERD, 2006: 69th session, July 18, emphasis mine)

This policy of distinguishing between students from European countries and "Third World nationals" creates a racial hierarchy in which immigrant students from Third World countries are entitled to fewer resources than ethnic Danes and other Europeans. For example, if a Spanish-speaking family moves to Denmark, the determination of whether the children will receive funds or not depends on their national origin. If the family is from Spain, the children will receive free instruction in Spanish for their entire educational career.[6] If the family is from Peru, the children will be denied native-language instruction (Horst 2010). This policy has affected a significant population of immigrant students; in 2005, 62,000 bilingual children of third-country origin lost their right to mother-tongue instruction (Timm 2008: 4). This is yet another example of policy technologies targeting particular populations, limiting Muslim and other "Third World" students' access to native-language instruction. Although the policy does not rule out the possibility of individual municipalities providing funding for mother-tongue instruction, the withdrawal of national funding led to the de facto elimination of such instruction in Danish schools.

Other changes in education policies ensure that schools emphasize Danish culture and religion. The Folkeskolen Amendments of 2000, 2001, and 2002 mandated that schools increase instructional time devoted to the teaching of Danish culture and religion. According to the Folkeskole Consolidation Act of 2000, a central goal of schooling is to "familiarize students with Danish culture and contribute to their understandings of other cultures" (Danish Ministry of Education n.d.). As a result of policy changes in the Folkeskole Act of 2006, Christian studies became one of the required high school exit exams and a required course of study in every year of the *folkeskole*. Other cultures and religions are taught and represented in schools, though as I reveal in other chapters, references to Islam and to the traditions and values of immigrant families are often silenced or contested in the space of school.

Ghetto Politics

A New Chance for Everyone launched a series of desegregation initiatives that sought to address the problem of "gender barriers" through the demolition of housing (such as the demolitions of the Engby houses mentioned in the opening of this chapter), the relocation of residents, increased surveillance and policing, mandatory language-learning opportunities for children, and reductions in government benefits. In a speech to the Danish Parliament, Prime Minister Lars Løkke Rasmussen commented on the problems of immigrant ghettos:

We must take determined action. The time has come to put an end to a misguided tolerance for the intolerance that dominates in parts of the ghettos. Let us speak openly about it: In areas where Danish values do not have a firm foothold, ordinary solutions will be rendered completely inadequate. It does not help to pump more money into painting facades. We are facing special problems that require special solutions. We will tear the walls down. We will open the ghettos up to society. (Rasmussen 2010)

While integration policies typically emphasize the benevolence of the government in supporting Muslim women to move beyond their oppressive families, Rasmussen's speech does not cloak coercive action in the liberal tropes of equality and democracy. He suggests that liberal societies have gone too far in their "misguided tolerance" and describes the problem of areas where "Danish values do not have a firm foothold." When riding public transportation, I watched as women wearing *hijab* were met with cold stares when they entered a crowded bus or a train (also see Khawaja 2014).[7] I heard narratives similar to Rasmussen's about immigrant takeover in Danish classrooms. For instance, in a class discussion about my life in New York City in an English class, Mathias, the teacher, asked me, "Do you have the same problem in New York with the kebob places taking over? It's hard to find decent Danish food anymore here in Engby." Moving beyond the cloaked language of liberalism and official humanism, Rasmussen signals to his public that it is time to take decisive action to restore Danish values and culture.

De-ghettoization policies produce notions of immigrant communities as sites of crime and deviance. They reproduce a racialized discourse about immigrant "ghettos" that reverberates through communities and schools. In Engby the local newspaper decried the problems of ghettos. One headline announced, "Engby Is a Danish Harlem"; the accompanying article indicated that the streets were no longer safe for the elderly because of crimes perpetrated by immigrant boys and announced that it was "grotesque" that Engby was "becoming like Soweto or Harlem." The media used notions of "ghetto" that in essence created a public call for de-ghettoization policies. When I first began my work in Engby, the Engby houses consisted of four buildings, with a grassy area with gardens and a playground in the center. At the end of the demolition discussed in the opening of this chapter, one building was torn down, essentially "opening" the housing complex to the outside community to expose the residents of those houses to Danish values. Thus, media representations and policymaking go hand in hand, reflecting particular "truths" about who immigrants are and what they require, justifying coercive action.

In discussions about the Engby houses at Engby School, teachers and students reproduced figured identities of immigrants and a culturalist view of the retrograde values of immigrant families. Lena, a teacher and assistant principal at Engby School, said:

They are quite violent, a lot of these ethnic minorities, and especially the ones living in the houses . . . and I think it is because we have a lot of students at this school where they still speak Arabic and Turkish in their homes and they do not speak Danish. Also because the mother is not speaking Danish and because mom perhaps has never gone to school. Some mothers have actually been taken out from poor areas in Turkey or Lebanon and been married to boys and put up here and they still do not understand what we are talking about.

In her narrative, Lena associates the Engby houses with violence, gender oppression, the failure to integrate (i.e., refusal to speak Danish), and the lack of education. Her words echo the language of integration policies surrounding the problems of gender barriers and the self-segregation of immigrants.

Several immigrant Muslim male students in my study described negotiating this racialized discourse on a daily basis in the Engby houses. Male

Muslim students explained that they were more likely to receive negative messages about their identities in the area surrounding the Engby houses and to be viewed there through the lens of the "criminal." Nadir, a Turkish student, explained that in Engby, "If someone sees an immigrant guy walking around, they are going to think he is going to get in trouble or fight. In Copenhagen they aren't going to think that." In an interview, a male Palestinian student, Jamail, drew an identity map shown in Figure 2.2, an image that reflected the messages he received about his identity in different spaces. In his picture of the Engby houses, he drew a person yelling, "Perker svin." Jamail and his friend Rahim explained that *perker* is a racialized term for Muslims in Denmark, a term that belongs in a class with the most denigrating of racial slurs.

On the other side of his map, Jamail draws a figure in Lebanon that calls out: "Habibi come." *Habibi* is an Arabic term of affection used between male friends. In the chapters that follow I provide a deeper analysis of how male Muslim students negotiate the features of their figured identities in the course of their daily lives, but I include this image here to show how integration politics amplify processes of racialization that move through the geographies of communities and schools and that are projected onto youth.

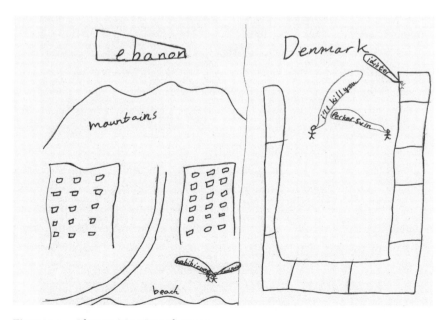

Figure 2.2.   Identity Map: Jamail, age 15.

Ghetto Schools

In 2009, sixty-four schools in Denmark were labeled "ghetto schools" because they had a population of more than forty percent immigrant students and were located near urban areas with large numbers of immigrant residents. The cities of Copenhagen and Aarhus developed programs to "improve" student performance by distributing immigrant students from ghetto schools to schools with large numbers of ethnic Danish students. These programs sought to improve educational conditions for immigrant students by increasing their exposure to the putatively superior values of ethnic Danish students, and also to help improve the public image of ghetto schools. In an article in the *Copenhagen Post*, a head teacher describes the success of the initiatives: "When registering, [ethnic Danish] parents don't ask as much about the number of bilingual students as they used to. . . . Today, they know that there are lots of ethnically Danish students" (*Copenhagen Post* 2012). While busing policies claim to be about improving outcomes for immigrant students, they are actually more addressed at easing public anxieties about Muslim immigrants and improving the image of Danish schools with large immigrant populations.

In 2010, as some Danish schools were embarking on busing initiatives to reduce the percentage of immigrant students, Tove Hvid Persson, the director of a teacher education institute, spoke about the importance of accommodating immigrant students. In an interview for a teacher education publication she explained that it is imperative that school leaders focus on "creating a school where we see diversity as a benefit." The interviewer asked her, "Where is the line? Is it a success if there are 80 percent bilingual students in a school?" She replied, "No, we don't want to be a ghetto school. The success in attracting bilingual students can also become a *death route* where they are the only ones who sign up. We want diversity, and we will train teachers for the Danish primary school. Therefore, there must be a great representation of ethnic Danish students" (2010 Roskilde, emphasis mine)). While Persson emphasizes "diversity" as a positive attribute, a sign of the openness of Danish schools and Danish culture, she also constructs immigrant students in large numbers as potentially problematic, a "death route." Like other discussions about immigrants challenging the "limits" of "our" respect and tolerance, Persson's comments invoke images of immigrant takeover, suggesting that it is necessary to carefully manage immigrant populations.

Several educational anthropologists have opposed the busing policies, citing the negative effects on young people who were bused. As Christian Horst argues, "The number of bilingual students doesn't mean anything in itself. The important thing is how well each individual school is geared to accommodate its student group. . . . Instead of spreading out the bilingual students, they should train the teachers and ensure that some schools specialize in handling the bilingual students and catering to their needs. We need to stop seeing bilingual students as a disruptive element" (*Copenhagen Post* 2012). Horst's critique highlights the nationalist portrayal of immigrant students in terms of their perceived cultural deficits and underscores the need for more reforms that expand the capacity of teachers and schools to educate immigrant students, a point I take up later in this book.

How Figured Identities Echo through the Spaces of Schools

Within Engby School, which is next door to the Engby houses, there were frequent discussions among teachers, students, and the outside community about the school's image as a "ghetto school" because of its high percentage of immigrant students. Teachers told me about the declining number of ethnic Danish students and the increasing numbers of immigrant youth from the local public housing project. As one Danish student explained, "When parents come and see all the brown faces, they don't think it's a good school." Over the years, as ethnic Danish families chose not to send their children to Engby School, teachers were let go and, as enrollment declined, the school budget was slashed. Teachers expressed nostalgia for the days when the school was a real "Danish" school. Within these politics there was a sense that Muslim students were a liability to the school's image and survival, bringing a heightened awareness of the number of girls wearing *hijab* in the school photo.

Through the course of my research I identified several school-based narratives about the importance of encouraging Muslim students' "proximity" (Anderson 1996) to Danish students. Teachers expressed faith that Danish modes of progressive education would help to enlighten and transform Muslim youth into ideal liberal subjects who "have their own opinions" and conform to Danish norms of belonging. They assume that the perceived social and educational challenges facing immigrant students at Engby School are a result of foreign, and especially Muslim, students' traditions and cultural values and that they live in the Engby houses. Throughout my interviews, teachers talked about their work to help students (particularly girls) to become autonomous individuals who embraced critical outlooks on the world. But within these discussions of individualism, I heard again and again that Muslim students, both boys and girls, were inherently not independent thinkers, and hence unable to take part in classroom debates, because of their upbringing and "traditions."

A number of teachers pointed out that Engby School was not a typical Danish school because of the presence of the Engby houses. As Birgitte, a ninth-grade teacher, suggested, "You should visit a school to the south of here, like in Velhaven. I think you'll find that the students are very different. Here we have this housing project and in the houses we have a lot of criminals and social problems." Mathias, another ninth-grade teacher, shared the same sentiment and associated the poor educational outcomes documented for immigrant students with the way they were socialized in their families:

> If you travel up the coast ten miles you will see that the students are completely different. I have a friend that teaches in Ryborg and it's amazing the things that his students cover. They know more, they have been brought up to ask questions, they speak their mind, as long as you just get involved in the conversation, then you'll learn something. Here in my class, there are like ten people in the class that don't say anything, they are at the point where they don't dare to say anything.

Here, Mathias contrasts the work of a teacher in a school with affluent ethnic Danish students to his own work with immigrant students. He constructs ethnic Danish students as ideal citizens, students who "speak their mind" and "have been brought up to ask questions." Mathias expresses ambivalence about working in Engby School with such a high percentage of immigrant students who complicate his efforts to foster inquiry in the classroom. It is clear that Mathias views the silence of Muslim students in his classrooms as evidence that their cultural and religious affiliations are antithetical to the development of critical thinking skills. [8] Two other teachers brought up the topic of "cousin marriage" to provide an explanation of the perceived social problems and cultural deficits of some immigrant students at Engby School. Hedda, an eighth-grade teacher, shared her thoughts after describing the challenge of dealing with an unruly immigrant boy in her class.

> Hedda: They are now talking about how in Denmark young people [immigrants] are marrying their cousins because they inherit not so good genes, and it is causing big problem. They tell the young people, don't marry their cousins. [*pauses*] Well, I should say, I am not a racist, that is not why I say it. They are very nice people and it is such a shame that they have those problems but it's because they only do what

their parents do or make the girls do. I think it is getting better because the more
[they are] educated, the more the girls will say no.

Reva: What is the solution?

Hedda: Democracy. Danish democracy. If you vote, you can be heard.

It is interesting that her discussion travels from her understanding of the
challenges facing an individual male student in one class to ideas about immigrant girls being forced into practices of cousin marriage to notions of Danish
democracy and the opportunities afforded to immigrants in Denmark. Cousin
marriage, discursively linked to forced marriage, is thought to be a common
practice in immigrant ghettos. Using the liberal tropes of democracy to insulate
herself from charges of racism, Hedda presents culturalist notions of oppressed
girls and deviant Muslim practices and frames schooling as a site of liberation
for these girls. Teachers at Engby School project images of "ideal" individual
subjects based on liberal ideas of a rational individuated subject who designs
individual relationships with culture and religion. This ideal is set in opposition to an Other who blindly accepts the orthodoxies of religion and tradition
(Brown 2006; Asad 2003).

Encouraging Proximity to Danish Values

The assimilationist regime of the Danish government from 1999 to the present
reflects deep societal anxieties about the perceived challenges of immigration.
Hedetoft argues that these anxieties are wrongly projected onto immigrant
communities. In his words, "It is globalization" that is the culprit and the larger
threats to Western welfare states such as "the loss of traditional sovereignty in
the context of growing globalization and Europeanization, de-industrialization,
and the transition from a service based to a high tech economy" (Hedetoft 2006:
425). Yet, anxieties about a contracting economy and an increasingly diverse
Denmark are obfuscated, channeled into technologies of concern that attempt
to regulate immigrant bodies and communities. As Lowe explains, immigrants
serve as "a phantasmatic site, on which the nation projects a series of condensed,
complicated anxieties regarding external and internal threats to the mutable coherence of the national body" (Lowe 1996: 18).

Under the banner of a noble struggle for equality and connecting to a long
tradition of liberal humanitarian action across the world, integration policies
neutralize cultural difference and make it more tolerable, whether through the
"opening" of immigrant enclaves to society or through the coercive assimila-

tion of immigrant youth who represent the next generation. But the liberal tropes of concern are not only exclusively deployed to justify and to preserve the good name of Western liberal nations; they are also deeply felt, lingering in the hearts of the concerned and in the daily lives of those who are the object of that concern. In the next chapter, I move to consider in more depth how figured identities and technologies of distribution and proximity are taken up within everyday interactions between teachers and immigrant students at Engby School. I offer insight into how some teachers understand their work in terms of liberating immigrant girls from the perceived confines of immigrant families and how their efforts to expose students to Danish norms of sexuality and intermarriage are enacted and experienced by the Muslim students themselves.

While much research in psychology and immigration confirms that linear models of assimilation that assume a shedding of one identity and a claiming of a new one do not reflect the experience of today's immigrant populations, current integration discourses and modes of immigrant incorporation still assume this as a goal. Within Danish and European discourses, there is an understanding that the failure of immigrants to adequately adapt to the host countries remains a serious problem and threat. Recently, I shared a cab with a German anthropologist who asked, "But where does it end if we let them keep their traditions? We will have countries within countries? We will have minorities telling us how we can live?" An American anthropologist chimed in: "And, how will we ever hold classes if we honor everyone's holidays? It would be chaos. We would never have time to teach." I often find myself in conversations like this that paint a grim picture of a chaotic, dark future. My interlocutors ask: "How much difference can we tolerate? At what point will 'they' threaten 'our' civilization and way of living? How do we get 'them' to blend in so as to retain our 'us-ness'?" The voices of young people in this book challenge this view, revealing dialogical subjectivities and possibilities for being both firmly rooted in particular national contexts where their expressions of identity need not undermine a "nation," while also a part of diasporic webs of belonging.

Shore and Wright argue that policies produce normative claims that present problems and solutions "as if they were the only ones possible while enforcing closure or silence on other ways of thinking or talking" (Shore and Wright 1997: 3). Western liberal understandings of the "problems" of immigration are tightly framed, focused on intervention into Muslim communities while ignoring broader forms of structural exclusion and the day-to-day realities of young peoples' lives, experiences, and desires. In order to deepen understandings of the challenges facing schools as they negotiate the increased complexity of demographic change, it is critical to look beyond the narrow framework of integration and assimilation to examine the multiple layers of policy and discourse and young peoples' complex experiences of migration and diaspora. The anthropology of policy allows us to see how the figured identities and narratives of policies move into and through the spaces of schools, shaping assumptions about the kinds of identities schools should foster and the strategies that schools should employ to cultivate those identities. This is the topic to come.

Chapter 3
Liberalizing Muslim Girls

CONCERNS ABOUT the integration of Muslim communities into the Danish na-tion influence teachers' everyday work with Muslim girls (Ball 2006). According to Holland and colleagues, "the new ethnographers of personhood describe how specific, often socially powerful, cultural discourses and practices both position people and provide them with the resources to respond to the problematic situ-ations in which they find themselves" (1998: 32). Teachers are not passive agents who merely absorb the knowledge contained within discourses—they adopt, resist, and adapt discourses as they negotiate their own identities and the cul-tural complexities of their students in the culturally constructed "figured world" of the school (Ball 2006; Holland et al. 1998; Shore and Wright 1997).

I noted earlier that, as a former teacher, I am uneasy about critiquing the work of teachers, especially given the current climate in which they are sub-jected to increasing surveillance and the global proliferation of accountability mandates. My research does not seek to engage in normative evaluations of individual teachers, but rather considers how nationalist discourses are carried and contested by individual actors. Teachers are reading the cues from the "air," the media, and the world around them as they define their everyday work with students. While my research finds common narratives that echo among teach-ers in school discourse and practice, there are also significant differences in how teachers position themselves in relation to immigrant students depending on their professional responsibilities within the school and their own histories and identities. It is critical to recognize the positionality of the teachers discussed in this chapter within the local context of a school that is faced with closing due to rising numbers of Muslim students and the declining population of ethnic Danish students, a situation in which the "threat" of immigrants is amplified.[1]

By exploring a series of interactions between teachers and immigrant girls from multiple perspectives, I aim to reveal how some teachers conceived of their work with Muslim students through the framework of concern—more specifically, their desire to share with their students the freedoms associated with Danish ideals of gender equity and democracy as an escape from what they believed to be a historical cycle of gender oppression in the Muslim community. I specifically focus on the experiences of female Muslim students in the classroom and examine the assumptions that some educators make about the lives and development of Muslim girls, such as: the presumed negative influence that Muslim families, ethnic enclaves, and religious affiliation have on female children; the belief that sexual liberation is a path to integration; and finally, the idea that intellectual and emotional development centers on becoming a free-thinking autonomous individual.

Impossible Love

In this section I draw on observations in an English language class and document how female Muslim students are positioned by peers and their teachers through the various interactions during classroom discussions. In my second week at Engby school, I observed an English language class in which students were preparing for the national exam. Lena, a Danish teacher in her mid-fifties, has taught sixth-through tenth-grade students in Danish schools for over twenty-five years and is also, as mentioned in the preceding chapter, the school's assistant principal. She had taught at Engby School for three years at the time of my research and before that she worked in schools with predominantly ethnic Danish students. Walking through the hallways of the school, Lena explained, "You should visit the school where I used to teach to see a 'real' Danish school. There, you'd see good girls and boys who do what the teacher says and always do their homework." She continued, "Here, the students are very different because we have the Engby houses here and we have a lot of social problems and criminality happening there."

Lena explained that this group of students, 9a, was unique: "In this class, we have a group of students with very high level skills and students with very low skill levels who are really struggling, who are from very low social backgrounds." On the day I observed the 9a English class, Lena was preparing students for the national exam in English. She expressed frustration about the difficulty of teaching students at such different skill levels: "It is really hard because we have these tests at the end of the year. I can't afford to be slowed down because then all of the strong students won't pass the tests . . . and I know that no matter what I do, it will be impossible for six of the students to pass those tests."

In the Danish *folkeskole*, all students are required to take English language classes in their third to tenth years, and there is a required national exam in English for entrance into upper secondary education. During the year that I conducted my fieldwork, the themes covered on the exam included "racism, isolation, religion, culture, love/friendship" (classroom handout, September 17, 2007). The curriculum of English classes is intended to promote intercultural awareness—an understanding of the English language and, as Lena explained, "the traditions of the English-speaking world."

When Lena and I entered the room together, a group of boys were playing with a soccer ball in the corner of the classroom while the rest of the students were seated and in the process of pulling their notebooks out of bags. The desks were configured in five groups of four. Eight ethnic Danish students sat together at the two groups of desks closest to the front of the room when Lena stood there to take attendance and seven immigrant students were seated at tables toward the back. I sat at the group of tables closest to the door with three immigrant girls, Sara, Dhalia, and Aliyah. Lena took attendance and asked, "Does anyone know where Aasif is? Have you seen him?" A group of boys laughed knowingly and spoke to one another in Arabic. Lena paused and then smiled and said, "Ok then, lets get started. We have a lot to do today."

The particular class I observed focused on the theme in the curriculum entitled "Impossible Love." Students explored instances when individuals from different cultures fall in love. Lena then asked students to silently read a story from the *Blue Cat Reader*, a Danish English-language textbook. The story, "Fatima and Saret" (McCarthy 2006), describes a Turkish-Muslim girl, Fatima, who works at home with her family. One afternoon, when she is taking a walk through the town with her baby brother in a stroller, Fatima stops to speak with Saret, a male friend from Cambodia. When Fatima's aunt reports to the family that she was seen talking to a boy, she is berated by her angry father: "Her father came towards her as if he were about to slap her across the face. 'You talk Turkish. Do you hear me? How come you think you can stand with any boy out on the street so everyone can see you like some common slut?'" (McCarthy 2006: 16). The story ends with Fatima's aunt suggesting that she should leave school to prepare for her impending arranged marriage.

After reading the story, Lena, the teacher, began a class discussion. Standing at the front of the room, she asked the class, "So when you think about what you could write about as a subject on the national exam, one thing would be inter-love.

You could write about all the people who are not supposed to love each other. How do we feel about Fatima and her problem?" An ethnic Danish student said that the story reminded her of the movie *Shakespeare in Love*. Then Lena asked again, "So what do we think of these problems with impossible love?" She asked two Palestinian students, Mohammed and Jamail, "What would happen if you brought home a girl who is Danish to your parents?" Mohammed replied, "It would be okay." She then asked a Danish girl, Majbritt, if her parents would approve if she dated a boy who was not Danish and she said, "It wouldn't be a problem." Then she turned to Dhalia, a Palestinian student who was sitting with two other immigrant girls, Aliyah and Sara. She asked, "Dhalia, could you bring home a Danish boyfriend?" Dhalia looked up at Lena seriously and said, "I would not." Lena continued, "But what if you fell in love with a blonde Danish boy." Dhalia responded, "I wouldn't." Lena repeated, "But what if you did?" Dhalia insisted, "I would not." Lena then asked another way, "But what about your own children, would you accept it if your child came home with a Danish boy?" Dhalia replied, "I would not," and added, "also my husband might not want it." When Lena heard this answer, she stepped back, looked at the rest of the class, and said, "And you would have to do what your husband says?" At this moment there was silence in the classroom. Lena then stepped away from Dhalia and asked the students to reflect on Dhalia's answer. "So [*pauses*] how can we help each other to understand these problems with impossible love?" There was silence in the room. Pernilla, a Danish student responded, "I think that it's a problem that she has to do what her husband says. It's very traditional. It's like during the time of Shakespeare—very traditional."

Throughout this interchange, I felt a growing tension in the room. Dhalia's eyes were serious and fixed on the teacher. I sensed the gravity of the interchange, but I didn't quite understand what was being communicated. I was in the midst of what Michael Agar (1986) calls a "breakdown moment" during ethnographic fieldwork, when one doesn't have a schema for making sense of events, when expectations of what should happen at a particular moment are not met. Why would this interchange about a choice of marriage partner invoke such strong feelings from the teacher? Why would the teacher persist in her questioning despite the student's growing discomfort?

It was in this early interaction that I began to see that Dhalia was cast as an outsider, a non-Dane, out of place within a country that conceives of itself as a paragon of democracy and gender equity. In the class discussion, Lena mobilized the characters of the "oppressed" Muslim girl and her violent father through a discussion of the story of Fatima and Saret (Wortham 2008). When Lena asked the class "so what do we think about Fatima and her problem," she introduced a set of normalized assumptions about the problematic nature of immigrant girls' relationships within their families. Throughout this unit, Lena mobilized beliefs about the inherent value of free and romantic love and religious "tradition" stifling these feelings. In this particular class session, figured identities were mobilized through the curriculum to fuel an assimilative critique of Dhalia's identity. Lena's questioning gained momentum as different actors were recruited to join the teacher in a commentary about Dhalia's identity. Other Muslim students who were present in the classroom later critiqued the teacher's questioning in the hallway. Sara said:

She didn't respect Dhalia's answer. She kept asking, and then she asked the Danish students what they think, and then she said, "Oh, that's like an old thing, like from the Middle Ages . . ." I think that she thinks that we can't do anything, we girls only go to school and go home and that's it, she thinks we are just at home and doing what our parents want us to do and only go to school. But it's not like that at all.

While Dhalia and other students were critical of how they were represented, they were not able to shift the ways their peers and teachers perceived them. Figured identities provided the dominant frame for understanding the meaning of Dhalia's response.

Other students, like Mohammed and Jamail, who had attended Engby School since preschool, were familiar with the figured world of the Danish school and the consequences of resistance. Mohammed explained that he chose to say "yes" he would marry a Dane, even though he explained that he plans to marry someone of the same religion. He said, "I come from Lebanon and it would not be okay for me to bring home a Danish girl. The Danes view the immigrants as different and they want to say that immigrant families are so strict." When I asked Akhil for his interpretation of the story of Fatima and Saret, he said, "It's meant to show the Danish people that Fatima is very unhappy in her family and that she can't go out and talk to men. It's a Danish story; like all other Danish stories, it's meant to show how we live." It was clear that the Muslim students in the class had a keen awareness of how the stereotypes of the oppressed Muslim girl and her male oppressor were present during the discussion; however, most only voiced a critique of the events in the safer space of the hallway after the class.

Immigration Discourses and Teachers' Work: "We Will Not See Any Light"

In a conversation two weeks later, Lena brought up the subject of the Impossible Love class. When I asked her about her work with immigrant students, she said the following about the girls:

They are still suppressed, if I could put it like that, in my opinion, and also I can see in the other girls' opinions. I mean, you saw, the other day . . . Dhalia sitting there and saying that she would never marry a Dane because her religion would forbid it or her parents would not approve or whatever. I think it is interesting that we have not come any further. I mean I think we try and try and try and many of them have been here for generations and still I am sure that we will not see any light within the next two generations. I think that it is tragic that it is like that . . . but I think that it is correct that it is like that.

While I had spent several days in Lena's class after the Impossible Love lesson, it was clear that the conversation with Dhalia held particular significance for Lena. She presented the interaction as representative of the problems with immigrant girls in Denmark and echoed the familiar trope of "oppressed" Muslim girls. What was clear in our discussion was that Dhalia's response carried significance far beyond that of an ordinary fourteen-year-old student offering up her opinion in a classroom discussion in English class. The event became amplified (Puwar 2004), representative of a larger story about Muslim immigrants who resist the values of "civilized" liberal democratic society. Lena was frustrated that despite the efforts of teachers who "try and try and try," immigrant girls remain mired in religious tradition, as they have been for generations. Despite all of her efforts, they refuse the "light" and the opportunities that are openly available in Danish society. Interestingly, Dhalia's response was not read by Lena as an act of agency, resisting the assimilationist discourses that were operating in the classroom, but rather as a sign of her oppression.

Lena's description exemplifies how teachers' desires to support the welfare of Muslim girls are inextricably connected to the nationalist discourse on immigration. By saying "I think it is interesting that we have not come any further," she suggested that Dhalia's refusal represented a problem on a number of fronts. In Lena's statement, it wasn't clear who "we" referred to. One interpretation suggests that it is "tragic" that despite the efforts of Danes to integrate the immigrants (over several generations), "we" Danes will not be able to integrate them in the future. It is also possible that she was suggesting that it is tragic that "we" women have not achieved more equitable status in communities across the world. Finally, she could have meant that it was tragic that "we"—a society of Danes and immigrants—have not come any further. The last of these possibilities suggests that Lena's image of Danish society, as one representing equality and democracy, was somehow tarnished by the presence of Muslim immigrants. While there wasn't a clear interpretation of Lena's intended meaning, these multiple readings reveal different narrative threads of the liberal discourse of concern. The image of the oppressed immigrant girl is one that invokes teachers' advocacy, anger, and collective anxieties about the integrity of the national community.

As Lena discussed her work with Dhalia and the other Muslim girls, she positioned herself as supporting the girls' positive integration and positioned the girls as requiring the intervention of teachers.

Of course we should [work with the immigrants to help them]. I mean that's a big part of our job and I know that a lot of our teachers are working with them very much. And also the education system is working to make them more a part of it. They have to be part of the jobs and the education system . . . and to . . . be open minded to what is . . . where I can no longer live in my little safe world where I did what my mother did, and she did what her mother did. . . . The more we can try to open them up the better it will be for their integration as a whole.

Lena sees her work in terms of supporting her female students to move beyond the perceived constraints of tradition and ethnic enclaves to join Danish society. It seems that within Lena's imagination, Dhalia's response about her choice of marriage partner is representative of the problem of generations of women who have been isolated in ethnic enclaves. Lena produces notions of Muslim immigrant communities as backward and oppressive, and Denmark as offering freedom and enlightenment—thus framing her work as bringing civilization to immigrant girls.

As Lena spoke about her work with Dhalia, Aliyah, and Sara, she reflected on experiences earlier in her career when she worked with women in Somali communities to start an educational campaign against genital mutilation. She casts her work in the classroom with Dhalia in the same light as her work with Somali women. When I asked Lena what she wanted for girls, she replied:

What do I want for the immigrant girls? For all of the girls, I want them to be assured in their inner self that they feel that they are something, that they are not dependent on a man's money. Of course they can earn their own money, but they also have an equality in possibilities of getting education.

Expressing a discourse of concern, Lena wants what most teachers want for their students, self-confidence and educational advancement. While Lena's concern draws on the figured identities and assumptions of the broader discourse on immigration, it is also connected to her own life experiences. In an interview in 2009, she shared some insights from her own experiences as a young woman growing up in Denmark and described how she was not able to pursue her own dream to become a journalist because her husband's career goals took precedence. In another interview, when I asked Lena about gender inequality in Danish society, she answered,

Yes, but I think it is important that you learn how to behave in a society, that you learn that you have exactly the same rights as all of the other persons in this society if you are a male or a female. You have to achieve as much as you can via your education because that will give you peace in your heart.

Consistent with other conversations, Lena portrayed Danish society unproblematically, as offering the same rights to men and women and she highlighted the importance of "learning to behave" in society, that is, by assimilating to Danish norms one will reap the benefits of Danish society.

In Danish schools, it is not uncommon for teachers to become involved in the personal lives of their students. The Danish head teacher, or *klasselæreren*, considered to be the "mother of the class" (Anderson 1996: 44), is responsible for the social and personal development of her students in addition to their academic needs (Anderson 1996). Perhaps this model, which allows for social intervention in students lives, is less complicated in a monocultural setting but becomes more difficult when teachers are navigating across cultural differences. Through her concern, Lena constructs a distorted image of Dhalia and the barriers she faces in her life that is removed from firsthand understandings of Dhalia's life. Further, as figured identities dance in Lena's imagination, she is the judging subject, scrutinizing the student whom she believes requires her help while she fails to consider how she is implicated in the social forces that are barriers in Dhalia's life.

Evident in the escalation of the discussion of Impossible Love and in Lena's reflections on this discussion, figured identities and policy narratives about the problems of immigrant ghettos are taken up in classrooms, drawing invisible boundaries between "us" and "them." Stereotyped notions of Muslim students are produced at the intersection of curricula, school-based discourses, and community discourses while they also draw on more global orientalist and postcolonial anti-Muslim discourses. Woven through all of these discourses is a set of assumptions about an inherent "clash of civilizations" as "enlightened" Western liberal societies confront Islam (Huntington 1996).

Within observations and interviews, teachers rarely made overtly Islamophobic references. Instead, their critiques were veiled within the curriculum or within questions like the one that Lena posed to the class: "So what do we think about these problems of impossible love?" Rather than engaging in direct critique of Islam, many teachers described Danish values of romantic love and Danish democracy as offering opportunities for Muslim girls to escape the confines of their families. Responding to social taboos against overtly racist language, teachers and policymakers frame their discussions of immigrant students in the benevolent language of individualism, equality, and progress.

When Dhalia said "No" she wouldn't marry a Dane, and Lena continued in her questioning, the lesson extended beyond its stated goals of preparing students for the national exam in English. In her work on the production of nationalism and citizenship through everyday schooling, the anthropologist Véronique Benei argues that "emotionality is produced, through, and feeds into, political, cultural, social, economic, and gender negotiations of nationhood and citizenship central to the everyday production of rights and entitlements" (2008: 5). As nationalisms move into classrooms, it is critical to examine not only how they are embodied and felt by different actors but also the material ways they inform the educational experiences of immigrant youth.

Teaching Danish Norms of Romantic Love

After my observation of the Impossible Love class, I interviewed Dhalia, who talked about other teachers who made her choices surrounding marriage and romantic love the focus of instructional practice:

This isn't the only time this happens. In extra-Danish class, the teacher said that it's okay to date and to have sex before you marry because then you get to know someone. Because she thought I would just be married to someone I don't know. This never happened before because before this I was in Islamic school. In the beginning when I came here it was very difficult for me. It's not fair, but I get used to it I guess.

Danish-as-a-second-language classes—or what are informally called "extra-Danish" classes—are relatively new in Danish schools.[2] They were created as a result of mandates in the 2001 Folkeskole Act that eliminated funding for native language instruction for students from "Third World" countries while calling for increased emphasis on the teaching of Danish language and culture. These classes are the only time during the school day that immigrant students are segregated from their Danish peers.

When Dhalia first told me that her teacher was counseling her to have sex before marriage, I was skeptical, thinking that perhaps Dhalia was exaggerating the message of her teacher. But in an interview the next week, Dhalia's extra-Danish teacher, Birgitte, told me that she was working to help the immigrant girls learn to fit in better in Danish society. Birgitte said she brought in an article from a Danish newspaper, "Falske jomfruer" (False Virgins) (Thorup 2007), that describes the case of Muslim girls in Denmark who choose to have hymen reattachment surgery so that they can engage in premarital sexual activity and then return to an intact state for their weddings.

Birgitte said that she brought in the article as a way of starting a discussion about Danish norms of romantic love.

They're very much struggling about . . . being Muslim girls in the Danish school. They can't really discuss being a virgin, if it's good, if it's fair that you have to wait until you get married. They can't really—they don't know their [own] opinion. They just know that it's not okay not being a virgin. And they . . . it's very hard for them to get rid of their background and say what they mean.

Birgitte contended that immigrant girls are caught between the values of Danish society and their families, struggling with negotiating their traditions in the context of a Western liberal society. She echoed a stereotyped narrative that was repeated in many of my interviews, the idea that Muslim girls were fundamentally not individuals, that they lacked the ability to think independently, to function in inquiry-based classrooms, and that they "don't really know their own opinion." Several teachers at Engby School understood their work in terms of helping Muslim girls to assimilate to Danish norms, as Birgitte says, "to get rid of their background" in order to become self-actualizing individuals. The teachers imagine an ideal autonomous liberal subject who designs his or her own unique relationship with religion and culture (Asad 2006).

Within extra-Danish class, Muslim girls were encouraged to scrutinize their own traditions. Associating the Danish values of sexual openness with increased freedom and autonomy, Birgitte describes using readings about forced marriage in the 1800s in Denmark to imply that Muslim students could overcome their "feudal" culture. As in the Impossible Love discussion, Birgitte mobilizes the image of the oppressed woman struggling to get her rights in order to imbue her work with a moral purpose (Wortham 2008). She conceives of herself as "helping" the girls to enjoy the more "enlightened" values of Danish society.

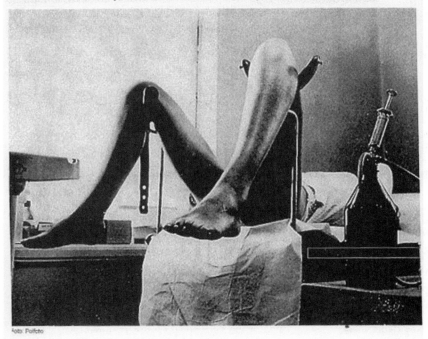

Information.dk

Politik & International

Falske jomfruer

Unge indvandrerkvinder bryder med familiens normer. De dyrker sex før ægteskabet og får flere provokerede aborter end etnisk danske kvinder. Men det er kun en halv revolution, for samtidig opsøger de klinikker for at få lavet en ny mødom. Vi fastholder dem i en undertrykkende tradition, siger overlæge

Foto: Polfoto

V. METTE-LINE THORUP

Figure 3.1.   False Virgins. Mette-Line Thorup, "Falske jomfruer," *Information*, September 27, 2007. http://www.information.dk/147084

In my discussion with Birgitte, she had a moment of reflection in which she paused and seemed to become uncomfortable with her description of her work with the girls.

But it's also hard. I mean, I shouldn't be the one to push them and say "Stupid, think for yourselves." I have to show them that I respect their home views, but I have to try to show them that they live here now, and when you choose your husband, I think it's important that you know who he is, and to tell them that in Denmark a way to learn about each other, to know each other is also to have sex, maybe, or whatever.

While Birgitte invoked the liberal trope of "respect," she contends that it was her job to help her female Muslim students conform to Danish norms of sexuality. In her explanation, she describes sexual liberation as a path to integration and the cultivation of a Danish identity. Other teachers in the school encouraged the assimilation of Muslim students; however, Birgitte was the only teacher I encountered to specifically mention openness to premarital sexual activity. Her moral agenda took up the specific elements of Danish national discourse related to sexual openness and gender liberation.[3]

Although Birgitte saw the Muslim girls as lacking their own opinions, the girls launched critical counter-narratives that disputed the idea that they lack agency within their families. Sara, who identifies as a Palestinian from Lebanon, participated in a focus group with Muslim girls who were critical of Birgitte's Danish-as-a-second-language class. She complained: "Because we live in Denmark, she [Birgitte] wants us to act like Danish people. She thinks that our parents decide what we do for us. She asked me if my parents will decide who I will get married to. I explained, '*No*, it's me who will decide who to get married to.' I feel like it is not her business." Sara challenged Birgitte's assumption that Muslim girls are victims of forced or arranged marriages. These students went on to describe that they experienced educators' "concern" as an assimilative critique of their identities and that being singled out and questioned in classrooms about their cultural and religious practices in front of their ethnic Danish peers made them uncomfortable. Aliyah recounted the conversation about the "Falske jomfruer" (False Virgins) that began in extra-Danish and continued in her regular class.

It was in extra-Danish class. It was just us three and then two other immigrant boys. And then another day, we talked about this with the whole class. Birgitte asked me and another girl to talk about it in front of the whole class, and it was really embarrassing to talk about it. She just said, "Now, Aliyah you talk about it." She also made us talk about women in the old time in Denmark before they had their rights. Other groups talked about issues that had nothing to do with this subject.

As in the Impossible Love interaction in Lena's class, Birgitte made Aliyah the focus of attention and extended an invitation to other students to comment on the "traditions" of Muslim girls. Aliyah describes her discomfort at being asked to make a presentation on issues related to immigrant girls and sexuality in Danish society when others made presentations on less personal topics. Other Muslim girls, who were not a part of the Danish-as-a-second-language class also remarked that Birgitte spoke with them about sex and dating. Hibo, a student who identifies as an Ethiopian from Somalia, said: "Birgitte talks a lot about girlfriends and boyfriends and comes over to us and says 'You gotta have a boyfriend.' It is so weird. It makes me feel kind of awkward and dirty."

Discussions with ethnic Danish students in the school revealed that the content covered in extra-Danish class specifically targeted immigrant students rather than all students as part of a broader school-wide sexual education and reproductive health curriculum. Danish students who were in the same ninth-grade class but did not attend extra-Danish classes indicated they did not have any sexual education in the ninth-grade year. In seventh grade they had a sexual education class where they learned about birth control methods and had discussions about "the right time" to have sex. Aliyah, Sara, and Dhalia spoke critically about extra-Danish class, indicating that it was not the subject matter that was problematic—they were accustomed to sexual education classes—but rather it was the suggestion that in order to be Danish they had to have sex before marriage.

In Birgitte and Lena's descriptions of their work with immigrant students they articulate the ways that stereotyped notions of the "oppressed" Muslim girl and the enlightened liberal subject "that she could be" represent an educational call to action; these discourses provide teachers with the authority to intervene in the personal lives of young women. Male teachers and administrators discussed the challenges facing immigrant girls in their families and communities; however, Birgitte and Lena were the only teachers to speak about their work to actively encourage Muslim girls to accept Danish norms surrounding sex and marriage. While these practices seem outside the bounds of what one would normally see within schools in Western liberal nations, a review of literature on Muslim students suggests that it is perhaps more common than one might expect.

Rescuing Muslim Girls: Comparative Insights

Sherene Razack observes that desires to liberate Muslim girls are likewise present in the educational agendas of NGOs in other Scandinavian countries. She explains that "rescuing Muslim women from their feudal cultures is considered an educational issue. Immigrant families are inherently dangerous places for young women" (2004: 139). Razack analyzes the work of the Human Rights Service, a private foundation in Norway that has been active in advocating immigration restrictions designed to protect Muslim girls from forced marriages in Norway and across Europe. The Human Rights Service published a self-help guide entitled *Forced Marriages—A Crisis Guide* (Storhaug and Human Rights Service 2004), which includes a chapter entitled "Life Improvement—You Deserve It" that urges Muslim women to accept the virtues of Western visions of romantic love and resist the oppression of their families (Razack 2004: 139). Similarly, Mannitz's ethnographic research reveals how the liberation of Muslim women is taken up in German schools. She documents a classroom in which a German teacher uses a feminist article on honor killings and asks a female Muslim student to explain the predicament of women in Muslim societies. Mannitz argues that "Muslim girls are in the position of having to defend themselves against the German majority that depicts Muslim women as puppet-like representatives of traditionalism" (2004: 247–48). Educational campaigns and practices such as these take up the narratives and figurings of the broader discourse, reproducing racialized notions of Muslim women without providing comfortable openings for Muslim women to enter into these dialogues. That the terms of the conversations about Muslim women are so overdetermined discourages a wider analysis of the structural barriers facing Muslim women and the actual conditions of their lives.

Other work by anthropologists explores the dimensions of educational concern for Muslim students in Western liberal schools. In her ethnographic research with Palestinian-American high school students in a large comprehensive school in the United States, Thea Abu El-Haj found that the production of everyday nationalisms leads to a view of education as "alternatively a liberating and disciplining force for Arab American youth" (2010: 242). The teachers in her study reproduced figured notions of Muslim women, evident in such statements as "they are subservient," "viewed as male property," "walk three steps behind their husbands," and "have no freedom" (2010: 251). Teachers in these schools, like those in Engby School, echoed desires to support Muslim girls to "have a voice." Abu El-Haj's work documents an instance in which Haneen, a Palestinian-American student, describes an encounter in which a teacher asks to see her hair and then states "you look more girl now." Abu El-Haj's analysis reveals that the brief uncovering of a Muslim girls hair is seen as an act of liberation. She concludes: "Thus, part of the American nationalist project aimed at Arab girls was one that sought to liberate them to be free individual agents imagined as the subject of American national identity—a project symbolically represented by the moment of showing one's hair" (2010: 255). I draw on these somewhat repetitive comparative examples to show that the teachers in my study are not unique but rather that they are acting as agents of a particular vision of Western liberal schooling focused on realizing a liberal future for Muslim girls. What are the affective dimensions of teachers' responses to their Muslim students? How do they reveal a blurring of liberal feminist agendas with nationalist anxieties about the changing demographics of schools and societies?

Teachers who engage in civilizing work express the desire for their female students to have access to education, jobs, and an individual identity while they also express broader concerns about the integrity of the national community. They take up the emancipatory language of democratic values to project an assimilationist agenda. As Wendy Brown argues, "The discourse of tolerance substantively brokers cultural value—valorizing the West, othering the rest—while feigning to do no more than distinguish civilization from barbarism, protect the former from the latter, and extend the benefits of liberal thought and practices" (2006: 203). In teachers' civilizing discourses, the language of helping ultimately slides into an insistence on assimilation as immigrant girls are invited to sever ties to family, religion, and community.

I believe that Danish teachers' concerns for their immigrant students are genuine. Birgitte and Lena are sincere in their desire to extend opportunities to immigrant girls to get an education and to land good jobs. Teachers conceive of education as providing opportunities for social mobility, higher levels of self-esteem, and independence. However, their work with these students concentrates on enforcing cultural assimilation rather than providing academic support. In short, they engage in culture work rather than academic work as they conceive of assimilation as a necessary prerequisite for academic success. In interviews with Muslim youth, many expressed that they feel that teachers have lower academic expectations of immigrant students and that it is difficult to access academic support. Furthermore, they describe how assimilative educational practices complicate their efforts to be fully involved in the life of the classroom and the school.

Mamdani (2005) critiques the liberal progressive discourse of gender equity that privileges normative notions of "free choice" and agency and justifies intervention in the lives of young immigrant girls. Some feminist scholars point to the limits of "imperial feminisms" that define Muslim women as "oppressed and backward" in relation to Western women, who are defined as "enlightened and progressive." This discourse emerges out of a colonial discourse that is established "on the basis of the 'inferiority' of non-Western cultures, most manifest in their patriarchal customs and practices, from which indigenous women had to be rescued" (Mamdani 2005: 190). The stakes are high in the education of immigrant girls as some teachers believe that if they are not successful in reaching individual girls, another generation will remain isolated within oppressive Muslim families and communities.

My data suggest that concern for the future of Muslim girls becomes conflated with concern about the shifting landscape of the national community. In a public talk, Talal Asad (2009) argued that the emotions of compassion and sympathy that accompany humanitarian concern are unpredictable and inevitably linked to national interests, a particular masquerading as a universal. Teachers' concern for the welfare of Muslim girls was frequently accompanied by statements about the negative influence of Muslim immigrants in Denmark, the growth of immigrant ghettos, and the growing presence of Muslim students in the school. As producers of the next generation and carriers of tradition, young women become especially amplified and the object of national concern (Yuval-Davis 1999). Muslim girls' attract the attention of educators who contend that they are rescuing young women from their oppressive families and culture and "liberalizing" the intolerant ideologies of Islam through exposure to Western liberal norms (Abu El-Haj 2010).

Policing Difference: Creating Liberal Subjects

While official discourses represented Engby School as welcoming of the cultures and traditions of all students, I observed an everyday politics of concern for and about Muslim students in the practices of the school. I documented instances in which teachers policed Muslim students' expressions of cultural, religious, and linguistic difference. Aysa, a Turkish teacher, described how teachers in the school encourage female Muslim students to take on "more Danish" identities: "There are some teachers who like [*pauses*] who get a big smile when they can see a Muslim girl is behaving like a Danish girl."

In interviews, teachers and ethnic Danish students frequently engaged in particular conversations related to immigrant students such as their decisions not to attend a school trip or to wear *hijab* in school. The class trip is a *folkeskole* tradition that involves traveling for several days with the class to another city or to the countryside. Several teachers complained about the absence since, in their eyes, class trips were particularly important for the Muslim girls because they provided opportunities for them to learn Danish ways of living and thinking. Muslim students explained that they didn't attend class trips because of their concerns about eating and sleeping arrangements. For example, a Turkish student who did go to Germany with her class described being pressured to eat food that contained pork during a dinner with a host family. Her teacher explained that it would be impolite to refuse the meal. In my own experience with my family during our year in Denmark, I found myself conflicted about my daughter's school trip. When my daughter was in the fifth grade at a Danish international school, her class went on a trip to a Christmas festival in Germany on the first three nights of the Jewish holiday of Hanukkah. Living far from our extended family, we felt that lighting our menorah in the dark Danish winter was important for our family. Moreover, it was a shock to me that an "international" school would not be aware of a Jewish holiday. I felt that there was a general assumption that all children, regardless of their religion (and there were Hindu and Muslim students in the class as well) should want to celebrate Christmas with their class. Part of what is not explicitly recognized in teachers' explanations of school trips is that they are developed as opportunities to socialize young people to learn about European values.

Birgitte, the Danish teacher, summarized the importance of the school trips:

Four of the girls, they are not allowed to go on the school tour. I think it's affecting their whole experience of how we all are. I mean to understand the social rules. They need to learn to be independent, to be able to sleep away from their family, to get their own opinion, to socialize playing games.

Here Birgitte suggests that trips are particularly important for the girls because they provide an opportunity for them "to learn the social rules." In addition, her statement that "they need to learn to be independent" is consistent with broader discursive narratives about immigrant girls' putative lack of agency within their families (Abu-Lughod 2002). Teachers position school trips as providing an opportunity for immigrant girls to be away from their "collectivist"-oriented families so that they can learn to be freethinking individuals. But at the same time, Birgitte's notions of individualism are very much rooted in specific national norms of behavior.

Henrik, a math teacher and soccer coach, was particularly upset about the absence of Muslim students from the same school trip:

There are some students that I think, Why are you here? Go back to your country. I say to myself, why are you here, you must leave the country if you are not going to follow the rules and know how to behave. Many of them think they can use special rules for themselves but they must use the same rules as I do. I will give you an example. With the girls, there are the four foreign girls who couldn't come with us on the school trip. My job is to take care of them and the parents must understand that, when you say "No" to not letting your girl come, you accuse me of not taking care of your girl, of not doing my job. . . . It's a problem, it's like they say, I follow the class as long as I like. I don't like to have to sleep outside. I told them, you are fifteen now and it's not normal and it's not good. They could learn, away from their home and be independent.

While it is understandable that a teacher might be irritated by students' lack of participation in a school-sponsored event, Henrik's anger about the girls' choice not to attend the trip reveals how the nationalist discourses and narratives surrounding Muslim girls are amplified and emotionally embodied within the spaces of classrooms (Benei 2008). In this description, Henrik's anger is clear as he positions himself as a caring teacher and positions the immigrant parents as refusing his concern—as he says, "you accuse me of not taking care of your girl." The discourse of concern slides into a discourse of exclusion as he suggests, if the girls aren't going to "follow the rules and know how to behave" they should leave Denmark. Feeling rebuffed by immigrant families that refuse his care and are denied the opportunities of Danish schools (and by extension society), Henrik argues that anger is a legitimate response, something that the girls brought on themselves, and he establishes an either/or scenario—either the girls conform to Danish notions of belonging and attend trips or they deserve exclusion.

Across my interviews, several teachers echoed this sentiment as they positioned the school as offering opportunities to Muslim immigrants who refused educators' "concern" and chose instead to maintain their traditions and beliefs rather than assimilating to Danish values. Peter Hervik (2004) analyzed Danish immigration discourses and identified a similar discourse of "hosts and guests" (Sassen 1999), i.e., the Muslim guest workers and refugees who arrived in Denmark (at the invitation of the benevolent hosts) and then never went home. "Since newcomers," Hervik explains, "have arrived seeking aid in the form of work, or for protection, they are like 'guests' and dependent upon the hospitality of the house (Denmark). They are supposed to be humble, undemanding, at best invisible, interested in Danish ways of living and willing to conform to these ways of living and thinking" (2004: 259). For those who choose to settle in Denmark, there is a social expectation that they should conform to Danish cultural traditions and values and if they refuse, exclusion is seen as a justified response.

The Material Costs of Concern

While an analysis of the educational outcomes of Muslim students at Engby School is beyond the scope of my study, my findings suggest that teachers' "concern" for Muslim students can complicate students' relationships with teachers and peers. Several of my participants reported that they lost teachers' support when they started wearing *hijab*. Aliyah described an instance in which Henrik publicly questioned her about her choice to begin wearing *hijab*:

Most teachers are like that, like the math teacher [Henrik] when I began to put my scarf on last year then he got a little bit angry at me. . . . He said, "Why did you put that on in the classroom?" when everyone [the other students] could hear . . . and he kept asking me why and why and saying, "are your parents making you put it on?" But I said, "No," I said, "It's not my parents, it's my decision what I do and what I choose not to do." He didn't believe what I was saying. He was like saying, "Oh yeah, it's your parents." Some teachers are like that.

In her recounting of the incident, Aliyah points out that it took place in the classroom in front of her peers, "when anyone could hear." Recruiting the figured identity of the oppressed Muslim girl, Henrik repeats the idea that Aliyah is forced by her parents to wear *hijab*. As in the Impossible Love incident, Aliyah is publicly and repeatedly "questioned," but she doesn't actually feel that she has an opportunity to present her side or to be heard. Henrik understands Aliyah's presence as a young woman wearing *hijab* in terms of available narratives about oppressed Muslim girls. Aliyah speaks back to these figured identities as she says, "It's my decision what I do and what I choose not to do."

Aliyah recalled the first day she wore *hijab* to school: "I remember the first day I put my *hijab* on; I was like really scared going to school, thinking, what they are going to say to me. But in another way, I felt really strong, like I was saying, I can do what I want." While Aliyah points to the strength that she feels in expressing her religious identity, she alludes to the ways this choice jeopardizes her positive relationships with her teachers.

In the sixth grade, I began to be really good in math and he was like my best teacher. And then in eighth grade, I didn't go to the camp because I was in Africa and he was angry that I missed the overnight. And then when I started wearing the scarf, he was like, he didn't like me. In the teacher-student meeting he told my parents that I wasn't doing well in math, I wasn't doing my homework. But I did. I *always* do my homework. Also the Danish teacher, that same year, said she isn't doing well, she is too quiet.

Aliyah felt that her absence from the trip and her choice to wear *hijab* led to a decline in her grades and her relationships with Henrik and the other teachers. She explained that the conflict with Henrik was particularly troubling because he had always been a supportive teacher, someone, as students said, you could turn to for help. In interviews, ethnic Danish students portrayed Henrik in a positive light. Catherina declared: "When I first got into his class, I wasn't good at math and I was really shy, he helped me so much and I wasn't afraid to ask him questions when I didn't know something." Although Henrik was understood to be supportive and attuned to the needs of his students, when it came to negotiating religious difference, he believed it was his role as a "good" teacher to show his disapproval of expressions of religious difference in his classroom in order to foster the integration of immigrant girls.

Like Aliyah, Nadifa, an eighth-grade Somali student, described a similar decline in her relationship with Henrik when she began wearing *hijab*:

Sometimes teachers too, Henrik is like that. He teaches us chemistry. When I just put on my *hijab* he looked at me differently, he talked to me in a really mean voice. When I started wearing *hijab* he changed from treating me sweetly, like before when I asked him for help and he would come and help. Then after I started wearing the *hijab* he was very strict, he would say, "No you can't do that." *I don't ask him for help anymore* [emphasis mine].

Nadifa notes a dramatic shift as she perceives Henrik to change from treating her "sweetly" to talking "in a really mean voice."

Just the sight of a girl wearing *hijab* or excusing herself from a class trip is understood to represent a challenge in the Danish space of the school. Yet while some Danish educators are not comfortable with the presence of Islam in schools, scholars find that immigrant students draw substantial support from their religious beliefs, which translates into higher academic outcomes (Suárez-Orozco et al. 2008; Zhou and Bankston 1994). However, some teachers I spoke with believed that Muslim girls' attachments to culture and tradition are barriers to their development. As such they felt it was their role to intervene and to show disapproval for those attachments and in some cases even withdraw educational supports.

Sabah, a ninth-grade student from Lebanon who had been in Engby School since kindergarten, spoke of teachers' changing perceptions of Muslim students as they moved up in grade level:

The thing about Denmark and the school is that you are really good in kindergarten and then when you come to eighth or ninth grade then, they begin to say "Oh, he's not good at that or she is not good at that." We have a Danish girl in the class and she is like really clever but she never talks, like her hand is always down when we discuss things. I talk more than her and then she still gets a better grade than me. When we have parent-teacher conferences they say [about me] . . . "She is not good at that."

Sabah's narrative reflects her perception that at Engby School racial differences inform teachers conceptions of successful and less successful students especially as the students progress over the years.

Some teachers perceive adolescence as representing a critical turning point in an immigrant girl's life that signals whether she will follow in the footsteps of her mother, embracing religious values, or whether she will join "democratic" society. This heightened scrutiny of adolescence and immigrant girls' behavior is uncharacteristic of Danish schools, which are otherwise antiauthoritarian and encouraging of adolescent experimentation. For instance, some forms of expression through dress are perceived to be unique displays of students' individuality, resonating with national ideals of "openness" and freedom, yet wearing *hijab* is taken to be a sign of oppression rather than a choice, a reminder of the captivity of Muslim girls and the perceived threat of Muslim immigration to Denmark.

"Trying Not to Be Different . . . Because We Are in Their Land"

In 2008 when Aliyah was in ninth grade at Engby School, she described how she learned to be private about her personal life because openness would invite scrutiny of her identity.

In school you have to be really private, they need to know nothing. They don't really know what I do at home. They don't know where I go home everyday. I have to be very careful in the school. If I say what I do at home they will think, "Oh, she is different than us, she is not like us." It's funny. They don't try to be like us, because we are in their land. But they think we should try to be like them.

It seems that in light of "concerned" teachers and peers, Aliyah learned to silence aspects of her identity in order to avoid being marked as different. She responds to the assimilative context of the school by holding back stories and visions of self that might invite critical questioning. As an African girl wearing *hijab*, Aliyah would always be recognized as different in the space of the school, yet she still silenced aspects of her identity in an attempt to blend in, to remain below the radar.

In his autobiography, Edward Said, renowned Palestinian scholar, describes a similar process of concealing his identity on his arrival to the United States:

Nationality, background, real origins, and past actions all seemed to be the sources of my problem. . . . So beginning in America I resolved to live as if I were a simple, transparent soul and not to speak about my family or origins except as required, and then very sparingly. To become, in other words, like the others, as anonymous as possible. (Said 2000: 137)

Similarly, Aliyah attempts to remain "anonymous" in order to avoid disrupting the Danish space of the school. While Aliyah sat in the classroom, parsing through which aspects of self could be safely shared and which needed to be held close, her teachers thought of Muslim girls as unable to be "individuals," in the words of Birgitte, who argued that Muslim girls, "don't have their own opinion." In the figured world of Engby School, teachers decry the problems of Muslim girls who can't be individuals because of their traditions while at the same time disallowing the girls to emerge as individuals in their own right. Aliyah, recognizing the futility of enacting her present sense of self, merely plays along, taking her cues from the air, squelching her own individualism by trying not to be different because "we are in their land."

The Muslim girls in my study revealed that in-class public scrutiny of their identities led them to withdraw from social interactions with teachers and peers within those classes and, in some cases, to stop seeking support from teachers. When they experienced the painful sting of misrecognition and surveillance in schools, they were less likely to feel that they could reach out to teachers and peers for support. Nadifa articulates this when she says, "I don't ask him [Henrik] for help anymore." Faced with this dilemma, the girls in this study employed protective strategies for developing a low profile and avoiding personal interactions with teachers and Danish peers. However, although these strategies express the agency of the girls, something that goes unrecognized in Engby, they also prevent them from accessing valuable resources and from fully engaging in the life of the school.

None of the Muslim girls in my study were subject to forced marriage or other oppressive practices within their families nor did they know of any friends who had been. My female participants described parents who wanted them to learn Danish, to be successful in school so that they would have the opportunity to attend upper secondary education and university in order to get good jobs. It would be naïve to argue that the practices of forced marriage or violence against women do not exist, or that they should not be the concern of teachers. However, I think one should consider that when that concern takes the form of coercive questioning and assimilative practices, when youth feel the sting of cultural and religious critique in classrooms, they are less likely to feel they can reach out to teachers and peers for support. Further, Razack (2004) shows that current European discourses on forced marriage, veiling practices, and genital mutilation have actually restricted conversations about antiviolence reforms and polarized communities in ways that limit women's access to supports. She argues that gender oppression cannot be addressed through racist policies and discourses.

The Promiscuity of Concern

Like a spark in kerosene, figurings of "oppressed Muslims girls" are easily taken up within liberal national imaginations. This spring, my fifteen-year-old son came home from his suburban New Jersey high school with a social studies assignment that asked him to explore the problem of gender oppression in "Islamic cultures." He described the class discussion that day, how the class debated women's positioning in "Muslim countries," exploring topics such as child marriage and the wearing of *hijab*. My son voiced his frustration with the stereo-types that flowed freely through the classroom. In thinking about this lesson, I wondered: Would a teacher in this racially diverse U.S. community ask students to debate the problems with African American or white "cultures," or engage in a debate about whether African Americans or whites are prone to violence? In my community, I would expect that there would be a collective understand-ing about how such lines of inquiry do harm. Yet, talking about oppressed Mus-lim women is viewed as a pressing issue, one that should be taken up in history classrooms. I believe that teachers need to have a more critical awareness that racial figurings and narratives propagated in classrooms can reproduce hierar-chies of racial difference.

In recent debates about talking about racial difference in Western liberal societies, there are always those who argue that "political correctness" silences substantive debate and discussion about difference in schools. Some take this argument even further to contend that political correctness fundamentally threatens democratic values. During the Mohammed cartoon crisis of 2005 in Denmark, proponents of "freedom of speech" argued that Muslims threatened Danes' right to freedom of expression. The explanatory text published with the cartoons states: "The modern secular society is rejected by some Muslims. They demand a special position, insisting on special consideration of their own religious feelings. It is incompatible with contemporary democracy and freedom of speech where one must be ready to put up with insults, mock-ery, and ridicule" (Rose 2006). Is this just a condition of belonging for racial or ethnic minorities in Western liberal societies? That is, should they be pre-pared to endure a certain amount of racialization? The publisher of the Mo-hammed cartoons, Flemming Rose, went as far as to argue that the cartoons were an effort to move Muslims toward equality: "And by treating Muslims in Denmark as equals they made a point: We are integrating you into the Dan-ish tradition of satire because you are part of our society, not strangers. The cartoons are including not excluding Muslims" (Rose 2006). Members of the United Nations Committee on the Eradication of Racism took another view, arguing "there isn't a hierarchy where freedom of speech is always at the top, it does not supersede the right to not be subjected to discrimination and hate speech" (CERD 2010). Educational anthropologist Andrea Dyrness reframes notions of "political correctness" and calls for a renewed "political conscious-ness" that includes "an awareness of how power relations shape our relations with others, and an awareness of how the others we speak about might react to our speech" (Dyrness 2014). I would add that it is essential to situate contemporary race talk within a historical context, to consider the enduring ways that racial tropes have emerged throughout history and the ways that they are imbricated with liberalism and liberal schooling.

The Problem with "Saving" Muslim Girls

In her elegantly argued essay, Lila Abu-Lughod (2002) addresses the question "Do Muslim Women Need Saving?" She suggests that the feminist secular humanist mission to save Muslim women is deeply problematic.

> When you save someone, you are implying that you are saving her from something. You are also saving her *to* something. What violences are entailed in this transformation, and what presumptions are being made about the superiority of that to which you are saving her? Projects of saving other women depend on and reinforce a sense of superiority by Westerners, a form of arrogance that deserves to be challenged. (Abu-Lughod 2002: 788, emphasis in the original)

In support of Abu-Lughod's premise, I illuminate the complex emotional dimensions of the discourse of concern for Muslim girls, revealing a blurring of national anxieties, national humanitarian commitments, and child-centered educational philosophies. It is critical that scholars and Western publics challenge the arrogance of technologies of concern to reveal the educational violence they enact, the burning shame and humiliation the discourses and their propagators inflict on Muslim students, and the failure of school systems to attend to the educational needs and desires of Muslim students.

This chapter reveals the contradiction in technologies of concern, which seek to foster the integration of immigrants but can actually encourage student disengagement and marginalization. The young people in my study speak to the importance of human recognition in schools, of being seen in terms of the fullness of their complex experiences and attachments rather than through reductive stereotypes. Their experience is corroborated by social psychologists who have described how the integration of immigrants depends on the social acceptance of their identities. For instance, Colette Van Laar and her colleagues, who studied Muslim women's participation in the labor market in the Netherlands, found that "many active debates about religious identity assume that religious identity will conflict with integration goals. The current research suggests in fact that making room for and valuing domains of importance to young Muslim women moves these women towards domains of concern to society at large, and towards integration, not away from it" (Van Laar 2011). The authors conclude that when young women feel their identities are accepted, they are more likely to be more engaged in their work environment and to identify with the broader society.

Though much literature points to the centrality of "caring teachers" and "caring relationships" between teachers and students, my work seeks to complicate the narcissism of this concern, the ways it projects very particular and national ways of being. My work calls for a critical analysis of how liberal educational discourses produce notions of barbaric Others who hold no regard for individual rights and ideal liberal subjects who embody enlightenment and modernity (Asad 2006; Foucault 1977). While immigration discourses and policies in Denmark and more generally throughout the West focus on reforming immigrant girls and families, the racial, political, and economic barriers that complicate the mobility of Muslim students are largely left unexamined.

Too often, the teachers I observed were resigned to the poor performance of Muslim immigrant students, ascribing their academic challenges to families' cultural practices or refusal to integrate. They complained about the lack of engagement and poor performance of immigrant students, believing that failure was inevitable. In Chapter 5, I explore how Muslim boys and girls are subjected to different processes of racialization and gendering in schools—girls tend to provoke sympathy and rescuing while boys require managing and containment. However, explanations about the academic outcomes of Muslim boys, like those of girls, tend to center on the problems of Muslim families. Resonating with the findings in my study, Gilliam's research in Danish schools finds that Muslim boys are positioned as "social problems" in schools by teachers who conclude that boys' challenges in schools are related to their cultural difference and deprived upbringing rather than their academic performance (Gilliam 2007). To address what they perceive as the core of the problem—the students themselves—teachers emphasize educational policies and practices intended to expose immigrant students to Danish ways of being rather than implementing inclusive and rigorous educational practices.

As nationalist policies and figured identities reverberate through schools, they limit the space for the development of culturally responsive educational practices and the recognition of immigrant students. Furthermore, educational policies that emphasize assimilation and the proliferation of standardized tests limit teachers' ability to fully witness and work with the immigrant students in their classrooms (Jaffe-Walter 2008). This is reflected in Lena's words of regret that she can't afford to be slowed down because then "the strong students won't pass the tests." In the next two chapters, dealing with the complex experiences of Muslim students in home countries and in Danish communities and schools, students express exasperation with their teachers' low expectations for their performance alongside educational desires for schools where they are supported and accepted. Their experiences call for an interrogation of technologies of concern, to consider how concern carries worry and advocacy, contradictory desires to reclaim the nation, to rescue poor oppressed Muslim girls, and to uphold understandings about the collective goodness of liberal societies. One must ask, what are the blind spots in liberal approaches to integration? And how is it that concern slides into coercion as it is mapped onto young peoples' bodies and biographies?

Chapter 4

Negotiating Relationships
to Hostlands and Homelands

IN THIS CHAPTER I explore how Muslim youth negotiate their construction within policy and discourse and their response to this figuring with creative improvisations of identity. How do they conceive of their connections to Danish citizenship and peer groups, as well as their relationships to home countries and ethnic communities? Through an exploration of the lives of my focal participants, I investigate how Muslim youth navigate adolescence, carrying the subjectivities produced amid the forces of globalization and nationalism, in their everyday experiences in schools, communities, and families.

The young people in my study forge connections that extend beyond cultural and national borders, developing new forms of consciousness and cultural production within transnational imaginaries (Smith 2006). I address the multiple subjectivities they create as they tiptoe across generations and geographies, negotiating a variety of raced, gendered, and classed topographies within families, schools, religious communities, and nations. Bhatia explores how life in diaspora involves "dialogical" negotiations between the complex circumstances of hostlands and homelands:

What is unique to the dialogical negotiations undertaken in the diaspora is that they are specifically affected by the culture, history, memory and politics of both the hostland and the homeland. Furthermore, these negotiations are not only affected by the incompatible and incongruent politics and cultural practices of the hostland and the homeland but are also embedded within, and fundamentally governed by, the asymmetrical power relationships between the cultures of the Third World and the First World, and the relationships of majority and minority cultures. (Bhatia 2002: 72)

The youth discussed in this chapter defined their own process of identification as one of constant negotiation, as they worked to maintain their real and imagined connections to their native countries, ethnic communities, and religious peer groups. Yet, these diverse connections are in dialectic tension with national identities in both host and home nations as young people come up against the rigid boundaries of gendered visions of citizenship and belonging.

Earlier chapters of this book reveal interactions in classrooms and communities in Western liberal democracies in which teachers, strangers, and policymakers consider young people's transnational and religious connections to be in conflict with national norms of belonging. Young peoples' multiple subjectivities are clearly unsettling to nation-states, producing anxieties about national purity and futures. Yet to the young people themselves, multiplicity is a given; it is the experience and life they know. Here I explore young people's understandings of their multiple selves produced in the diasporic spaces between nations and communities.

Bhatia theorizes that for immigrant children and their families, crafting cultural identities is essentially a "dialogical process that involves a constant moving back and forth between incompatible cultural positions. . . . Such negotiations involve multiple mediations with a larger set of political and historical practices that are linked to and shaped by the specific circumstances of one's 'homeland' and 'hostland'" (Bhatia 2002: 58). Many of my participants and their families fled homelands struggling with civil war, military occupation, and poverty to live in hostlands where their presence is contested. Immigrant youth are often subjected to intensive forms of nationalist policies and technologies because society views them as representing the next generation, the future of the nation. While their parents are the "unintegrated," the "problem" created by lax policies, Muslim youth represent an invitation to imagine a different future.

In this chapter I explore how youths' processes of identity negotiation are shaped by issues of race, gender, nationalism, and power. How do young people negotiate particular identities and subject positions in tension or conflict? How do they carve out their identities within complex figurings, webs of history and global change, and the racialized and gendered politics of host countries? Through an exploration of the lives of three focal participants—Aliyah, Dhalia, and Sara—I offer insights into what it feels like to negotiate everyday exclusion as a Muslim immigrant in a Western liberal democracy, and more significantly, I show how young people pursue fragile webs of belonging and recognition in the context of transnational imaginaries.

Creating a Counter-Public:
Conversations with Aliyah, Sara, and Dhalia

Although I had met Aliyah, Sara, and Dhalia a few weeks before, the events in the "Impossible Love" class (discussed in Chapter 3) marked the beginning of my relationship with the three young women. When I asked Dhalia to talk about how our relationship began she said, "I like Americans and I like to speak English. Also you were very sweet when you asked me about that time in Lena's class when she kept asking me if I would marry a Danish boy." It was in the discussions following this class that I established an "implicit contract" with the girls, which, according to Josselson, allows for "the development of the individual, personal, intimate relationship between researcher and participant . . . the terms of which are difficult to foresee or make explicit" (2007: 539). Josselson goes on to point out that this relationship becomes an "arena for differing assumptions, expectations and contingencies" (2007: 539). Our relationship developed through a conversation about the everyday injustices experienced by Dhalia in Danish schools and deepened over time. In addition to engaging in long conversations, in our early work together, I asked the girls to complete identity maps, visual depictions of the messages that they received about their identities in different spaces.[1] I used these maps to acquire information that might not emerge in the course of traditional focus groups. As my relationship with Aliyah, Dhalia, and Sara matured, our focus groups and meetings provided space for the girls to speak back to everyday processes of racialization. The exchanges constituted what Fraser (1995: 291) calls "counter-publics," areas where young people challenge the ways public discourse represents their race, ethnicity, gender, and religion and stumble into the stew that is self, imagining subjectivities that incorporate multiple histories, desires, and belongings.

My ability to be a part of this space, to establish rapport with the girls, was largely because I was an outsider in Denmark, a friendly stranger. When I asked if I could bring a Danish researcher with me to one focus group, the girls suggested that they would not be comfortable with this, because "she would probably defend Denmark and we could not say how we feel." During our second focus group, Aliyah said the following about our discussions:

Reva: What does it feel like to be talking to me in this way?

Aliyah: I like talking to someone that I don't really know because I can really talk about how I feel. No one ever really asks how I feel. It would be really different to talk to a teacher or to someone that I see every day. Also, I like speaking in English.

My position as an outsider afforded Aliyah the space to talk about how she feels without the fear of judgment. All of the girls mentioned that they learned to express different aspects of their identities depending on the spaces they occupied. They explained that there was particular information that could be shared with teachers and peers, with sisters, parents, and friends. They selectively revealed different aspects of their identities and experiences in different contexts and to different people. It is poignant that Aliyah feels that in school "no one really asks how I feel" yet she reports being the object of much attention and conversation.

In another interview, Dhalia described the risks associated with criticizing teachers or school leadership.

If you were my teacher I wouldn't speak to you like this. My teacher would give me bad grades if I criticized Denmark or the school. Maybe she wouldn't want to let me speak or wouldn't want me in the class.

Eighteen months after our first focus group together, Aliyah spoke of the complicated feelings that emerged through our work together.

It feels good to talk to get our problems out. But I didn't think about these problems before we began to talk. When we began to talk, I began to think about what we are going to do to stop this. I didn't even think about anything before. I just thought why are they doing this to us and then I just stopped thinking about it. When I think about it now, I begin to hate living here more.

All three of the girls mentioned that talking together brought up a variety of emotions. While it both felt good to tell their stories and to be heard, it also unleashed feelings of anger and frustration. Increasingly, the girl's growing awareness and growing critical consciousness revealed the fault lines between the many worlds they navigated.

As I became aware of the girls mixed reactions to our work together and their growing anger about the treatment of immigrants in Denmark, I felt a responsibility to them—to at least make myself available to talk, even if I didn't have the power to influence difficult circumstances. After I returned home to the United States, I kept in touch via email and telephone and I spent time with them during return visits in 2009, 2011, and 2014. There were difficult phone calls when I was not sure how to counsel the girls through conflicts with teachers and principals in new schools. Of the three girls, Sara kept in the closest contact via email and Facebook and expressed the most frustration about her life in Denmark. In one email in the fall of 2011, she wrote:

Hey Reva,

I want to thank you because you're the only one who really bothers to listen to our stories. I also think that it would be a good idea to share them internationally, so everyone can see the truth. I hope I can see you again this year because I've missed you so much and so we can continue our conversations together.

I will be graduating this year; it's my last year I am really looking forward to be finished here in a month. Then I will hold summer vacation in Lebanon and my sister is getting married. But I don't really know what I have to do after I can't find any work, but I wish to continue my education abroad and try new things, there are no opportunities in Denmark to immigrants you can't get a proper education or work especially when you have the scarf on :(

Love & Hugs,

Sara

After this email, Sara and I had a conversation via Skype in which she expressed frustration about the lack of opportunities available to her. I listened and encouraged her to keep working to finish her degree. But ultimately, I felt that my responses were inadequate. From my former work as a teacher, I was accustomed to having solutions, to helping guide young people through difficult times. But in the case of Sara, with the distance and my lack of connections and knowledge about the inside workings of the Danish educational system, there wasn't much I could do. I sent several emails to colleagues in Denmark, trying to find an internship site, but these emails never materialized into opportunities.

Throughout our work together, I have struggled to respect the implicit contract we developed, the terms of the space that allowed Dhalia, Sara, and Aliyah to speak freely and openly. This meant that I allowed them to tell me what they wanted to tell me and at times I did not pursue questions that might have provided more in-depth understanding of their lives. As they described growing up under the interrogating gaze of "concerned" teachers and community members who wanted to know the details of their personal lives, I did not want to be perceived in those ways. And so I avoided probing that might violate the trust that we had built and the terms of the space our dialogue created. It is my hope that the girls were able to strategically use our relationship as a distinct space for speaking from, about, and against their local contexts. I don't think I created this space. It was in my bearing witness, an outsider, a teacher sitting alongside them in classrooms, being present during moments of coercive assimilation in schools that anchored our discussions. This chapter provides different kinds of insights into each of the girl's lives, based on how they chose to narrate their own stories to me and represent the various aspects of their selves.

A Sketch: Aliyah

Aliyah stands taller than her peers and dresses fashionably—the first day I met her, she was wearing a bright orange *hijab* with a matching print dress. In our early discussions together, Aliyah appeared to me to be more confident and outgoing than any of her friends. At times she acted as a translator when Dhalia and Sara struggled for words—she would jump in with a word or she would clarify a point in Danish and then explain in English. She tended to be the most active member of discussions, always ready with incisive analysis that would make an important point while bringing her friends to laughter. Although she described herself as sometimes "shy" as a young girl, in our conversations she was self-assured and spoke firmly and directly. She appeared to be comfortable in the school and frequently spent time between classes and after school hanging out with other students in lounge areas. Aliyah had strong Danish skills because she had attended Engby School for her entire academic career.

One day, after we had been working together in the library for several hours and then moved outside, Aliyah grabbed my camera from me, took pictures of her friends and then asked one of them to take several pictures of her posing under a tree, looking serious in one picture and then smiling broadly in another. She handed the camera back to me when she realized she had received a text message from a friend on her phone. She smiled at the screen and texted back. After hours of hearing her describe difficult and painful experiences of discrimination and missing her family in Ethiopia, it was reassuring to see Aliyah comfortable in her teenage identity as she relaxed with friends in the late afternoon sun, playfully taking pictures, seemingly pleased with her image as she looked at the camera screen and smiled.

Coming of Age: "I Began to See Things That I Didn't See Before"
Aliyah summarized how she came to live in Denmark:

I was born in Somalia. My mom and my brother and I went to Italy and then there were some people who helped them to get to Denmark when there was a war in Somalia. My aunts already lived in Denmark. My dad came one year later. I go back to Ethiopia sometimes. It's the same thing, Ethiopia, Somalia, because of the war the name of the country changed but my family's homes stayed the same. When I am in Ethiopia, I feel that I am home and I can be me.

Aliyah noted that she has family "everywhere" because of the violence in the region of Ethiopia where she lived. Aliyah's family is from Qabridahar, a town in Ogaden, in the Somali region of Ethiopia. While the Somali Muslims in this area had elected an independent government in 1992 and sought to remain independent, the Ethiopian government sent in the military to suppress the independence movement and launched several bloody military campaigns in 1993 and 1994 to gain control of the region. During this period, Aliyah's family dispersed around the globe, to Canada, the United States, Denmark, and Germany. Aliyah's parents fled to Qatar with Aliyah and then moved to Denmark to be reunited with family members who had moved there earlier. Aliyah described her strong connection to her grandfather's farm in Qabridahar. She explained that while national boundaries shifted through war, her "family homes stayed the same." Despite the violence in the region, Aliyah's description of her grandfather's farm suggests a rootedness in place where "I feel like I am home and can be me." As we spoke, it was clear to me that Aliyah's sense of self and personal history knit together experiences that spanned temporal and national boundaries. Her image of her grandfather's farm remained frozen in time, an anchor of the notion of family and self that was central to her own identity. For Aliyah, coming of age in Denmark was not a straightforward process of accepting a Danish identity and shedding an Ethiopian or Somali or Muslim identity. It involved a dialogical process of negotiating her multiple selves within the contexts of the various communities in which she participated.

School Experiences
Aliyah's first school experience in Denmark was an intensive year-long language immersion preschool class that she attended with Rahim and Jamail, boys who

were in her class at Engby School. Aliyah described her early years at Engby School and her close relationships to her ethnic Danish peers:

Aliyah: I started Engbyskolen in kindergarten. In the lower grades, I always thought that I was one of them. I thought that I was Danish. I didn't have problems with them. . . . We would laugh and play around together and my best friends were Danish. But when I grew up, it was different. At the end of ninth grade, I went to Ethiopia and when I came back, when summer vacation was over, I felt like I was a different person, like we were different people.

Reva: Was the change within you or in the way your friends treated you?

Aliyah: I think both them and me. We didn't have the same things together anymore. I began to talk more to Sanaz, the Turkish girl who wears *hijab*. We were always friends before, but after seventh grade it was different. Sanaz and I were best friends and then Sara and Dhalia came from Islamic school and we were all together as immigrant girls.

From her experiences in preschool through her early years in *folkeskole*, Aliyah felt attached to a Danish identity and felt that she fit in with her peers. The trip to Ethiopia coincided with a critical period of identity development in Aliyah's life. When she returned she faced conflicting feelings about her position in her community of peers. Her view of herself transformed from feeling Danish or "one of them" to feeling like she belonged more within the group of immigrant girls. The camaraderie she had felt with the Danish girls dissolved, as she explains: "We didn't have the same things together anymore." Below, she describes a shift in her perceptions of her peers after the trip.

That trip made me begin to see how the Danes are. Before, I thought I was Danish and then I saw where I was really from. Before the trip, when immigrant girls would say bad things about Danish girls, I would get angry, because I felt like I was Danish. When I left, I was speaking only in Danish. When the Danish girls would say negative things about immigrants, I would laugh. I didn't take it seriously. But when I came back, I began to see things that I didn't see before.

Though Aliyah felt accepted within her ethnic Danish peer group and "one of them" for the first nine years of her education, she began to see the limitations of the local context of her Danish peer group.

Returning from her trip, she describes a significant change. She suddenly felt more comfortable at the immigrant girls' table in the lunchroom. As with other youth in my study, the more Aliyah became aware of her ethnic identity and the ways it is contested within the community of her Danish peers, the more she seemed to identify with her immigrant peer group. She reveals how this period during adolescence represents a critical time of racial identity formation that is influenced both by her own emerging sense of self as a Somali and a Muslim as well by as an increasing awareness of the negative views of her Danish peers (Cross 2012). I am not arguing that it was the trip itself that led to Aliyah's exit from her Danish peer group but rather her realization that she no longer could tolerate the anti-immigrant views that circulated in her that group. Perhaps if there had been more room for Aliyah to express her Danish and Somali selves at Engby School without scrutiny by teachers or peers, she might have been able to negotiate relationships across peer groups; but in the figured world of the school where one is either a Dane or an immigrant, it seems this wasn't possible. In Aliyah's upper secondary education at an international school, she describes being able to move more easily between diverse groups of friends.

In 2011, when Aliyah was seventeen, I spent a day with her at Dhalia's apartment in the Engby houses. She was critical of government integration policies and the anti-Muslim attitudes of the current Danish government but she cast her new school, an academic high school with an International Baccalaureate program, in a very different light from Engby School.[2] Aliyah noted that she didn't experience the same kind of anti-immigrant sentiment in the schools that she attended after the tenth grade and that she felt supported academically. She told how the new school had a more "international" feeling and that she had friends who were from China and India as well as from Denmark and other European countries. In this educational space she felt she had more freedom to express aspects of her identity that she had to keep concealed in other schools.

Even when she was in a more inclusive school, Aliyah felt that people made assumptions about her identity. She described how her fellow students teased her when they found out she was from Engby: "They would say, 'Oh, wow are you from gangster-town? Does that mean that you are a gangster?' I would just say, 'Yeah, you better watch out.'" Aliyah also complained that being open about her Muslim identity in her Danish peer group meant that she was often called upon to answer questions about Islam (Zaal et al. 2007). "Sometimes I meet people who ask why I'm wearing *hijab* and what it's like to be a Muslim because they only know what they hear in the media. So sometimes I have a discussion with them and I tell them how I feel. Most people are like, 'Oh I didn't know it was like that.' They are surprised. Sometimes I get tired of it." Several of my participants expressed their frustration over having to educate others about Islam, either in response to others' curiosity or in order to justify their presence.

Bridging Communities: "I'm Not That Person Right Now"

During a phone conversation with Aliyah two years later in May of 2013, she explained that her view of herself and of Danish society was changing. She had finished her studies at the academic high school and was in the midst of studying at a university to become a social worker. Her voice was full of energy as she told me about her program and the government stipend she received to support her while she was in school. She described her plans to be a social worker serving immigrant communities in Denmark: "Danish society needs people who are immigrants to work with immigrants because the Danish people can't figure out what to do about the immigrants. They need people like me. I'm like a bridge between these two worlds to help people understand each other."

As our conversation continued, Aliyah went on to explain that she felt more of an attachment to Denmark than she had in the past.

A lot of me changed since then, since we last spoke. I'm not that person right now. I think that there are Danish people who will accept immigrants. The younger generation is more accepting of immigrants because they grew up with them. The older generations have heard all of the bad things about immigrants in the media and on the news. But with the younger generation, we have a lot in common. We all want to study, we want to work and get a good job.

I don't have the same view of Danish people that I had when I was in Engby School. But it's still the same at Engby School and there are still a majority of people there who hate the immigrants. I just spoke to my friend's younger sister who was very upset because Birgitte was talking to her about how she should have sex. Some things never change. I think the teachers at Engby School wanted something better for us but I just think they didn't know how to give it to us. I still have my friends from childhood who are immigrants and I have made new friends where I have been in high school in my IB class. There are a lot of people from India, China, and America and I also have a lot of new friends who are also Danish. . . . Will I stay in Denmark? I can imagine living here for the rest of my life. I'd like to visit another country for a year or so, study in another country but I think Denmark is the place where I'll always live.

A scan of the photos on her Facebook page reveals images of Aliyah, with her family, in Denmark and Ethiopia, with groups of Danish friends and immigrant friends, images of European rock bands and a blood-stained Somali flag that reads "Justice for Somalia in South Africa." By the age of seventeen, she is firmly rooted in her various affiliations and as a result she seems more immune to processes of figuring and the gendered narratives that are projected onto her. Aliyah spoke out against the brutal violence experienced by Somalis in South Africa and explained that it is important "because people don't really know about it." Aliyah's awareness of the precarious situation of Muslim immigrants in Europe and around the world has led her to become active in the fight for the rights of immigrants. In addition, she has managed to fashion her diverse experiences into a resource as she engages her various selves in working between Danish and immigrant communities. She explained that being successful as an immigrant in Denmark required that she persist in the face of discrimination: "Just because people have looked at you wrong or said no to you because of your *hijab* doesn't mean you have to stop there; without fighting, you can't get what you want."

A Second Sketch: Sara

Sara was born in the Bourj el-Barajneh refugee camp in Lebanon and came to Denmark as an infant with her parents. She explained the circumstances surrounding her family's decision to move:

My parents came to Denmark when I was one year old. They were born in Lebanon but their parents were born in Palestine. They had a very difficult time in Lebanon because they had three girls. In Lebanon there is no help from the government and we had no money and so they decided to come here. It was very difficult for my mother when she first came to Denmark because she had to start over in a new country, learn a new language, and take care of three little girls. My mother was always sad and crying all the time when she first came here because she left her father and her siblings. She never had the chance to meet her mother, who died when she was a baby, so she was raised by her siblings. She was scared of people when she first came. It wasn't easy for her to forget what she saw in Lebanon during the war. There were dead people in the street and my mother's best friend died right in front of her eyes. My parents were the only ones from their families to leave Lebanon. During the war, when life was very difficult, they came to Denmark because it accepted refugees. My parents thought they could provide a good life for us there. When they first arrived in Denmark, they moved to Engby to the same house in the Engby houses where we live now.

Like many other refugees and immigrants, Sara's parents escaped the hardship of war and refugee life to access education and a better life for their children. But Sarah struggles to deal with the racial politics of Denmark and the legacy of generations of exile from Palestine.

In conversations with Sara, images of family closeness are set against the pain of family separation that her parents experienced.

My mother has had a hard time this year because her father died in Lebanon and she didn't have the money to go there to see him. She would talk to him on the phone and I would see her crying. He was having a difficult time because he lived alone. It is good because it's different for me. I live here together with my parents and when I get married, I will live close to my parents so that I can take care of them.

After witnessing family separation, Sara feels fortunate that she lives together with her family and will be able to help them in the future. She recognizes the stability and continuity that her life in Denmark affords her. On a late spring afternoon in 2009, as Sara and I sat together on a picnic table on the playground of Engby School, she talked about her sadness over the challenges her parents have experienced:

I am going to tell you about me and my parents. We are seven children at my house and we can't get what we want. I have two big sisters and I am the third born. I always want to help my parents because things are very difficult now. [Sara stared off into the distance at children playing on the swings and her eyes filled with tears. She paused and then continued.] It is better that we live here rather than in Lebanon because both of my parents are sick and here we can get help from the government. My parents can't work and so I don't know what I would do if we were in Lebanon. When my father moved here he did a lot of work in construction. He had a hard time finding another job because his Danish skills weren't so good but then he got sick and he couldn't find any work. If we were in Lebanon, we would have to work so we could eat and I wouldn't be able to go to school. Sometimes I think that I want to move to Lebanon, but here there are opportunities.

Sara narrates various life trajectories in Lebanon that are all imperfect: connection but not enough money to survive and a lack of opportunity to work and go to school. While it seems that Sara feels that she has more opportunities in Denmark, her father has struggled to find work. Throughout my interviews with Sara, she repeatedly described her strong attachment to Lebanon and her feelings of racialization and exclusion in Denmark. In 2008, while Sara was attending Engby School, she created an identity map that reflected the messages she experienced with friends, family, at school, in "my land," and with Danish people.

In talking about her identity map, Sara said, "I don't think Danish people hate us because we come from another country; it is because they want Denmark to be one language and they are afraid there will be more immigrants than Danish people." Sara represented herself feeling at home with family in her land and had mixed emotions about her experiences in Denmark. In the time I spent with Sara, I felt that the negative messages she received about her identity penetrated her to the core; too often she saw herself through the eyes of others. This is evidenced in her articulation of her experiences in her map. "I feel that I'm crazy [and] I don't know what I'm going to do." In discussing her map Sara explained that sometimes with friends she is very happy and sometimes she is very upset. "With the Danish girls," she said, "I think they are boring and if you don't talk to them, they don't talk to you." Aliyah chimed in to the conversation: "They think Sara is crazy if she does something funny. They are like [*mocking*] 'Oh my God, Sara.'" Sara then added, "Yes, when I'm happy and acting silly, they look down on me." I asked, "So you don't feel like you can be yourself in school?" Sara replied, "No, I feel like I am crazy, as a newcomer to the school and as a

Figure 4.1.   Identity Map: Sara I, age 14.

Muslim girl wearing *hijab*." Sarah thus lingered on the margins of the class that had been together since kindergarten.

Sara attended Islamic school for the first eight years of her education and then transferred to Engby School because she felt that Islamic school was not adequately preparing her for higher education and work. Her parents had hoped that after leaving Engby School she would be able to attend gymnasium, the academic high school that prepares students for university studies, but Sara lacked the linguistic skills to pass the ninth-grade tests required for admission to gymnasium. After leaving Engby School, Sara attended a high school where she pursued training to become a secretary. When I visited with her in the summer of 2010, she seemed happier than she had been while she attended Engby School. She told me about her experiences in a tenth-grade class: "I am better now. Like now when Danish students judge me, I'm not sad like before. I'm good and I know what I'm going to do with my life." She beamed as she told me of her plans to be a secretary. While she seemed hopeful about the future, she also described one particular Danish teacher who didn't know her name and frequently called her by the name of another student who wore *hijab*. She expressed disappointment with the teachers' low expectations of immigrant students and described being given the lowest level of work even when her grades were higher than those of her Danish peers. When I suggested that things still seemed challenging, she said that the current treatment she received was different from her experience in the ninth grade because "teachers in the tenth-grade class are not getting into my personal life like teachers at Engby School. They leave me alone." She felt that being in a school where teachers were intruding in her private life and encouraging her to assimilate to Danish norms was more difficult than navigating a school with low expectations for immigrant students.

When I spoke to Sara in the spring of 2012, the cheer in her voice seemed forced. She expressed relief over having finished her classes and was looking forward to summer vacation in Lebanon. But after a few minutes her voice lowered as she said, "I really don't know what I'm going to do here now that I'm finished with school. I can't get my degree until I get an internship and it's impossible to get an internship if you wear *hijab*." She described an endless stream of unsuccessful interviews and one instance in which the interviewer told her that he was worried that having a secretary who wears *hijab* would scare clients. When I spoke to Aliyah about Sara's situation during a phone conversation, she was critical of Sara's choice to pursue a career as a secretary: "I think it's tough to be an immigrant and a secretary in Denmark. To get a job as a secretary, people are really looking at you. Most of the secretaries are blonde haired and blue eyed. I think as an immigrant in Denmark you have to think about where you can get a job, especially if you are a girl who wears *hijab*."

Unable to complete her degree, Sara took a job in the kitchen at a local bakery. After a few months she wrote to me, saying that the job was "off the books" and that her boss refused to pay her and so she stopped working there. With debt and frustration building, Sara is more pessimistic about opportunities in Denmark, but continues to search for work. As of mid-2015 Sara was still looking for work. It seems that in shaping her multiple selves, Sara has had limited opportunities to develop notions of self that radically depart from the scripts and narratives of the figured world of Danish immigration.

A Third Sketch: Dhalia

In 2007, Dhalia told me the following about her family:

My parents were born and lived in Lebanon and fell in love there. My father came to Denmark as a teenager and went to school in Denmark up until he was in the tenth grade. My mother moved to Denmark when she was twenty-one. It was very hard for her in the beginning because she couldn't speak Danish. When my parents first came here it was hard for them because they didn't have work. Now, things are much better for them because six months ago they opened their own shop selling food from other countries. Now things are better for them. But some things are still difficult. . . . My mother has also been trying to get a Danish passport since she moved here. She still can't travel out of the European Union. They do not accept my mother because she is an immigrant and they think there are too many immigrants in Denmark.

Dhalia asserted that while there are more opportunities in Denmark than in Lebanon, she will always feel like an outsider in Denmark. On many occasions, Dhalia repeated that even though she was born in Denmark and lives in Denmark, she does not consider herself Danish. She considers herself Palestinian, and expressed anger at her parents for moving to Denmark. Like Aliyah and Sara, Dhalia describes how her family is spread out across the globe:

I have family in Germany and Switzerland, my uncle lives there, in Sweden and in Lebanon. I am going to visit Beirut during the summer vacation. I was there last in 2006 when there was war. When I was there [I was] at a party and I met my boyfriend Wallid. This summer I am going back. I have a lot of family there and the sun is perfect. My cousin's daughter is going to get married and I am going to the wedding. It will be very beautiful. I feel very different there.

In summer 2010, Dhalia described how she left her current school, a well-known private gymnasium where she was the only immigrant girl in the school. She explained that despite her efforts, she couldn't make friends in the school and she ultimately found the isolation to be too much. She described how she was often called upon to speak about Islam in the school. "My teachers were always asking me to make presentations about Islam. One time when I was giving a presentation at the gymnasium this Danish boy started asking me questions about Islam, like about why women were forced to have children and all of this stuff, then he asked questions that I didn't know the answer to and everyone was just staring at me. I felt sick." Dhalia felt alone at the gymnasium, seen in terms of narratives about Islam, asked to speak for her culture but not understood. When she chose to leave the gymnasium, she had a contentious meeting with the headmaster, who wanted her to explain why she was leaving. She said, "He was like, 'Haven't we done enough here for you?' I felt like he was mad that I was making the school look bad. My leaving made them feel like racist or something." For a prestigious private gymnasium, Dhalia was evidence of the school's openness and enlightenment. From the perspective of the administrators, that she would want to leave was a stain on the school's reputation. After leaving the gymnasium in 2010, Dhalia took bookkeeping classes but ultimately got a factory job assembling boat lanterns.

On several occasions, Dhalia expressed her anger that her parents had chosen a life in Denmark. In 2008, she described a conversation she had with her mother: "My mom sometimes says to me that I am born in Denmark. She says that I am Danish. When we watch TV and the queen is on, she will say, 'See, there is your queen.' I say, 'No, I'm not Danish. I'm Arab. You gave birth to me here; it's not my choice.'" Throughout her life, Dhalia positioned herself as an internal exile (Sirin and Fine 2008) in Denmark, physically living in and legally attached to Denmark, while feeling psychologically excluded and positioned as an outsider. Although Dhalia was the only one of the three girls to have been born in Denmark, she seemed to distance herself from a Danish identity even more than Aliyah or Sara.

In our meeting in 2010, Dhalia first told me of her dream to live in Lebanon. Two years later, when I returned to Denmark, she had exciting news: she had become engaged to her boyfriend and was planning to move to Lebanon with him. "I've been in love with Wallid for such a long time," she exclaimed. "I'm glad that we will be together. I'm now excited that I can finally be in Beirut, as I have always wanted. . . . I've always known that I would leave Denmark someday. I want to continue my education but that has always been a little bit stressed with me in Denmark." After her wedding in the fall of 2013, Dhalia wrote to tell me that she was studying Arabic language and culture at a university in Beirut. "I started university here," she wrote, "and it is so much harder than school in Denmark. I am so busy but I love it and I would fight for it."

Transnational Connections

In the beginning, when I first went to Ethiopia, I was in different clothes than them. Someone on the street was like looking down at me but most people said "Mannn, I heard you are from Europe." When I am there I feel more European but here I feel that they are looking down on me.   —Aliyah

Even though Dhalia, Aliyah, and Sara described home countries that were torn by civil war and upheaval, suffering from shifting borders and exclusionary policies, to the girls these countries represented safety and a rootedness in place where as, Aliyah says, "I feel like I am home and I can be me." Visits to home countries allowed the girls to see themselves outside of the light of the figured world of Danes and immigrants, us and them. Aliyah describes herself as feeling "European" in Ethiopia, casting her difference in a positive light, whereas in Denmark she feels that "they are looking down on me." Through their attachments to native countries, immigrant youth are able to envision versions of self that are protective, sustaining them through experiences of discrimination in hostlands. But notions of home are complex for youth of diaspora, for while there may be acceptance and recognition, there is also longing for the "home" of Denmark, for the familiar tastes and smells of childhood. For instance, Aliyah mentioned that on a summer trip to Ethiopia, she missed her friends and Danish *rugbrod* (rye bread).

Creating narratives about experiences in home countries, young people described idealized visions of themselves in home countries. In a discussion about a visit to Ethiopia in the eighth grade, Aliyah did not mention the challenges she described in her native country at other times, such as feeling like an outsider or struggling to find words in Somali. Her experience of this place was also insulated from the bloodshed and war that her parents had witnessed.

It was such a good trip; it was two months. I spent time in my father and mother's hometown. It was fun getting to know my big family. My granddad has a camel farm and he has all kinds of animals like little lambs. And I loved being with my cousins.

Aliyah portrays an idealized journey to a homeland she is "really" from, where she plays with cousins and lambs and visits her mother and father's village. In many cases, young people narrated selective idealized accounts of life in home countries when talking about the racialization and exclusion they felt in Denmark.

In a focus group in 2008 in which Aliyah, Sara, and Dhalia were drawing identity maps, as Aliyah began work on her map she asked, "Reva, can I say how I feel when I go home back to my country? Can I draw how people see me in Ethiopia and in Denmark?" She drew a line down the middle of the page and proceeded to draw maps that illustrated stark contrasts between the messages that she received about her identities in her native country and in Denmark (see Figure 4.2).

In 2011 Aliyah said the following about her map:

This is me in Denmark. The black symbolizes that they hate me. I don't like to be here. Here I wrote I am not a human but an animal. And like the heart means, like my heart is black I don't feel anything. People hate me because of my *hijab*. I think that I am nothing. [In Ethiopia] I drew a sun because I am happy and there is a lot of sun there [*laughs*].

Figure 4.2.   Identity Map: Aliyah, age 15.

Aliyah's descriptions of racialization and exclusion in Denmark are set in stark contrast to the acceptance she feels in Ethiopia. In describing her map, she said: "When I'm in Ethiopia, I feel like I belong, but here, I feel like they hate me." Like Aliyah's descriptions of her experiences in Ethiopia, she creates an idealized vision of Ethiopia and a vision of herself that is very different from the self she describes in Denmark where "I think I am nothing." On the left side of her map, in Denmark, she drew a black heart with the words, "people hate me because of my *hijab*" and on the right in Ethiopia, she drew a red heart with the words, "I am human." Perhaps, not being able to "feel anything" in Denmark is a reflection of the tight spaces in which she is forced to negotiate her identity.

Like Aliyah's map, Dhalia's depicts a self in sunny Lebanon in contrast to the "dark/night" of Denmark.

Here this is in Denmark and this is me and here they are thinking that we immigrants only come here for money. They think that immigrants are going to destroy Denmark because there are some immigrant boys who are criminals. It's dark and night and I feel *ensomhed* [alone] and nobody wants to speak to me. This side is in Lebanon and

Figure 4.3.   Identity Map: Dhalia, age 14.

I feel very happy and the green color symbolizes hope and everybody likes me and nobody would look down on me. And all in Lebanon have the same traditions but it is also hard because sometimes there is war and you can't get money if you don't have work. But there is love and family.

Dhalia's images of the dark night on the right side of the map convey the negative messages and isolation she feels living in Denmark. In particular, she takes up the discursive narrative that immigrants are "uninvited guests" (Hervik 2004: 258), laborers who come to Denmark "only for money" and overstay their welcome. The left side of Dhalia's map shows a sense of happiness and well-being in Lebanon despite the challenges of economic uncertainty and war. Although Dhalia was born in Denmark and has visited Lebanon only for visits in the summer, it seems that she, like Aliyah and Sara, narrates connections to a "home" country" that insulate her from the negative messages she experiences in Denmark. Above the figure of herself in Denmark, Dhalia asks, "Why [do] I live here?"—thus expressing her struggle with psychological assaults in a place that she didn't choose to live.

Dhalia's description of Lebanon as a place where "everybody likes me and nobody would look down on me" is similarly idealized. Her description includes a discussion of the political and economic challenges her family experienced in Lebanon: "because sometimes there is war and you can't get money if you don't have work." Across all the girls' many descriptions of visits to Lebanon and Ethiopia, there was a clear sense of how they were strengthened by their connections to home countries. As the anthropologist James Clifford finds, "The empowering paradox of diaspora is that dwelling *here* assumes a solidarity and connection *there*. But *there* is not necessarily a single place or an exclusivist nation. . . . [It is] the connection [elsewhere] that makes a difference [here]" (1994: 322, emphasis in the original). Visits to "home" countries become crystallized in the imaginations of the young women, representing visions of self that are frozen in time. Yet, at the same time, home countries also represent a place where young women can return to access a more authentic self. In her memoir, *Lost in Translation*, Eva Hoffman describes her deep nostalgia for her home country, Poland, after her family moved to Canada:

Loss is a magical preservative. Time stops at the point of severance, and no subsequent impressions muddy the picture you have in mind. The house, the garden, the country you have lost remain forever as you remember them. Nostalgia—that most lyrical of feelings—

crystallizes around these images like amber. Arrested within it, the house, the past, is clear, vivid, made more beautiful by the medium in which it is held and by its stillness. (1998: 115)

Listening to the girls' recollections of childhood visits to home countries, I heard a similar kind of nostalgic recollection of an idealized home, frozen in time, where they could be themselves. But the girls' connections to this idealized home entailed less of a feeling of loss—or, as Hoffman puts it, "a phantom pain" (1998: 115)—and more of a sense that the home county was a lifeline and a place where they could assert a version of self free of their disciplined and truncated identities in Denmark. The girls' narratives reveal the nostalgia for a home where life is simpler and where they feel they belong. This nostalgia is not unlike the nostalgia of Danish teachers and policymakers who describe their longing for an idealized past before Muslim immigration.

Home visits or "re-education" trips have been the subject of government policies that construct notions of such visits as impeding the integration of immigrant youth. In 2006 as part of nationalist reforms such as the elimination of national funding for mother-tongue instruction, the government passed a series of restrictions on trips to home countries in order to facilitate the integration of immigrant youth and to prevent absences from school. However, the government has not viewed Danish students' absences for family vacations and trips in the same light. Its discriminatory policies have been part of a constellation of policies that seek to erode young peoples' transnational attachments and parents' efforts to preserve their own cultural and religious traditions. While these policies frame home visits as harmful to young peoples' development, the girls' narratives reveal that these visits help them to ground themselves in positive visions of self as they move into adulthood.

Like Aliyah and Dhalia, Sara also maintained close connections with her family. In an interview in 2011 Sara explained, "I'm so excited because this summer I'm going to take a road trip in Lebanon with my family. We try to go to Lebanon to see our family every year if we have money. I feel very welcome there, like I'm with my own people, my own family." But Sara also points out that in Lebanon, people know she is not Lebanese: "When I walk on the street they can see that I'm not from there, they know I'm not Lebanese but they welcome me there. But I feel like I'm home and I'm one of the people who lives there." In Sara's identity map and in her descriptions Lebanon is "home," a place where she belongs and where she is welcomed. However, in other instances she had a much different view of Lebanon, describing how Palestinians have lived in a tenuous state of belonging in Lebanon.

I am very grateful that my parents came to Denmark to give us a better and good life, especially when I see how my family in Lebanon lives. Palestinians in Lebanon are not treated as Lebanese. It is very difficult for Palestinians to find work in Lebanon, especially Palestinians without education. Most Lebanese hate Palestinians, and I can even see when I go down there, they are treated badly; my parents' families live in very old houses that have been built a long time [ago] and are about to fall apart. Their houses are quite small and dirty, even the water is polluted and they can't drink it.

Sara was born in the Bourj el-Barajneh Palestinian refugee camp in a southern suburb of Beirut, which was created in 1948 to provide housing for Palestinians displaced by the creation of the state of Israel. The camp houses approximately twenty thousand residents in an area of less than a third of a square mile. Palestinians in Lebanon live in a permanent state of non-belonging, barred from most skilled professions and not permitted to own land. Despite generations of residency, they have been unable to gain the basic rights of citizenship. These exclusionary policies are generated by fears that granting Palestinians rights in Lebanon could lead to their naturalization (Wood 2013).

In June 2013, Sara traveled to Beirut by herself to see her family and attend Dhalia's wedding. Although thrilled to see her family and cousins who were visiting from the United States, in a message to me she admitted she was tired of being there because of the poor conditions. "There isn't always power or light," she wrote, "and it's really hot and smells of something dirty (if you know what I mean)." She shared a picture she took on that visit (Figure 4.4).

At first Sara portrayed life in Lebanon in different ways, so different that are at odds with one another. She moved between descriptions of Lebanon as the home where she was accepted and then as a place marked by the stark realities of war, poverty, and the tenuous belongings associated with being a Palestinian in exile. Nonetheless, Lebanon was the place that Sara considered home and experienced acceptance within a large web of family. It was also where she was able to experience, as she describes it, "a Palestinian community where I can be surrounded by other Palestinians." She posted images of herself on Facebook wearing zebra-striped pants and a bright blue *hijab*, laughing with cousins at a Beirut café in the late evening. No doubt Sara relishes these moments when she can be herself and still be accepted, and doesn't have work so hard to assert her own belonging.

Although Sarah and Dhalia spoke of their connections to a Palestinian identity, they did not talk about connections to the Palestinian territories. To Sarah and Dhalia, "home" is Lebanon, though being Palestinian is also central to their identities. Sara explained that in her family, her parents and grandparents talk more about Palestine and have a strong place-based identification with the Palestinian territories.

We don't talk about it [Palestine] so often anymore. My parents' parents had a house in Palestine, my grandfather kept the key since they went to Lebanon, but they could never return because the house was taken from them. My aunt's daughter traveled to Palestine a few years back and she went and took a video of the house. She showed us the house and the big farm that was planted by trees of fruit and olives.

Figure 4.4.   Image of Bourj el-Barajneh Palestinian Refugee Camp. Published with the permission of the photographer.

There are clearly differences in how individuals from different generations look back on experiences of diaspora. Given that Sara had never been to Palestine, these stories and connections became a part of her own diasporic imaginary in which grandparents' and parents' memories are woven together with her own, crystallized in images of fruit trees and keys to locks that no longer exist.

Negotiating Schooling in Hostlands or Host(i)l(e)lands

Given the cultural discontinuities of living in diaspora, Dhalia's and Sara's parents wanted their daughters to attend Islamic school in Denmark so that they would learn Arabic and remain faithful to their cultural and religious values. Whether to send children to Islamic or public schools is often a difficult decision for immigrant families. On the one hand, parents want their children to have the skills to be successful in host societies, but they also want to preserve traditions and values that have sustained diasporic families for generations. In addition, many immigrant families see religious schools as a way to buffer their children from anti-immigrant attitudes and assimilative practices.

In describing the positive aspects of her experience in Islamic school, Sara explained that she felt fortunate to have had the opportunity to learn Arabic and to maintain connections to her culture. However, she was critical of her academic experience because it failed to provide her with the Danish-language skills that she needed to be successful in the Danish educational system.

It is difficult for me because I went to Islamic school as a young child because my parents wanted me to learn the culture and to learn Arabic. In Islamic school, I feel like I didn't learn Danish. When I came to Danish school in seventh grade, I feel like I was just beginning. It felt much better to be in Islamic school because we learned about our religion and our culture and it meant a lot to our parents. Also, I didn't have teachers telling me that I should be Danish and I should have sex and all these crazy things. But it caused problems for me because we spoke Arabic all the time and then my Danish skills were not strong enough when I went into the Danish schools. There are some students who go to the Arabic school who go into the gymnasium but most of them drop out because they don't have the language skills they need.

Dhalia's experience was similar: "In the eight grade, I stopped going to Islamic school because it was far from my house and I feel like I didn't learn anything from the fourth grade to seventh grade. When I was there I didn't learn Danish and there we spoke Arabic because all of the students were Arab." But after commenting on the academic limitations, Sara also reflected back on her experiences in Birgitte's class and in other classes at Engby School. "At least in Islamic school, I didn't have teachers telling me that I should have sex and be Danish." She reveals how accessing academic resources required that she negotiate the gaze of concerned teachers.

Eva Gulløv's (2008 personal communication) research among preschool parents in Engby found that despite some Muslim parents' perceptions that Danish schools were academically superior to Islamic schools, some parents chose Islamic schools because of concerns about the sexual content in the curriculum and the fear of negative views of immigrant families. Per, the principal of Engby School, confirmed this and explained that after nationalist shifts in education policies and the elimination of mother-tongue instruction in 2001, increasing numbers of immigrant parents chose Islamic schools over Danish schools. This raises significant questions about schooling and integration that linger internationally. Some Latino families, for example, and some immigrant groups in the United States choose parochial schools over supposedly better schools in order to maintain cultural, linguistic, and religious identities.

Research on Muslim students in secular public schools details the obstacles these students face in negotiating their religious values in the context of pressures to assimilate to the dominant Eurocentric frameworks of Western liberal schools. Zine's research finds that anti-Muslim discrimination coupled with peer pressure can lead to a loss of Islamic identity and disengagement with the home culture (Zine 2001). Zine demonstrates that Muslim students can resist marginalization by joining Muslim organizations in schools. At the time of my observations, there were no such organizations in any of the schools with significant immigrant populations that I visited and any attempts by Muslim students to gather were treated as a threat. While teachers and the principals at the schools where I observed did make accommodations for Muslim students, such as not serving pork in the school cantina or providing changing rooms for girls for gym classes, there were no extracurricular activities created for Muslim students. At Engby School it was understood to be a problem when Muslim students were together in groups without ethnic Danish students. There was a sense that allowing Muslim student groups would exacerbate the "problems" of self-segregation as well as a fear of the risk of potential terrorism.

As discussed earlier, while Per insists that Danish schools are secular and do not allow religion, a factor that underlay his decision to deny an exclusive

Muslim prayer space, a number of Christian traditions and rituals, such as preparation for confirmation, are a taken-for-granted part of Danish schools. I cite this example again not to suggest that the school should have a dedicated prayer room, but rather to underscore that Islam is contested and treated as a threat in the everyday practices of the school. While Per and the teachers conceive of the school as tolerant and respectful of difference, Muslim students point to the multiple ways their identities are scrutinized in Danish schools. Perhaps, as Zine's (2001) research reveals, creating opportunities for Muslim students to support one another might actually promote schools' goals of encouraging the engagement of such students. Given the current immigration discourse and the conflation of Islam with terrorism, however, school administrators view Muslim student organizations through the lens of risk and, as Per suggested, fear that their members might pressure their peers to become "real" Muslims. However, there are numerous examples that reveal that the more immigrant youth experience acceptance of their identities, the more likely it is that they will be engaged in schools (Barreto and Ellemers 2002).

When Dhalia and Sara left Islamic school and started at Engby School, they had a very difficult transition. Dhalia described the challenges when she transferred to Engby School: "In the beginning it was very hard for me at Engby School because I didn't know anyone but Sara." In a conversation with the three girls, Aliyah described how Dhalia and Sara's treatment was different from the way she was treated because she had attended Engby School since kindergarten: "I feel like they hate Sara more because I have been in the class since kindergarten and so when Sara started, the girls didn't want to talk with her. But when Dhalia started most of the girls wanted to talk to her because she didn't wear *hijab* so she was accepted more than Sara because she wears *hijab*." Aliyah added, "It was the same when I started wearing *hijab*. It was like some girls just said 'Okay, I'm not going to talk to you anymore.'" Though Dhalia and Sara, who entered Engby in the ninth grade, clearly had a different experience, the reaction to Aliyah when she began to wear the *hijab* exemplifies the public scrutiny of signs of Muslim religious and cultural life. Beyond that, the girls reveal how difficult it was to move from Islamic school, where wearing *hijab* and being Muslim was the norm, to a Danish school, where they were expected to conform to Danish liberal values. In thinking about how young people position themselves within the schools and communities of host societies, it is critical to examine the messages they receive about their identities and the ways those messages might complicate or enable their participation. I have focused here on the ways that young people develop multiple subjectivities through their experiences of diaspora and the ways they are required to check particular identities at the door when they enter state-sponsored schools.

Challenging Integration Paradigms

In these young women's stories we hear of multiple selves formed at the intersection of the different historical circumstances of homelands struggling with civil war and occupation and a hostland where they are positioned as outsiders. In their depictions of their experiences in home countries they describe being at peace, at "home." As the girls struggle to create tenuous webs of connection across geographies, they reveal the fundamental human need to belong, to be known, and to be accepted. The girls' narratives acknowledge the many opportunities open to them in Denmark, such as social benefits, some jobs, and free education, but their lives in Denmark are filled with constant reminders that they don't belong.

Aliyah's story speaks to the importance of recognition as she was able to access higher education and social contexts where Danish, Muslim, and Ethiopian traditions were not assumed to be in conflict. Although Aliyah felt she had to silence aspects of self at Engby School, at the school with the International Baccalaureate program, as she explained, she had more freedom to be herself and more space for the expression of difference. Aliyah took advantage of this flexibility to move between Danish and immigrant peer groups and communities, crafting a vision of self that selected from various threads. Contrary to the assumptions of the figured world of Danish immigration, Aliyah was able to claim an authority based on her unique experiences as a Danish Muslim woman in order to work toward improving relations between ethnic Danish and immigrant communities. In the next chapter I consider the experiences of the larger group of young people in my study and explore how Muslim students saw their own identities in relation to Danishness and how they negotiated their multiple selves in schools and communities.

The complex experiences and narrations of the youth in my study call into question popular notions of what it means to integrate "into" host nations. Young people cannot simply shed their cultures and legacies to replace them with more liberal, Western identities. Policies that propose "integration" as a process of unlearning and learning culture silence the multiple, contested, and sometimes contradictory voices that immigrant youth experience when they are living across multiple worlds simultaneously. And young people's stories also reveal that negotiating "cultures" is not simply an act of learning to be bicultural, happily holding sanitized and acceptable parts of one's legacy alongside the traditions and values of host countries (LaFromboise et al. 1998). In the complex terrain of globalization, young people are not merely moving out of one national cultural context and into another; instead, they are negotiating multiple national, religious, and cultural identities. In the next chapter I introduce youth who identify as Palestinian from Lebanon who are living in Denmark, others who identify as Iraqi Bulgarians, and still others from immigrant families who identify as Danish. These youth live across unique spaces of diaspora that are produced through the political forces of labor migration and political occupation and dispossession. Unlike immigrant communities of previous generations that moved across oceans on ships to never see their homelands again, through international travel and digital technologies, these youths enjoy living, breathing connections to homelands.

Chapter 5

Somali by Nature, Muslim by Choice, Danish by Paper

Narrating Identities

I was happy to see Sara approach as I waited at the bus stop near the school. I planned to meet at the bus stop with Aliyah and Sara and then to travel to the library where we would meet with Dhalia to talk. It was difficult to find a space in Engby where we could talk and work privately. When we spent the day in the gardens at Louisiana, people would linger near us, smiling, listening. I feel like we are being watched. At the library we had reserved a private room where we would have time and space to work. Sara and I stood in the early spring sunlight just outside of the bus shelter when a woman approached. She had a white substance around the corners of her mouth, smelled of alcohol and wore a red baseball hat that covered her nearly hairless head. She kept speaking to Sara and then to me in Danish with a pleading look on her face. She asked Sara over and over, "Why don't you go into politics?" "Are you happy here?" The people waiting for the bus with us just watched as the woman's voice grew louder and louder. We walked away from her and she followed us. My hands were shaking and other people standing at the bus stop began to stare at us but no one intervened. I was relieved to see Aliyah approaching and I asked if we could get a taxi to the library. Aliyah laughed and said, "There are no taxis in Engby." So we waited and the woman finally drifted away from us. When the bus arrived, Aliyah, Sara, and I boarded it and sat near the back. The woman sat in the last seat next to two boys who had short dark hair, were of medium build and appeared to be about 12 years old and of Arab descent. When the woman began yelling loudly at one of the boys, Aliyah threw her head back in reaction and rolled her eyes. She translated for me. The woman said to one of the boys, "Why do you hate me? Why are you angry at me?" The boy did not answer and she repeated the question several times during the ten-minute trip to the library. Finally the boy quietly said, "I wish I wasn't born here." The woman yelled back at him, "You could never be born here."

—Field notes, Engby, 5/1/2009

WHILE THIS WOMAN was clearly unstable, she gave voice to the narratives about Muslim youth that linger in the air in the figured world of Danish immigration. Sara and Aliyah's response to this incident suggested that they had grown accustomed to public scrutiny of their identities. The woman makes certain assumptions about the youth she encounters based on their physical attributes and dress—Sara's *hijab* and the boys' dark hair. The woman continued to urge Sara, "You should go into politics," as if she required some encouragement to participate in Danish society. The message is positive, but the woman probably would not have approached an ethnic Danish young woman in the same way. Her questions to the boy, "Why do you hate me? Why are you angry at me?" echoes the stereotype of the criminal immigrant boy. In the end, she reminds the boy that he will always be seen as a foreigner: "You could never be born here."

While both boys and girls are subject to routine policing of their identities, there are significant differences in the ways they are positioned within the figured world of Danish immigration. Girls are objects of concern, deemed worthy of sympathy and care; boys are "troublemakers" and "criminals." It is clear that the woman considered both the boy and Sara as bodies out of place—bodies that invite comment in the public space of the bus stop—unlike ethnic Danes, who belong naturally. In interviews, students described other incidents of being approached in public by strangers. In an interview, Aliyah shares another encounter on public transportation.

There are so many immigrants in other lands but they don't have it like this. They don't want us to be here in Denmark. Especially the old people. I was getting out of the train with my aunt and she had the stroller. I was helping her carry the stroller down and I had the bottom of the stroller and I took it with me and an old man pushed me and said "get out of my land." I said if you don't want me here you can say that but you can't stop me.

This incident is one of many stories shared by the youth in my study, a moment on a staircase that echoes countless other experiences. While I experienced the interaction at the bus stop as shocking and disturbing, it was clear that the girls were accustomed to encounters of this sort, reflecting what Solorzano and colleagues (2000) describes as "microagressions," the subtle (and sometimes not so subtle) insults that people of color experience in their daily lives.

Although young people receive constant reminders of their outsider status, society expects that they should still want to embrace Danish norms and values and cultivate Danish identities to become properly integrated citizens. This expectation is based on the assumption that of course immigrants should want to take up the putatively superior traditions and values of Danish society, to enjoy the benefits of their host country. This chapter examines the complexities of negotiating Danish identities in the context of a world where immigrant youth are understood to be bodies out of place, bodies that never truly belong.

Hyphenated Identities

Interviews with my participants revealed that the messages they received about their identities influenced how they conceived of their own relationships to Danish identities. In my discussions with students, I introduced the idea of hyphenated identities, that is, an identity that blends aspects of Danishness and other national affiliations. I was interested in knowing to what degree the students felt Danish and Palestinian, Iraqi, or Turkish. In his research on globalization and acculturation, the social psychologist Berry (2008) developed a model of acculturation which explored the extent to which individuals are willing and allowed to participate in their host societies and home culture simultaneously. His work explores how immigrants create hyphenated or blended identities that encompass elements of host and home countries. Sirin and Fine (2008) examine how Muslim youth in America have negotiated their identities following 9/11 and explore how they negotiate hyphenated selves. It was largely the work of Sirin and Fine (2008) that inspired me to ask my participants to create identity maps such as those shown earlier encompassing their experiences in homelands and hostlands. I hoped that these representations would help me understand how the immigrant youth in Denmark conceived of their identities. Sirin and Fine (2008: 136) considered youths' identities to be "integrated" if their affiliations with home and host cultures were blended in a nonconflicting way, "parallel" if both identities were represented as existing in separate worlds, or "conflictual" if their attachments were conflicting or irreconcilable. The majority of the Muslim youth in Sirin and Fine's study described membership in U.S. mainstream society as well as a Muslim community. The authors explain:

When we looked at the correlations among the three domains of the scale across the Muslim and American affiliations, there was a positive and significant relation between how they view their membership to American mainstream society and the Muslim community at large. The more the participants saw themselves as members of the Muslim community, the more likely they also saw themselves as a member of the mainstream U.S. society. Together, these findings suggest that Muslim and American identities were not mutually exclusive, and on the contrary, were highly compatible. (2008: 147)

Some of the Muslim-American participants in Sirin and Fine's study described personal experiences of surveillance and anti-Muslim discrimination in school and community in the wake of 9/11, but overall the majority depicted identities that represented their affiliations with both the United States and Muslim communities.

One of the maps in Sirin and Fine illustrates the ways a student experienced the American/Muslim/Afghani aspects of his identity as distinct but also integrated in the "highway" of his life (Figure 5.1). Sirin and Fine's research critiques claims about the incompatibility of "Muslim" and "American" identities and reveals that embracing one's Muslim identity *encouraged* affiliation with the national community. This is in stark contrast to the logic of U.S. and European integration regimes that frame Muslim values as a barrier to cultivation of national identities.

Unlike Sirin and Fine's participants, the Muslim youth in my study explained that it is essentially not possible to be a Muslim Dane. They depicted "conflictual" identities in their maps and explained that being Danish means having the physical characteristics of ethnic Danes and celebrating Christian holidays. In addition, many emphasized how experiences of surveillance and exclusion reinforced their feelings that they could not be Danish. They explained that being a Dane means belonging—i.e., having the right to participate in Danish society without being the object of suspicion or concern. In interview after interview,

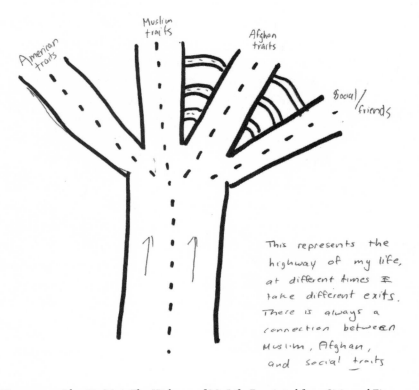

Figure 5.1. Identity Map: The Highway of My Life. Reprinted from Sirin and Fine (2008) with permission of NYU Press © 2008.

first- and second-generation youth (and one second-generation immigrant teacher) used the same words to explain that being Danish involves "eating pork, having blue eyes, celebrating Christmas and Easter." When compared to the responses of Sirin and Fine's participants, these findings invite questions about differences between how Muslim's are received in the United States and Europe. A number of scholars have documented that Muslim youth in the United States have experienced Islamophobia and racializing discourses following 9/11 that has led them to be positioned as outsiders and subject to forms of everyday racialization (Abu El-Haj 2015; Maira 2009). Dorah (age twenty) a participant in Sirin and Fine's study (2008) vividly depicts how her life changed dramatically after the events of 9/11 (see Figure 5.2).

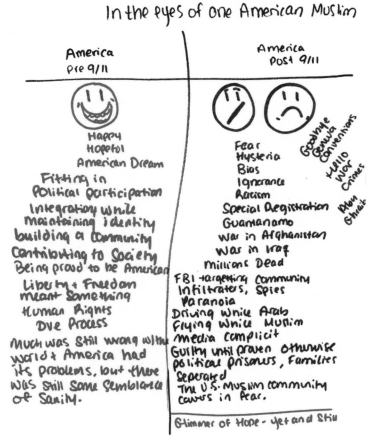

Figure 5.2.   Identity Map: In the Eyes of One American Muslim. Reprinted from Sirin and Fine (2008) with permission of NYU Press © 2008.

While Muslim youth in the United States experience racialization, the context is somewhat different in that there is a more expansive view of what it is to be American. Perhaps there is more potential for Muslim, "home country," and American identities to exist together, that is, the development of one identity is not understood to require the muting of the other. In Denmark, on the other hand, there is a collective idea of what it means to be Danish and an expectation that immigrant children should want to embrace that ideal. However, looking across national contexts reveals that violent events such as 9/11 and the Hebdo attacks have led to national anxieties that influence how young people are positioned and the messages they receive about their identities. In the current integration discourse, there is much attention to the degree to which young people see themselves as members of the national community and are willing to declare themselves to be, for instance, French, American, or Danish. Yet, there seems to be a lack of awareness of how the tide of messages and experiences of everyday surveillance and racialization might influence young people's identifications.

On What It Feels Like to Be a Problem

Just as the woman at the bus stop in the vignette that opens this chapter says, "you could never be born here," immigrant youth in Denmark are told that their identities conflict with Danish values in myriad ways that echo through policy, the media, and the stares and comments of strangers. Moustafa Bayoumi explores W. E. B. Du Bois's well-known question "How does it feel to be a problem?" in the context of the experiences of Muslim Americans following 9/11:

Profiling Arabs and Muslims has in reality expanded far beyond the realms of law enforcement. Arab and Muslim Americans are now routinely profiled in their places of employment, in housing, for public opinion polls and in the media. Yet they remain curiously unknown. Broadly speaking, the representations that describe them tend to fall into two types, the exceptional assimilated immigrant and the violent fundamentalist, with very little room in between. The questions that are asked in the media and in real life constantly circle simplistically around the same frame of reference—terrorism, women, and assimilation—fixations that may be understandable in this age but that frequently overlook the complex human dimensions of Muslim-American or Arab-American life. (2008: 4)

The male Muslim students in my study poignantly described the difficulty of negotiating these kinds of fixations in their daily lives in their communities and in schools. They reported on the multiple ways they were told that they didn't belong. Danish psychologist Iram Khawaja's research documents how Muslim immigrants experience stereotyping gazes in Denmark, what one of her participants described as the "second class stare" (2014: 2). Despite the presence of these exclusionary discourses that emphasize the ways that Muslim youth don't belong within Denmark, the discourses surrounding the integration crisis posit that it is an even more significant problem when young people take up these narratives themselves, when they say that they don't consider themselves to be Danish. Jamail and Mohammed, male participants who identified as Palestinian from Lebanon, explained that it is not possible for them to be Danish because Danishness is ultimately biologically determined. Having dark hair means that one will never be accepted as Danish by others. Several other male participants also explained that being labeled as Danish suggests that they reject their connections to their home countries and religion, their "real" identities. Nadir explained:

We see being called Danish as a negative thing. If my mother and father say, you live in Denmark and you are Danish, I say, "No, I'm not Danish." And when we are with kids our age we don't like being called Danish because we are different. If someone Muslim is trying to be Danish it looks like he is hiding who he really is. People *can see* that I am from another country and will probably think that I am a jerk and have lost the meaning of life. There is a lot of reason, I have a lot of family and traditions and I can't just stop that.

To Nadir, being Danish means rejection of family and tradition.

While Nadir, who identifies as Turkish, says he would never consider himself Danish, he does refer to Denmark as "home" and points to the advantages of living in Denmark. "I have lived here all my life and home is here. I would also call Turkey my home but they don't have the same transportation, they drive on the wrong side of the road, and there is a better chance here to get a good education and a good future." Many of my participants referenced the advantages of living in Denmark—access to jobs, education, and the basic necessitates of life—and described their "legal" rights given that they were born in Denmark or held a Danish passport. But while they reference their connections to Denmark in terms of rights and benefits, they contend that their selves are fundamentally not Danish. Bashir, who identifies as an Iraqi Bulgarian who was born in Denmark, said the following about his identity: "I would say that I am

Iraqi Bulgarian. Yes, I still have the Danish part of me, I was born here and I have the Danish passport and papers, but inside—my traditions, my culture—they are different from the Danish."

Bashir's statement concludes that to be Danish one must be ethnically and culturally Danish. While he says that "inside" he is not Danish, he presents himself as having a blended national identity that includes two identifications, Bulgarian and Iraqi. He emphasized that in Bulgaria and Iraq he feels comfortable because he can speak his native language and "because everyone looks like me." It seems that in the figured world of Danish immigration, it is clear that having black hair, celebrating Muslim holidays, and being Muslim are not understood to exist easily alongside Danishness, which is constructed in terms of Danish ethnicity and Danish traditions.

When I asked Jamail and Mohammed what it means to be Danish, they replied:

Mohammed: It's to celebrate Christmas on the holidays and to eat pork, that's Danish.
Jamail: Yes, they want me to be Danish in this school.
Mohammed: I'm proud of being an Arab and I don't want to be Danish.

I asked if it is possible to be both Danish and Arab.

Mohammed: It's just as it is. You can't be both. The Arab people can never be Danish because of our black hair; we look different and no one will treat us like a Dane.

Although male and female Muslim students' responses to the question "Do you consider yourself a Dane?" were similar in some ways—i.e., they focused on specific physical attributes and on celebrating Christian holidays—the boys pointed out that they were viewed through the lens of risk as criminals or "potential terrorists." They emphasized that they would never consider themselves Danish because they feel they will never be accepted as full citizens.

Rahim, a second-generation student from Iraq, gave the following reasons for why he doesn't consider himself a Dane:

Reva: Would you consider yourself a Dane?
Rahim: No.
Reva: And you were born here. Why is that?
Rahim: Well, because I don't have the traditions they have. I don't eat pork. I don't celebrate holidays they celebrate. I don't feel like I'm welcome in many locations, for example disco. And you're going out to parties they always double check you for weapons when you have black hair.

Reva: Even if you wanted to be a Dane, it's not possible?

Rahim: It's not possible. And if they don't accept me, I don't want to be one of them. And I don't feel like I'm one of them.

Rahim calls attention to how his feelings of social rejection inform a desire *not* to belong to a Danish community: "If they don't accept me, I don't want to be one of them." And he explains that to be Danish is to be one who is understood to belong naturally: "They are, of course, in their own country and they are looked at as one of themselves and they are always welcome everywhere." In contrast, he is treated with suspicion in public spaces: "If you go somewhere and something happens, people will always point at you even if you didn't do anything." Growing up in the figured world of Danish society where Danish people "belong naturally" and Muslim boys are "hostile outsiders," youth like Rahim respond by distancing themselves from Danish identities.

Despite being positioned as outsiders, male Muslim students' claims of non-Danishness arouse public scrutiny. In a focus group of ethnic Danish students at Engby School, Thomas, a star on the school's soccer team, summed up the views of other students in the focus group:

Some of them [immigrant students] will say, "I am from Palestine and not Denmark," even though they have never lived in Palestine and were born in Denmark. They have to marry someone from the same country and the same religion. I won't say they should marry a Danish person, but they shouldn't say, "I'm a *perker*," they should say, "I'm from Denmark."[1]

In this instance, Thomas is critical of the multiple affiliations expressed by immigrant youth at the same time that he projects on them the racialized label "perker." Within the discourse of Danish immigration, Thomas interprets the statement "I am from Palestine" in terms of the available figured identities of male immigrants, not as a statement of pride in one's heritage. In addition, Thomas's statements reveal that Muslim students' refusal to claim their social ties to Denmark are particularly provocative. Within the Western liberal imagination, it is as if the immigrant "guests" are refusing the benevolence of their hosts and the opportunity to be European and embrace a better life. From the perspectives of the Muslim male students in my study, Danish society excludes them in a multiplicity of ways, and hence the idea that they could ever truly belong is an illusion. It is understandable then that they turn to affiliations beyond Danish society in the search for a sense of belonging.

The male participants in my study experienced both implicit everyday racialization as well as explicit exclusion. For example, to avoid "troublemakers,"
the owners of a nightclub in a community near Engby barred the admission
of young people whose identifications revealed they were from the town of
Engby and another nearby town with a large population of Muslims. This is yet
another example that reveals Muslim youth are considered what Puwar calls
"space invaders": "Some bodies are deemed as having the right to belong, while
others are marked out as trespassers, who are in accordance with how both
spaces and bodies are imagined (politically, historically and conceptually), cir-
cumscribed as being 'out of place'" (2004: 8; see also Ríos-Rojas 2011). Rahim not
only described the multiple ways his identity was figured in narratives about
"criminal" Muslim boys, he also suggested that there are Danish people who see
him in more complex ways. In our discussion, I asked him what advice he would
give to a younger cousin who was coming to live in Denmark for the first time.

Well, I would tell him to first of all try to get along with the Danes that welcome you and
see you as a friend and not just as a guy always looking for trouble. Well, if they don't accept that, well, family is the second best thing because family is family and they accept
you for who you are. If your friends don't accept you, get your strength from your family
in each and every way.

Rahim acknowledges that there are some Danes who will "welcome you and
see you as a friend and not just as a guy looking for trouble." But he also describes his strategy for coping with racialization, turning to family where "they
accept you for who you are." In Rahim's words, the more his identity is figured
as "a guy always looking for trouble," the more he turns toward family. Gilliam's
research finds a similar pattern, concluding that as Muslim boys become aware
that they do not fit the criteria for being considered Danish, "their own national
identity—Palestinian, Albanian, etc.—has become a family identity through
their immigrant experience. It relates them to a concrete and significant place
and access to a legitimising national discourse" (Gilliam 2007: 2).

This is consistent with research in social psychology that suggests that experiences of discrimination weaken young peoples' identification with their host
societies and strengthen their affiliation with their own families and communities (Sirin and Fine 2008). Barreto and Ellemers (2002: 629) find that "when
people are treated in ways that neglect their self-identities, they will affirm
their self-identity and resist expressing identification with externally ascribed

groups" (2002: 630). Young people are less likely to identify with Danish peer groups and communities when doing so requires that they accept negative messages about their identities as immigrants. Coercive integration policies and racialization complicate young peoples' ability to forge social ties with Danish peer groups and others in Danish communities. As revealed in Chapter 3, young people respond to scrutiny of their identities by withdrawing from social interactions and adopting a defensive posture. Yet Rahim seems to leave the door open, asserting that there are possibilities for recognition within Danish society by those "who see you as a friend."

Lamya Kaddor, A German-Syrian teacher of religion in German public schools, alludes to the ways that the social exclusion of youth can slide into alienation and even violence. She describes the case of five of her female students who hadn't expressed strong connections to Islam but left Germany to wage jihad in Syria. In an interview with National Public Radio she discussed how these students were vulnerable to recruitment:

There are very difficult conditions in Germany, one being that Germany doesn't understand itself as an immigrant nation. . . . Number two is Islamophobia. It's gone so far that in Germany every second German will say that he or she has an issue with Muslims and those are scary figures. There is still a discrepancy between being a German and a Muslim. You can't be both. There is no concept of being German and Muslim. (NPR 2015)

While one must wonder about the societal risks of having a generation of young people who feel so excluded, not feeling strong connections to either homelands or hostlands, it is important not to assume that alienation and social marginalization lead to acts of terror and violence. Following the violence in Paris and Copenhagen in 2015, media commentators and academics have reached overly facile conclusions that link violence to young people's alienation. This can contribute to processes of figuring and stereotyping. For most young people like Rahim, social exclusion and alienation take the form of a quiet violence that doesn't make the headlines, but is instead felt in the hearts and bodies of youth who struggle with the reality of social rejection.

Negotiating Figured Identities at Engby School

The male Muslim youth in my study described how the figured identity of the "violent, oppressive, criminal" Muslim followed them into schools from their communities. At Engby School, there were several variations on this theme—

some teachers used the term "criminal" while others spoke of immigrant boys "making trouble" (Gilliam 2007). Aysa, the second-generation immigrant teacher, described how teachers spoke about Jamail: "A lot of the teachers will call him *criminal*. I know that. For me he's not criminal. He's just a kid that needs a role model—a good one that can give him a push and give him the feeling that he is something good." Aysa is critical of the negative cycle in which immigrant boys—rather than receiving emotional and pedagogical support—are too often subject to surveillance, labeling, and disciplining. Many teachers spoke of Muslim boys as disruptive within the community of the school (Gilliam 2007). This pattern is consistent with Gilliam's findings that teachers tend to categorize male Muslim students as "trouble makers": "far from treating the boys as individuals, they see them as children of a specific gender and ethnicity." They are not afforded any leeway for being "naughty boys," but are ascribed "pathological characteristics, social problems and criminal inclinations" (2007: 4). Rather than being treated as individuals engaging in "normal" teenage activity, Muslim boys are figured with the narratives and categories of the wider discourse.

Given the amplification of Muslim boys' behavior in school and how they are positioned in the racialized and gendered national discourse, Muslim students are more likely than their ethnic Danish peers to experience disciplinary actions (Ferguson 2001). As Gilliam (2007) argues, rather than viewing the individual infractions of Muslim students through the lens of normative male adolescent behavior, teachers see them through the lens of criminality and cultural deviance. Jamail describes his perception that disciplinary infractions by Danish youth are treated much differently than those of Muslim youth. "Well, we are kind of known for fights and stuff, so if the teacher sees two Danish boys wrestling and fighting and hitting each other, they know they are just having fun. But if we are seen fighting and stuff it's, we're being sent up to the principal. They make up huge case out of it."

In my own observations, I noted incidents where Danish students acted out in classes but were not disciplined by teachers. In the midst of Birgitte's class, I watched as a Danish student forcefully bounced a soccer ball off the head of another Danish student, yet the teacher, who was grading papers nearby, said nothing. I also observed many instances where ethnic Danish male students called male Muslim students "terrorists" in front of teachers who did not comment or intervene. Danish schools are known to allow students considerable freedom in behavior in school; it is common to hear students use profanity in classroom discussions and there is a tolerance for Danish boys roughhousing as it is seen as developmentally appropriate behavior that should be allowed. I frequently observed ethnic Danish students wrestling in the halls between classes, obliging me to pause to let them pass to avoid being struck, but these instances rarely attracted the attention of educators. In the context of broader fears of criminal activity and terrorism, the behavior of male Muslim students is amplified and subjected to a higher level of scrutiny.

At Engby School, the majority of students in special education classes are immigrant boys. The Organisation for Economic Co-operation and Development (OECD) review of migrant education finds that immigrant youth are much more likely to be placed in special education classes than their ethnic Danish peers (CERD 2006). In the midst of my work with Dhalia in 2008, she described her parents' struggle with the administration at Engby to keep her second-grade brother, Abed, from being placed in a special education class. The family felt that while Abed was active, he didn't have any disabilities that warranted this placement. The parents resisted the placement because they knew that once it was made, he would never have an opportunity to return to regular classes. They also understood that this would prevent him from accessing most avenues of higher education. In 2010, Dhalia confirmed that her brother had been moved into special education classes and in 2014 she told me that he had dropped out of school. I am sure there are special education placements that are necessary and appropriate, but I wonder if figurings of Muslim boys as deviant and criminal quietly influence decisions in cases that are unclear and on the border.

"Shaking the Goalposts": Scrutinizing Male Students' Beliefs

Within the figured world of the school, female Muslim students described how they experienced a discourse of assimilative concern while boys (and teachers) typically described the ways that boys were understood to require disciplining and control. However, in one interview, an English teacher, Mathias, told of questioning a male student about his religion in order to "loosen up the discussion" and to encourage the student to think critically about his own religious views.

I have a very relaxed attitude towards religion, but if I flash that, I will always sugarcoat it to say that other people might think something else. This is Denmark; it is the cornerstone for freedom of speech and so I respect people's views but I also feel that it is my right to scratch the surface because if you don't have any self-irony it is going to be hard for you. You do that best where *you create a situation where you shake the goalposts a little*. There was this guy in my class, and we were talking about the idea that you get seventy-two virgins in heaven if you pray five times a day. . . . He said, "I don't pray five times a day," and he said every time you skip a prayer you spend three hundred and fifty days in purgatory, and I told him, it doesn't really matter. In my mind, that helps to loosen up the discussion and makes it more easygoing. [Emphasis added]

As in the incidents in the Impossible Love class discussion, Mathias engages in an exchange that involves scrutinizing immigrant students' beliefs in order to encourage the student to embrace liberal values. In this description, he conceals his critique of Islam in the liberal tropes of "freedom of speech" and "respect." He explains that while he respects others' views he also feels it is his right to "scratch the surface" in order to "loosen up the discussion," to question the religious beliefs of immigrant youth. Ultimately, he dismisses the student's explanation of the importance of prayer by saying "it doesn't really matter." It is surprising that Danish teachers dismiss the traditions of others given how central specific traditions and rituals are to Danish culture. This is another example of contesting Islam in the everyday practices of the school, of positioning it as "backward" and retrograde when viewed against the implicit norm of Christianity. Mathias characterizes this conversation as part of a democratic debate where individuals should be able to have "self-irony"; he doesn't see his strategy as singling out a student about his beliefs but rather as encouraging his students to engage in critical thinking and supporting a good classroom discussion.

I observed other instances in which Mathias engaged in assimilation work, policing students' use of native languages and repeating stereotypes of "oppressed Muslim women" and "criminal men" in his teaching. However, it's also important to add that despite this, Mathias was described by a Muslim student, Fahed, as a supportive teacher:

Fahed: I respect him a lot. Because the way he teaches, makes you understand, makes it so easy for you to do things. You don't look at it like, "Oh my God I'm not gonna do that; I don't know how." He has helped me a lot along the years. And I feel like he doesn't look at me like other teachers do; he doesn't assume I can't do it because I'm Muslim. He looks at me like all the other students.

Well of course, when you feel, when the teachers talk to you it's not like how they would talk to a Danish student. It's like we're being treated very specially.

Reva: In what way?

Fahed: They underestimate us in many ways. Because we don't speak Danish at home . . . so even if we are very good at school and maybe even better than many of the Danish students they still underestimate us because . . . because we have black hair.

While Fahed describes Mathias as a supportive teacher, he also voices his feeling that he received less support from other teachers. A number of male and female participants said that they felt that Danish teachers expected less from their immigrant students. Asli, a female Turkish student said, "They [the teachers] expect less from me. The teachers expect more from Danish students. If a Danish student doesn't do her homework then the teacher will be very upset but if an immigrant student doesn't do her homework the teacher will be like 'Well, okay.' I think that they could give us more support academically." Despite his feelings that his teachers had lower academic expectations of him, Fahed was able to move into an academic high school and eventually to the university. Clearly, some students are able to distance themselves from the figured identities and racialization that echo throughout the school to establish relationships that help them access the resources they need to be successful. It seems that they are able to develop a kind of porous buffer that allows them to defend themselves against negative stereotypes while at the same time remaining open enough to access the resources they require for educational mobility (Cross 2012).

Living in the Shadow of Stereotype: Counter-Narratives

As the youth introduced in this chapter describe interactions with peers, teachers, and strangers in their communities and schools in which they are positioned as "outsiders," we witness the psychological and material consequences of this exclusion. We hear their complex reactions—from frustration and alienation to anger, to feeling "crazy." Carola Suárez-Orozco and Marcelo Suárez-Orozco assess the costs of living in the shadow of figured identities: "When facing toxic levels of cultural violence, children will tend to spend much of their psychic energy defending against these assaults on their sense of self" (2001: 95). But beyond this psychic energy, youth also describe the material consequences of exclusion, such as their limited access to support in schools and limited prospects in the labor market.

At the same time that youth described the limitations they experienced within the figured world of Danish immigration, they also sought to reframe the messages they received to critique and reassert visions of self that upset the rigid assumptions of figured identities. In one focus group, Sara and Aliyah joked about the problematic nature of Danish liberal views of sexual openness and drinking:

Reva: What does it mean to be Danish?

Aliyah: To celebrate Danish things like Christmas, Easter, to behave like them. When you are a teenager you can have sex. You don't get married until you're like 30. You have like two children. [They both look at one another and laugh.]

Sara: You go out with boys, you have sex before you are married.

Aliyah: When you are thirteen you drink and drink, like every weekend. You say, "Oh, I just went out last night and I drank so much and got so drunk." I have a friend she says [*high voice*], "I was drinking like so much, like five beers and I was throwing up so much, oh my God it was so cool."

Sara and Aliyah turn the spotlight that has been so often been trained on them, illuminating social problems in Danish society that are rarely discussed in the media and public discourse—e.g., problems with high rates of youth alcoholism, eating disorders, and teen suicide. In their conversation, they challenge Danish notions of "freedom" and "openness" while questioning the implicit values that are so frequently projected onto them. In other conversations, the girls spoke of Danish adults asking questions such as "How many people live in your house?" in ways that were implicitly critical of large immigrant families. In this conversation, Aliyah jokes about Danish traditions of delayed marriage and her perception that ethnic Danes have small families.

Just as, in the opening of this book, Aliyah mocked the voice of a newscaster talking about "problems with immigrant girls," here she mimics the voice of a Danish girl bragging to her friends about her night of drinking. Aliyah speaks through a voice of "Danishness" directed precisely at the official gendered discourses imposed on her. She uses what Bakhtin (1981) calls "double-voicing" to replay others' voices so as to challenge the common discursive notions of Danes as morally superior and immigrants as inferior and backward. Aliyah's double-voicing punctures the authority of concern—as if to point to the image of her drunk friend to ask, "Is this who I should become?"

In a society where immigrant girls must navigate stereotypes on a daily basis, double-voicing allows Aliyah to critique Danish norms rather than accept her social positioning as "less than." Engaging in this kind of contestation of meaning in a figured world isn't easy work given that liberal values are ossified and protected within a discourse of concern that produces notions of enlightened Western women and oppressed Muslim women. Wendy Brown (2006: 188–89) suggests that while Muslim values are always a topic of controversy and debate, Western liberals pay little attention to the reality that Western women's lives are also guided by particular social norms:

When Western liberals express dismay at (what is perceived as mandatory) veiling in fundamentalist Islamic contexts, this dismay is justified through the idiom of women's choice. But the contrast between the nearly compulsory baring of skin by American teenage girls and compulsory veiling in a few Islamic societies is drawn routinely as absolute lack of choice, indeed tyranny, "over there" and absolute freedom of choice . . . "over here."

Young peoples' counter-narratives shed light on conversations about Western liberal values that are often silenced by nationalist discourses.

In the summer of 2010, Dhalia drew an identity map that challenged the coercive assimilation she experienced in schools. She drew figures of teachers at Engby School and at her current gymnasium and wrote in the caption: "Our mission is to change the immigrants." On the other side she wrote, "My dream is to be myself, to have the chance to speak out about how I feel, whatever I feel, but NO!!!" But while Dhalia was critical of the discourse of concern for immigrants in Danish society, she ultimately seemed resigned to the idea that she would not be able to be herself or be accepted within Danish communities. She ultimately chose to move to Lebanon, where she felt that she would have more opportunities for recognition and belonging.

As immigrant youth come up against the rigid boundaries of nationalist visions of belonging they engage resources of family, community, and religion and insist upon their own hybrid imaginings of their identities. In a map that Aliyah drew in July 2010, more than two years after her initial drawing, she was critical of the multiple labels attached to immigrants in Denmark. She drew a Danish flag with an "X" over it and wrote, "I'm not Danish, I'm not New Danish. I'm not a second generation. I'm Somali by nature, I'm Muslim by choice, and I'm Danish by paper." She rejects the labels "New Dane" and "second generation," which have been commonly used in public discourse to refer to the children of immigrants. "New Dane" (*Nydanske*) emerged in public discourse in 2009–2010 as a coined term that escapes the negative social implications of "immigrant" and represents Denmark as an open and welcoming country. Sara also commented on the term "New Dane" and explained that it seems to endorse forced assimilation to a Danish identity. "I hate it that they are always calling us that because I have my own background and traditions. They think they can make us like them, they think that we should have to practice their traditions and holidays because we live here in Denmark."

Aliyah resists being forced into the rigid categories in the figured world of nationalist discourses whereby one is either Danish or an immigrant. Instead she asserts multiple visions of self, helping me to understand her relationships to different aspects of her identity, from ethnicity (Somali), to religion (Muslim), to legal identity (Danish). Her statement "Muslim by choice" speaks back to figured identities of "oppressed" Muslim women and the idea that girls are coerced into observance of Muslim traditions. In her map she asserts her multiple selves, refusing to have her identity collapsed into the categories in the figured world of Danish immigration.

Similarly, when in a conversation with Jamail and Mohammed about their identifications, I asked Jamail whether it was possible to be both Danish and Palestinian, he leaned back in his chair laughing and said, "*No way*, because I'm Arab, I can't be Danish. It's cool to be Arab, it's gay to be Danish. My blood is Arab." In a commentary on a group he feels excluded from, Jamail critiques notions of Danish masculinity and emphasizes his connections to an Arab identity that allows him to occupy a space of connection and belonging. Young people resist adopting identities that require them to accept negative messages about themselves and in turn strengthen other identifications that provide them with greater legitimacy (see Mir 2014).[2]

From "Crazy" to "Connected":
Insulating Oneself from Processes of Figuring

The preceding chapter revealed how Sara struggled more than Aliyah and Dhalia with the negative reactions to her identity, mentioning several times how she felt "crazy" in the vortex of the hostile messages that swirled around her. In 2010, Sara drew another identity map, this time more clearly and distinctly separating her self-representation from the negative constructions forced on her (see Figure 5.3).

In Sara's identity map, she addresses nationalist discourses and policies through a series of short statements that challenge the labels attached to Muslim immigrants. Unlike her earlier map, which illustrated the ways she was affected by these saturating discourses, in this map, she represents a buffered space that she has created for herself, producing an image of herself standing on green grass under a yellow sun, separated from the negative voices by a layer of blue clouds. In this map, she has produced a positive vision of a self that is Palestinian and Muslim and growing up in Denmark. This image reflects her own conception of her hybrid belongings and insists on her right to cultivate her own traditions.

Her image solicits questions about the ways young people's counter-narratives provide opportunities to escape the overdetermined meanings of discourse, to resist figuring. These counter-narratives provide young people with the ideological space to draw together the various threads of attachments they hold, to imagine positive visions of self. Moreover, young people's counter-narratives question taken-for-granted discourses. Once again, Sara turns the lens to ask, "Can you forget your culture? Coz I can't!" and "Look at your Life!" Danish discourses of concern present an ideal to which Muslim girls are expected to aspire: they should want to enjoy the "freedoms" of Western society and hence display "appropriate" ways of being and behaviors. Their counter-narratives reveal a grappling with this discourse of power. As Bakhtin suggests, "the importance of struggling with another's discourse, its influence

Figure 5.3.   Identity Map: Sara II, age 16.

in the history of an individual's coming to ideological consciousness, is enormous. One's own discourse and one's own voice, although born of another or dynamically stimulated by another, will sooner or later begin to liberate themselves from the authority of the other's discourse" (1981: 348).

Yet while young people's counter-narratives challenge the authority of figured identities, they are limited. In the perceived safety of focus groups and casual conversations, young people openly shared their counter-narratives and critiques of nationalist discourses. However, in official school spaces, they silenced these views and shared only what was necessary to get by. They explained that they were afraid to be openly critical in schools about their experiences as immigrants in Danish society because it might jeopardize the support of teachers. Students implicitly understand that teachers are gatekeepers, controlling access to educational and social capital. Similarly, potential employers, like the ones who chose not to hire Sara, are also gatekeepers, denying access to the labor market. While young people's counter-narratives were helpful in distancing them from deficit discourses and challenging teachers' "civilizing" work, they do not get far enough to challenge the broader exclusionary forces at play. While some may argue that encouraging young people to voice critiques of host societies promotes a kind of dissonant citizenship that runs counter to the goals of integration, creating spaces that welcome these views will support youth to be more a part of conversations in schools and society, ultimately supporting their broader engagement.

On Blended Identities in Rigidly Figured Worlds

The literature on immigrant acculturation suggests that the most successful immigrant students are those who are able to synthesize elements of their identities that draw from both home countries and host countries (Suárez-Orozco and Qin 2006). This implies that being successful in host countries is a function of students' ability and willingness to choose aspects of self from a menu of options. This view, however, fails to recognize that this menu is limited within particular national contexts. In the figured world of Danish immigration, how can young people freely blend attachments to Denmark with their other selves? Immigrant youth believe that being Danish involves a rigid set of physical attributes and beliefs—which clearly position them outside of the norms of Danishness—making it impossible for them to be Danish. As Aysa explains, "I am [as] Danish as I can be," yet she is still positioned as an outsider by some.

The youth discussed in this chapter reveal that there are differences in their ability to resist figuring. Muslim boys spoke to the difficulty of feeling a connection to a Danish identity in the face of surveillance and exclusion. Frequently boys echoed the discourse about the criminality of Muslim boys. For instance, Rahim declared, "We, the *not Danish students* . . . well *we* sometimes make trouble and stuff and the school has a very bad reputation now." Rather than challenging the integration discourse that labels Engby a "ghetto school," Rahim attributed the school's problematic image to the behavior of immigrant boys. There were several instances when boys seemed to accept the labels of criminals and terrorists as a regular part of everyday discourse. A fifth-grade Muslim boy explained that he believes that one particular teacher is supportive. He said, "She asks me, are you going to be a successful student or are you going to be a criminal?"—seemingly unaware that the teacher was producing the figure of the Muslim criminal. Although female Muslim students also at times reproduced the discourse that Muslim boys are criminals, in our discussions they didn't reproduce the stereotype of the oppressed Muslim woman.

It is unclear how to read the differences in student responses. It could be that girls are able to be more strategic in engaging their multiple selves as resources in negotiating exclusionary discourses. Studies in the area of gender, psychology, and immigration suggest that immigrant girls have more flexibility when it comes to cultivating identities that represent their various attachments (Waters 1997). In her study of Caribbean girls, Waters (1997) found that they were less likely to take on racialized identities and more flexible in defining their own identities. Even though my data seem to corroborate these findings on the surface, I'm skeptical about presenting results with such broad strokes. My findings may be related to interviewer/subject affect. I spent much more time speaking with the girls and they felt comfortable with me and had more space to verbalize counter-narratives.

However, it did seem to me that boys had less room to navigate their multiple selves as the figured identities surrounding them were more rigid and unyielding than those directed at immigrant girls. Further, boys were more frequently subjected to disciplinary technologies that contain and limit the perceived threat they posed. Immigrant girls are more often subjected to technologies that seek to develop and transform them into liberal subjects, bringing them into the fold of Danish society. But with the boys, there is a desire to neutralize the threat they pose. This raises questions about why figured identities of

Muslim boys as potential terrorists and criminals are more durable, saturating, and therefore difficult to escape than those of oppressed immigrant girls. Are boys positioned in such a way in the figured world of Danish immigration that it is difficult to claim their right to belong? Despite these differences, this chapter suggests that in order for young people to create positive ties to Danish society and to be successful in Danish institutions, there needs to be a softening of what it means to be Danish so that immigrant youth can define new, more flexible forms of citizenship.

Chapter 6

Teachers' Counter-Narratives and Comparative Sites of Possibility

THROUGHOUT MY TIME at Engby School the discourse of concern was palpable, reproduced through educational practices and simple gestures, as when a male teacher walked into a computer room where a group of fourth-grade boys were speaking Arabic and laughing, raised a finger and said "danske!" The boys instantly switch to speaking Danish. Teachers police young people's cultural and linguistic identities in a variety of ways, both direct and indirect, sometimes with cues, like a finger in the air, that young people learn as they are socialized into the world of the school. Aysa, the Turkish teacher, was critical of the policing of Muslim students' identities at Engby and described the sometimes subtle ways teachers encouraged assimilation: "There are many teachers here who believe that Muslim students *have* to behave like Danish students. That means doing everything in accordance with Danish culture and not showing that they are Muslims. When the Muslim girls show their Muslim traditions, the teacher's eyes go down." As Aysa spoke, she looked away from me and down at the floor. Though strategies of disciplining immigrant students identities seemed inconsistent with the child-centered commitment of Danish schools, it was clear that school-based discourses echoed the broader national imaginary as different actors took up the call to action reproduced in policy and discourse.

Despite the durability of the cultural schemas and assumptions within particular figured worlds, there is always room for improvisation, for the authoring of new meanings and imaginaries (Holland et al. 1998; Bakhtin 1981). This chapter presents the voices of teachers at Engby School who opposed the nationalist discourses and figured worlds of Danish immigration, producing new assumptions about who immigrant students are and what they require. It then moves into the spaces of schools in the United States that explicitly seek to promote the achievement of immigrant students. As a researcher with a commitment to social justice, it is my responsibility not just to document exclusionary practices but also to present what "could be" so that we might collectively envision more equitable modes of schooling for Muslim and immigrant youth that in the long run improve education for all youth.

One afternoon when I was sitting at a table outside the teachers' room writing field notes, I met Karen, a 25-year-old special education teacher. Karen is the lead special education teacher for a group of eight seventh-grade boys (six out of eight of whom are Muslim). As she spoke about her students' learning disabilities, she did not concentrate on cultural factors.

Karen: Their culture isn't the problem at all. I have a deep respect for their culture and they know that. I don't think that they should assimilate—they don't need to forget who they are. In my class we celebrate Ramadan and the festival of Eid. When they don't eat, I cancel all of the cooking classes to respect that they are not eating.

Reva: Could you imagine a time when there would be a celebration for Ramadan in the school?

Karen: [*Pauses and smiles*] Now, that would be real integration, if we took some days away from the winter holiday and gave the Muslim students a real holiday for the feast of Ramadan and we all had a party together in the school.

Perhaps Karen welcomed diversity because most of her students are Muslim and she doesn't have to contend with the pressures of preparing students for high school examinations. Her students spend the entire day in class with her, where they complete basic academic work and then also learn daily living skills, cooking, and handcrafts. In comparison, I observed groups of third- and fourth-grade Muslim students who were fasting for Ramadan sitting together at lunchroom tables watching their peers eat their lunches because of a policy that required that Muslim students remain with the class. In addition, Muslim students were required to participate in gym classes even if they were fasting.

Still, there were teachers like Karen who believed that "culture isn't the problem." When I asked Jaan, an ethnic Danish teacher of math, to describe the challenges facing immigrant students, like Karen he too did not provide an answer limited to cultural differences or discursive stereotypes. Instead, he pointed out that immigrant students "have the Danish skills to talk to each other but they don't have the academic Danish skills required to be successful on the national exams."

Jaan spoke to the need for more support for immigrant students' language development. He also stressed that the curriculum should reflect the interests of Muslim students: "In our school we have so many Muslims and we have learned that when there is a war in Palestine we discuss it. We talk about it, because we have a lot of Palestinian students." These types of discussions position young people and their experiences in homelands in very different ways than the Impossible Love discussion presented in Chapter 3. They encourage participation by creating openings for students to discuss experiences and feelings about homelands rather than scrutinizing students' values and requiring them to defend their culture and identities.[1] In addition to voicing his acceptance of cultural differences and his conviction that the academic needs of his immigrant students must be met, he spoke about his work with his colleague Aysa. "My colleague Aysa, we are together and she wears *hijab*, we are equal. She helps me to communicate with families. She can translate when we are sitting with families. Especially with the girls—they speak to her because she has the same background." It seems that Aysa's and Jaan's classrooms provide a space for counter-narration as they create new notions of belonging.

Aysa's War

It was difficult to find time to speak with Aysa because she was often deeply absorbed in her work. When I did manage to find time for interviews, she was very open, which I attribute in part my own identity as an American, an outsider in Denmark. In our conversations, Aysa volunteered stories about her growing up in Denmark to provide insight into the experiences of her immigrant students.

Aysa was the most discussed teacher in the school and came up frequently in interviews with students and teachers. Immigrant students often cited Aysa as "one of us" and a teacher to whom they could turn for support. The principal cited Aysa's position in the school as a point of pride, a symbol of the schools multiculturalism. Lena, the English teacher, explained that Aysa had an important role in the school and helped teachers to mediate issues with immigrant families. And then she leaned over to me and whispered, "Although Aysa looks like one of them, she is one of us." Aysa described how her colleagues frequently moved her between the category of "Dane" and "Muslim": "Sometimes they say 'She is a Dane.' Like Stieg, he says to me, 'If you talk with me on the phone I would think that your name is Luisa or Maria because it isn't important when I hear you. But if I saw you, I would say, oh, you are just a Muslim.'" Her presence in the school stimulated a lot of talk about what category she belonged in—Muslim, Dane, Teacher, Immigrant. Aysa seemed to strategically engage this ambiguity, to challenge others' assumptions about the ascribed meanings and values associated with these categories, to "show" through her example. "I chose this school and this work," Aysa said,

because I want to show something through my example. I could be in an office too. But who would see me there? I'm different from all the other teachers here. I know it's not something I say to be bigger or something. All the pupils know me with my name. I don't teach them [all] but they know who I am and they know how to talk with me. So that's really, really great. They come to me and they say "Why don't you have lessons with us?"

Aysa embraces her heightened visibility in the space of the school as she emphasizes the importance of being "seen" and proving her competence to others. She spoke with pride about the many times she "met angry faces" and the subsequent times that she managed to prove her abilities within Danish communities. She explained that when she first came to the school, several parents called to question her ability to teach Danish as a Muslim woman wearing *hijab*. Even though Aysa felt she had gained the respect of most of her colleagues and the students in the school, she noted that there are those who still question her position:

It is a war. The woman in the cantina is always asking me, what are you doing in this school, what is your work? She thinks that I am just nobody. When I explain that I teach the ninth-grade class, she says, "Ohhh . . . " She makes a negative face because she can't see me in my position. She has her own ideas about who I am. I can't be more Danish than I am; I do everything.

Defending herself in the face of figured identities was not new to Aysa. As the only Muslim girl in her gymnasium, she frequently encountered the questioning gaze of her peers. "That has been my war—yeah, all my life, to show that I didn't have to play Danish." Aysa uses the metaphor of war to describe different types of threats she had to negotiate throughout her life as an immigrant girl, a teacher, and a mother. "We can't stop; we can't stop the other people's eyes on us. You can be yourself, but you have to show and say something. You have to show that your knowledge of language, religion, and culture is better than theirs." It is clear that this war is ongoing, in skirmishes and battles that Aysa has fought throughout her life. Like the female Muslim youth in this book, Aysa describes the ways her identity is subject to surveillance and public scrutiny.

The female Muslim informants in John Bowen's book *Why the French Don't Like Headscarves* describe a similar kind of hypervisibility. Fariba, a Muslim resident of France and a native of Algeria, explains:

Sometimes even when I have not been listening to the news, I know what has happened by watching how people regard me. On September 11th [2001,] I returned home from work, turned on the television and saw the catastrophe. I was shocked like everyone else. The next morning, Wednesday, I had almost forgotten what had happened, I took the train to work, and the looks I got from others reminded me that it was the 12th, of what happened the day before. At first I did not understand, I looked myself over, to see if there was something wrong with my clothes, what did I do? And then I made the connection . . .

The other time that happened to me, it was when there was a French ship blown up, I had not heard about it, and I saw a great deal of aggression and people stared, and [I] said to myself I had better read a newspaper right away, and I saw the explanation. I function as a barometer of the popularity of Muslims. When there were sympathetic looks it was between the two votes for the president, . . . when Jean-Marie Le Pen had done well, they felt guilty, and so if in the subway I was jostled a bit, people would say "Oh excuse me ma'am," as if to say, "I did not vote for Le Pen." So in some sense, I've never been spit on or struck or yelled at but I see a lot in those looks. And with the polemic on the voile [veil] there has been a lot of electricity in the air. (2007: 79–80). [2]

Muslim women's identities and bodies can become, as Fariba puts it, a barometer of national sentiment. Aysa similarly speaks of how her identity was amplified in the spaces of Engby School and within her community, explaining how she is frequently stopped on the street by strangers who tell her to "speak Danish" or who comment on her wearing *hijab*.

When I am in the street and I am speaking to my children in Turkish, I get confronted by Danish people on the street who say, "Speak Danish!" I meet people that when they look at me, they think I don't know a shit, they are so wrong. When I am talking to my daughter and when someone says, "Oh, speak Danish!" I always choose words that are very difficult in Danish, to show the person that I know more than them. It is a war.

In these words she describes her defenses against processes of figuring. Her "war" to insist on her belonging involves asserting both her Turkish and Danish identities, speaking Turkish with her daughter while also deploying sophisti-cated Danish vocabulary. In a way she attempts to show how she is more Danish than those who question her. Her narratives reveal both the possibilities and the limitations within the figured world of Danes and "others." Aysa said the following about her own Danish identity:

I don't say I'm a Dane. I say I can't be more Danish than I am now. I am a Dane too, but you can't say that I have blue eyes or that I think like you. We can't always say that we are Danish because we are living here. But I don't joke about sex and swear like the other teachers and I'm not always hugging like the other teachers.

Aysa's response to the question "Do you consider yourself Danish?" echoes the responses of young people who explain why they cannot consider themselves Danish. Aysa references physical criteria for belonging and distances herself from Danish values of "openness." In interviews, she described her discomfort with the culture of liberal "openness" in the school, the ways teachers spoke openly about sex and were physical with one another. In other conversations, she was critical of the idea that this climate of openness supported students' development. She explained: "In Denmark we have this idea that students should be able to say 'shit' and 'fuck' to their teachers." She was also critical of the lack of rules around students' dress "like, I know I'm not supposed to say anything but I just don't want to see your green underwear. Sometimes I want to say, 'I don't want to see your ass as you walk down the hall.'" Aysa defined her own belonging in terms of her own work as a teacher, not in terms of her ability to conform to Danish norms and "liberal" values. By announcing that "I can't be more Danish than I am now," she asserts her belonging and insists on her right to belong.

Aysa: Creating Space for Herself and Others

When I talked to Aysa about immigrant students navigating assimilative discourses, she didn't speak about particular teachers or particular incidents that I mentioned to her such as the Impossible Love discussion. However, she did not seem surprised when I asked her about my own findings related to teachers' expressions of assimilitive "concern" for Muslim girls. She indicates she believes it is important that girls not give in to the pressures of "playing Danish":

The most successful girls will be the girls who can stand up in the classroom and show that it's not their hair color that's important but it's their brain and their heart. I think what's most important is that when the girls play at being Danish, they are not being themselves and they're using their energy to be another person and instead [they should be] using their energy for their homework and to be successful.

Aysa spoke to the importance of creating space within the school for immigrant students to openly express their views: "I give them a lot of space to
show that they are coming from another land, they have another language, they
have another religion. They can't show it to the Danish students because they
think it is wrong to talk about that." Aysa knows all too well the energy that
youth expend trying to keep a low profile in school to avoid public scrutiny, as
Aliyah described in Chapter 3. However, there are also students who choose not
to assert their Muslim identity in school, who are "trying on" a Danish identity
or who come from more assimilated families.

Aysa revealed her concern that some Muslim girls were giving in to pressure
to assimilate by "playing Danish" and that she struggles with her own desire to
police Muslim girls' dress:

When I can see that they're doing something wrong—against their religion for
example—I think, "Should I say something or not?" And when I think in terms of my religious values, I want to say something, but when I think like a teacher, that's not my business. It's very difficult. Sometimes I say, "Oh, I can see your stomach," for example. I'm
just saying it in a nice way because it's not my job. Because I am a Muslim I feel like I have
to say something because I know their parents wouldn't want for them to dress that way.

Aysa is enacting her own notion of what it is to be a "successful" immigrant
student—projecting her own ideals and expectations that her immigrant students must negotiate. In this, she is like Birgitte and Lena, who also present
their students with a picture of what success looks like, except that Aysa's depic-
tion couldn't be more different. She interprets the behavior of more assimilated
Muslim students as succumbing to the pressures of the Danish space of the
school, citing examples of Muslim students who dress in provocative clothing
or talk about sex in order to fit in the liberal atmosphere of Danish "openness."
When teachers are deeply engaged with their students, they project their own
desires, fears, and hopes onto their students and can obscure students' actual
lives and experiences. Just as Aysa works to expand the space for the recognition of students' diverse experiences and traditions, she also reproduces the
rigid binary of Dane versus Muslim, positioning many Danish values as being in
conflict with signs of identity that immigrant students improvise with.

Although young immigrants in Denmark create critical counter-narratives
that challenge the authority of nationalist discourses, to some extent they must
conform to the social expectations of the contexts in which they operate. So

while youth were clearly aware of the coercive nature of the events in the Impossible Love discussion, they were not able to disrupt processes of figuring. In comparison, Aysa is uniquely positioned and has the institutional authority to create space for the expression of difference in Engby School. In a sense, she claims the space, disrupts the Danish and Christian fabric of the school by asserting her right to make her own (and by extension her students') traditions and values visible.

Yes, yes, I know this, we have a holiday too this Thursday [her voice grew louder and she looked directly at me]. I say it a lot, *you have to show them that it is okay*. I'm not coming to school, it is my holiday and it is okay. *We are all the same because we all live here, we all work here together in the same school, they have to understand me as I understand the other children and the parents, you understand?*

Aysa strategically engages her multiple positions to claim her right to recognition. She references her identity as a Muslim who is observing a major holiday and then positions herself within the group of teachers seeking to understand all children and parents, implicitly leaning on her status within the school to justify her rights. It is interesting that in comparison to students' "rights-based" discourse rooted in legal citizenship or "Danish by paper," as Aliyah says, Aysa claims her right to recognition based on her experience of living and working with her colleagues.

Aysa resists the nationalist discourse that reverberates through the school by encouraging the use of multiple languages in her class and she expands the curriculum beyond a focus on Danishness and Christianity. In interviews, she was critical of the politician Pia Kjærsgaard and his call for more attention to Christianity and Danishness in the curriculum. Aysa explained, "The test only asks questions on Christendom. But I can also ask questions about other religions in my class." Aysa challenges processes of figuring and expands the space for alternative representations of students' traditions, cultures, and languages.

Aysa also brings attention to the political and economic barriers facing her immigrant students. She explained that few immigrant students attend the academic gymnasium; the majority end up working in low-wage service jobs in pizzerias and the like and in construction.

They work from ten a.m. to ten at night, twelve hours. They don't get paid well and they don't have the same opportunities as us. I can say that I'm free when the school is closed. I have my days when my children are ill. . . . When my old teacher sees me and asks

"What are you doing now?" I can say, "I'm a teacher" and then she can feel pride in all that I have accomplished. I want that feeling too for my students.

Although many of her colleagues attribute the challenges facing their Muslim students to the supposed cultural deprivation of immigrant families, Aysa voices a discourse of concern that shifts the lens to the political and economic challenges facing immigrant students. She challenges the racialized hierarchy of the Danish economy and imagines a future where her students will have professional jobs that will make both them and herself proud. Like Nancy Fraser, who advocates a framework of social justice that integrates recognition and redistribution, Aysa challenges both the representation of immigrants in Danish society and the school as well their economic marginalization, that is, that they are confined to poorly paid service work (Fraser and Honneth 2003).

Aysa softens the rigid borders of these figurings as she briskly walks through the halls of Engby School, demanding her space and insisting that "I am as Danish as I can be." She opens up new spaces for the recognition of difference through her own personal example. When she is confronted by those who challenge her status, she turns to her defenses, working diligently to ensure that her students have the highest test scores in the school. However, Aysa expresses the vulnerability that she feels as one of the few Muslim teachers in the school.

In her first few years at the school, she recounts, she argued with teachers who refused to make accommodations for students observing Ramadan, but eventually she grew tired of being the lone voice defending the rights of Muslim students and stopped. She expressed her frustration that the school does not have a policy exempting students from gym and from being required to sit at lunchroom tables while fasting during Ramadan, and that these issues have to be debated by the staff every year. She also fears that challenging the culture of Danishness in the school might be understood as a betrayal and might threaten her belonging there:

Sometimes I have to be careful because I am new. All of the teachers who are sitting there, they have been a teacher for five, ten, twenty-five, thirty years, so I have to, I know that, I am beginning. I don't want to be seen as the teacher who is sitting by myself and trying to make the school a Muslim school.

Though Aysa has experienced challenges and burdens—resisting the exclusive focus on Danishness and taking on the added responsibility of educating Danish teachers about Islam (Zaal et al. 2007)—she has gained legitimacy within the school through her work. Aysa invokes the metaphor of a "war" to prove herself in the face of deficit views, yet she ultimately points to a victory of sorts in gaining the respect of Danish members of the school community.

It's a war to show them that I'm a person and I speak Danish as well as them and I do a great job. I know that because I love this job. I love the job to teach children. The most fun is the Danish parents who used to complain that I was teaching in the school who now write to the principal and want me to teach their children.

Ultimately Aysa argues that the school needs to do a better job of providing academic support to immigrant students. She also expresses concern about the toll taken on youth who are trying to fit in and "use their energy to be another person instead of trying to be themselves and using their energy for their homework." Aysa argues that the corrective for the obsession with cultivating national values in immigrant students should be the vigorous development of the academic skills they need to be successful in Danish society.

In order to reach diverse students, teachers need to interrogate their own beliefs and racial and ethnic attachments, the "sociocultural consciousness" that guides their approach to the cultural differences of the students in their classrooms. Villegas and Lucas (2002) argue that teachers need to recognize that their own views about race, gender, and culture shape their perceptions of "good" students and "problematic" students and the myriad messages they implicitly and explicitly send to their students about their own identities. Furthermore, in order to foster the achievement of immigrant students, teachers should see these students as capable learners. Being fully proficient in the native language and adopting national traditions and culture are not prerequisites for academic achievement.

Although I believe Danish schools are in some ways better positioned than those in places like the United States that struggle with deep inequities in funding between schools with majority immigrant populations and those without, in other ways there is something fundamentally challenging about adapting the fabric of Danish schooling to reflect Denmark's changing demography. Engby's teachers spoke extensively about the importance of time-honored rhythms of Danish schooling and collective celebrations of Christian Danish traditions in schools and expressed dismay when Muslim students didn't embrace these traditions. In addition, teachers idealized Danish educational traditions and expressed faith in Danish schools' abilities to produce social equity without an awareness of how these conceptions might be tied to their own fears about the changing nation (Gilliam 2007). In several interviews, teachers met my questions about Muslim students with the statement, "This is Denmark and we are a Danish school." These statements resonated with the rhetoric of policymakers who call for "establishing a limit" and "drawing a line" in order to prevent the erosion of Danish values.

Deficit Thinking and Teacher Accountability

In the colorful words of Frederick Erickson, a prominent educational anthropologist, "deficit thinking is like zombies and vampires—it just keeps coming back" (Erickson, personal communication 2013). Indeed, I believe that many of the problems in immigrant education are largely the result of deficit thinking, which "blames the victim" for school failure and underachievement rather than examining the ways schools are structured to prevent immigrant and minority students from reaching their potential (Valencia 2010). In the following discussion, I offer a comparative perspective from public schools that exclusively serve low-income immigrant youth in the United States, schools from the Internationals Network for Public Schools (the Internationals). In exploring the case of the Internationals we encounter teachers who resist the kinds of deficit thinking present in U.S. political discourse in order to develop schools that are more responsive to the needs of immigrant students.

I do not suggest that U.S. schools ensure more equitable outcomes for immigrant and minority youth. Educational research confirms that most immigrant students in the United States attend under-resourced schools that offer limited educational opportunities, are overcrowded, are staffed by inexperienced teachers, and have high drop-out rates (Lopez 2003; Suárez-Orozco et al. 2008). In addition, U.S. education and immigration policies construct immigrant families and youth as "in need of intervention" and a drain on state resources. As these policy discourses are reproduced through schools, many immigrant students encounter institutional practices that engage deficit perspectives, devaluing their native languages and cultures (Lee 2005; Valenzuela 1999). Furthermore, instances like the recent arrest of fourteen-year-old Ahmed Mohamed, a Texas student who was suspended from school and arrested when his homemade clock was assumed to be a bomb, are a reminder of the pervasiveness of the racialization of Muslim youth in schools. Like zombies and vampires, deficit thinking is not unique to U.S. or European contexts; it is found throughout schools across the globe (Suárez-Orozco and Qin-Hilliard 2004).

At Engby School several teachers attributed the challenges of immigrant students to living with families that are "less fortunate," don't engage in critical discussions at home, and fail to participate in Danish ways of thinking and living. Mathias explains the problems with immigrant parents who lack knowledge about the requirements of schools.

Mathias: If you ask the immigrant kids what they want to be when they grow up, they will say doctors and lawyers. They will never in a million years be a lawyer. They want to make good money, to bring prestige on their families.

Reva: Why are they struggling?

Mathias: The parents think the kids are taking it seriously but they don't. The first two years they all pay attention. Then at fourth grade they don't do well. The parents say, "You have to do well in school, you have to listen to your teacher," but they don't have a grasp of what is required.

Here Mathias expresses his belief that immigrant parents have high educational expectations for their children, but that they lack the skills and knowledge their children require to be successful. In Danish schools, teachers frequently discuss the problems with resource-weak (*resourcevahed*) families (Gilliam 2007). The teachers' explanations for students' poor performance are similar to the cultural deprivation explanations of the putative deficits in African-American families in the United States (Lewis 2003; also Valdes 1996; Lee 2005 for critique). "Culture of poverty" narratives contend that minority students have poor school performance because their parents lack the "right" orientation toward education, are not sufficiently involved in their children's advancement, and do not prepare their children for school (Valdes 1996). This argument obscures that it is the Eurocentric norms in Western liberal schools that disadvantage immigrant and minority students.

In ascribing the challenges facing immigrant students to their families and to resistance to integration, Engby's teachers in effect are declaring that the academic outcomes of their students are somehow beyond their control, thus abdicating their responsibility as educators. On many occasions, teachers told me about immigrant students' lack of engagement and poor performance. For example, Lena said, "A big group of those kids in 9c are never going to ever be able to pass the tests; they just sit there every day." As I witnessed in discussions and observations, most teachers reacted to the poor performance of immigrant students with resignation. These teachers made no effort to adjust instruction to meet students' needs. I did not observe any use of teaching strategies commonly applied with immigrant students, such as scaffolding or breaking down tasks, presenting material in multiple ways, or providing targeted supports.

In a class discussion of a short story about Catholicism in English class, Lena asked Jamail about a reading assignment.

Lena: What do the neighbors think about the teenage girl becoming pregnant?
Jamail: I read it, but I didn't understand it.
Lena: It was too difficult?
Jamail: Yes, it was.
Lena: Aaah, okay.

Lena turned away from Jamail and continued teaching the lesson. Throughout the rest of the class, Jamail remained in his seat with his book open to the story but his attention appeared to be riveted on sending text messages on his telephone.

Lena's passive acceptance of Jamail's lack of engagement reflects, I would argue, a common assumption among Engby's teachers, namely that poor academic performance is a result of the student's culture, lack of motivation, or family background. As I have mentioned, some participants, both male and female, acknowledge that they feel that Danish teachers expect less from immigrant students. However, I don't think these teacher and student narratives reflect a lack of care among teachers. Rather, I think that there is a guiding assumption operating in Danish schools that because Danish modes of education concentrate on producing social equality, they should be effective for all students. Schools take a one-size-fits-all approach to education and have a historical faith in Danish schools affording equal opportunities to all students. When a student falls short of expectations, it must be due to the "choice" of that student.

Following this one-size-fits-all approach, the teachers I interviewed had very little training in working with bilingual and immigrant students and operated in a policy environment in which deficit notions—that culture and linguistic difference were barriers to be overcome—were the norm. Thus, teachers' deficit narratives are a reflection of the broader discursive landscape. Beyond that, the teachers I spoke with lacked the structural supports needed to change their narratives about Muslim youth. In the next sections I explore how teachers and schools serving immigrant youth can work together to change the narratives on immigrant education.

The Internationals:
Images of Internal Accountability for Immigrant Students

The nonprofit International Network (the Internationals) includes public high schools in New York City dedicated to serving the academic and emotional needs of recently arrived immigrant youth. The Internationals are designed to create a nurturing environment that supports students in making a successful transition into the educational and social life of the United States. Their educational model emphasizes learning English through content and also encouraging students to engage their native languages and cultural experiences within an interdisciplinary course of study. Students at the Internationals come from over seventy countries and speak over sixty languages. In addition, the majority come from homes with low incomes; in 2009, 92 percent of students were eligible for free lunch (New York City Department of Education 2009). To qualify for admission, a student must have lived in the United States for less than four years, qualify as an English language learner (ELL), and live in New York City. A study of the outcomes of the three oldest Internationals high schools in New York City reveals that for students who entered Internationals schools in 1998, the final graduation rate was 88.7 percent, compared with a 49.6 percent graduation rate for ELLs citywide (Fine et al. 2005: 27). It is important to emphasize that the Internationals are not typical American schools in any sense. Rather, they serve an exclusively immigrant population, they recruit staff who are oriented toward working with this population of students, and, as the NYC graduation rate reveals, they exist within a broader educational terrain in which immigrant students are vastly underserved.

In a student focus group from an Internationals high school in Brooklyn, New York, Abhik, a Muslim student from Bangladesh, said the following when asked if there was anything else he would like to share: "I want to thank the school for giving us the feeling that our culture is not bad. . . . Most of the time in American schools they want you to forget about your culture; they are always putting down other cultures. It's really helping me to trust in myself and trust in my roots and to take that to go forward not to cut them off, chop them off." Abhik's narrative provides insight into the ways the school's recognition of his cultural and linguistic identity was central in helping him to be successful in high school and going "forward" into his adult life. The Internationals create space for students to trust in and express their diverse forms of cultural knowledge while also imagining future selves. They foster transnational imaginaries providing students with the resources they need to be successful in an increasingly globalizing world; they encourage the cultivation of the knowledge and skills to navigate schooling and careers in host countries as well as the development of students' critical consciousness to critique and reframe nationalist and exclusionary discourses; and they provide safe spaces where students experience recognition and a sense of belonging. In contrast to nationalist modes of schooling that constrict students within narrow channels of inclusion in school and society, transnational imaginaries respond to young peoples' diverse participation within and across diasporic webs of belonging.

In interviews, students and graduates described the Internationals as "safe spaces" where they felt recognized, connected to others, and experienced a sense of belonging (Fine et al. 1997: 13). Several graduates recounted experiences attending middle schools where they "stayed quiet" because they feared the humiliation often endured on the soccer field and in hallways. In contrast to these narratives of non-belonging, the descriptions of the Internationals were positive: they were places where students could use their newly emerging language skills because "everybody has an accent here" (Jaffe-Walter 2008: 2048). One graduate found his school to be a second home: "It was such a comfort zone for me, you know. I didn't know any English. Didn't know where to turn. . . . I would come in early in the morning and go home probably at eight o'clock at night." (Fine et al. 1997: 27)

The Internationals schools take a team-based approach in which groups of teachers work together on building academic and emotional skills, cultivating what Ricardo Stanton-Salazar calls "actively explicit agendas geared toward the transmission of institutional support to minority children and youth" (1997: 22). Teachers' narratives about their students reflect an awareness that immigrant families often lack an understanding of how to navigate schooling in the United States and that immigrant students face hurdles because of varying levels of education in their native countries and the psychological strains related to migration and adapting to life in a new host country (Suárez-Orozco et al. 2008). In a focus group, a teacher explained that one academic challenge for many students is that they have to do their schoolwork without the support of parents. He believed this is often because of different living situations and the economic demands of living in a new country: "A lot of kids don't live with their parents—they live with cousins [or other relatives]. Even if they do live with parents they don't see them because they work night shifts. Our students are very independent; they have to be." In other schools in the United States I have heard teachers describe immigrant families in terms of deficit constructions of "absent parents," however, this teacher formulates a more positive notion of his students' skills of "independence."

Teachers sometimes report feeling overwhelmed by the diverse educational and emotional needs of their immigrant students, but the team-based approach at the Internationals provides them with support through working together to determine how to meet students' individual needs. Teams hold weekly guidance meetings to discuss students who are particularly vulnerable. In a guidance meeting I observed, teachers brainstormed about how to prevent a female undocumented student from dropping out of high school and how to access community supports for a male student from Yemen who was living in an apartment with an older brother. Implicit in their discussions about their students was the belief that teachers are collectively responsible for supporting all of their students. It is important to acknowledge that there were rare instances when I heard teachers echo deficit figurings of immigrant youth within the Internationals, but interestingly, I also witnessed how other faculty members would shift the conversation to try to encourage their peers to see these students in a more positive light, emphasizing their strengths.

The literature on immigration and education points out that immigrant and bilingual students are often denied academically rigorous coursework because of the assumption that they must first become fluent in the dominant language (Callahan et al. 2008). Internationals' pedagogy is based on principles of language and content integration in which students develop language skills through an interdisciplinary course of study. The language practices of the schools are student centered, as García and Sylvan argue. "Rather than having a structure where language practices are controlled by a rigid external language education policy, the students use diverse language practices for purposes of learning and teachers use inclusive language practices for purposes of teaching" (García and Sylvan 2011: 390). Students at Internationals engage in what García, Flores, and Woodley (2012) describe as "translanguaging," flexibly using language to make meaning of their worlds. Freely moving between languages in the spaces of classrooms, students are able to build academic and linguistic skills and also forge a sense of belonging and community in the school.

Students spoke in focus groups of how the teachers worked to tailor instruction to their needs (Jaffe-Walter and Lee 2011). In a focus group at an Internationals, a student from Mexico praised the teachers: "The teachers are really good here because they teach you separately if you don't understand something. They will help to explain it in your own language. If they see that you don't understand, they will put you in a group with others who speak the same language. This is better than being in a group where you just sit and don't understand anything." Internationals support the majority of their students to make successful transitions to college by offering students of all levels of linguistic and academic achievement a rigorous and challenging curriculum that draws on their cultural background. For example, students in an English class wrote personal narratives about their immigration experiences. A Chinese student wrote about a flashback to her life in China after seeing a billboard about China's one-child child policy. In another class students worked in groups to analyze a video on global sweatshops and then generated explanations about the causes of economic exploitation. The teacher said the following about her goals for this class: "This unit supports students to develop a civic consciousness. It encourages them to take a critical stance on mass media and to be aware of the connections between what governments do and how people around the world are affected" (Jaffe-Walter and Lee 2011: 288).

Furthermore, the Internationals' curriculum encourages students to address social injustice (Jaffe-Walter and Lee 2011: 288). Helping students to develop a critical consciousness of the political and economic inequalities facing immigrants in host societies provides them with the skills to navigate everyday exclusion, helping them to understand that exclusionary practices are structural rather a reflection of their own personal merit or worth. In addition, developing critical perspectives on social injustice promotes students' engagement in school and society. As Ladson-Billings (1995: 162) reminds us, "if school is about preparing students for active citizenship, what better citizenship tool than the ability to critically analyze the society?" She argues that critiquing the norms, values, and institutions that produce inequities helps students to be more engaged in society.

Although the curriculum of Danish schools also encourages exploration of issues of discrimination and social inequality, discussing racism and exclusion in Denmark and in Danish schools is strictly taboo. It is thought to be polarizing, challenging the community within schools by creating social divisions between immigrant students and ethnic Danish peers. There is an understanding that equality is achieved through a color-blind approach in which everyone is treated equally. In the United States, this color-blind stance has been used to ban the representation of immigrant groups and critical dialogue in schools. For instance, in 2010, the Arizona legislature passed a law that in effect prohibited programs in Mexican-American studies that, conservatives charged, promoted discrimination against whites and the "overthrow of the U.S. government." Two years later, under pressure, the Tucson Board of Education ended an innovative curriculum in Mexican-American studies despite evidence that it increased the graduation rates and enhanced the achievement of immigrant students (Planas 2013).

Scholars in globalization and education remind us that "education's challenge will be to shape the cognitive skills, interpersonal sensibilities, and cultural sophistication of children and youth whose lives will be both engaged in local contexts and responsive to larger transnational processes" (Suárez-Orozco and Qin-Hilliard 2004: 3). In contrast to nationalist modes of schooling, the curriculum within transnational imaginaries emphasizes that students have unique transnational perspectives on their worlds. Furthermore, such a curriculum recognizes that through participation with transnational networks, immigrant youth develop cultural flexibility and skills to broker between the various communities in which they participate. Through the cases of Aysa, who has become a teacher promoting immigrant belonging and success, and Aliyah, who plans to work with Danish and immigrant communities as a social worker, it is clear that transnational youth are in a unique position to support nations to envision more responsive practices and policies.

Making schooling more responsive to the needs of immigrant students isn't a matter of just including "other" cultures in mono-cultural nationalist classrooms, it's about cultivating transnational imaginaries that are based on the meeting of different peoples and cultures and the creation of ever evolving notions of community and belonging (Guan et al. 2014). Encouraging young people to engage their transnational experiences and global understandings not only benefits immigrant youth but also encourages native-born youth to examine life from multiple perspectives, a precondition for democratic citizenship in a globalizing world (Dabach 2015; Malsbary 2014).

Buffering Nationalist and Incoherent Policies

Teachers in Internationals schools understand that to be accountable to their students means actively resisting policies that frame immigrant student's language and culture as "deficits" to be overcome, and instead developing practices responsive to the needs of students (Jaffe-Walter 2008). In this way, these schools resist the logic of the figured worlds in which they operate. For example, in April 2014, teachers at the International High School in Prospect Heights refused to administer a New York City assessment on the grounds that it was traumatic and demoralizing for their students who are developing English language skills. This protest was part of a long history in the Internationals of resisting standardized tests that are inappropriate for English language learners (Menken 2008).

Resisting educational policies in the United States that reify test scores as a signifier of success, the teachers at the Internationals define success in terms of supporting students to sustain hope. Aware that high-stakes testing translates into the drop-out of immigrant students, five schools in the network have managed to negotiate a waiver from New York State that limits the number of high-stakes tests their students have to take (Jaffe-Walter 2008). This is an example of how the leadership of the schools and the network work with city and state organizations to promote policies and accommodations that buffer the negative impact of policy and to support teachers in cultivating transnational imaginaries (see Jaffe-Walter 2008).

While there isn't adequate space to provide an extended discussion of the structures and practices that promote immigrant students' success, the example of Internationals schools in New York City provides a glimpse into how schools can cultivate spaces of recognition and deep engagement for immigrant students. At a talk in November 2014 at the American Anthropological Association Meetings, educational anthropologist Marjorie Orellana explained that moving beyond deficit thinking isn't just a matter of committing ourselves to stop thinking in those ways. It requires new practices and structures that allow us to see immigrant students in a different light.

A comparison of the cases of resistance at Engby School and at the Internationals reveals how various actors in schools can buffer nationalist and incoherent policies to create spaces of recognition in classrooms. However, it also reveals the limitations and fragility of individual acts of resistance. While Aysa and Karen are able to limit the flow of figured identities in their classrooms, they are fighting the gravity of an institutional culture of assimilation that reads immigrants in terms of their deficits and that is focused on transforming immigrants into good liberal subjects. The case of Internationals reveals how resisting deficit discourses isn't just a matter of "not thinking" in particular ways. It involves intensive collaborative work to create schools where teachers have a profound sense of accountability to their immigrant students. While individual actors may have the institutional power to challenge the assumptions circulating in the broader figured world, transforming educational contexts and outcomes requires deeper and more established alliances and networks.

Conclusion
Interrogating Liberal Blind Spots and Silences

BY "STUDYING THROUGH" the multiple sites of discourse, policy, and everyday interactions in schools, I explore how the reforms, technologies, and ways of seeing produced within policies reverberate through communities and public institutions as well as the hearts of teachers and citizens who respond to the call that "something must be done" about the problems of Muslim immigration. I also consider how nationalist discourses are felt in the lives of Muslim youth and how presumably well-intentioned acts of "helping" are experienced as coercion. Thus, I reveal the troubling persistence of exclusionary practices cloaked within concern.

Concerns about immigration move between an explicitly racist and exclusionary politics and one that is cloaked within the sentiments of care and liberal values. Analyzing Danish integration politics from the 1990s to the present reveals a shift in political discourse away from an explicitly racist politics toward an emphasis on the values of freedom, equality, and unity. However, while there has been a shift in political rhetoric, there hasn't been a parallel movement toward policies that actually address the barriers facing Muslim and immigrant communities in Europe (Dominus 2015). European politicians' stances on immigration flow with the tide of public opinion and pressure from conservative factions. As of the writing of this book, far-right anti-immigrant groups are leading in the polls and gaining ground in elections in many European countries. In the 2015 Danish election, the far-right Danish People's Party promised tougher immigration laws and won a fifth of the vote, a doubling of its popularity from the 2011 election (Gani 2015).

The politics of concern, whether enacted in xenophobic policies or in everyday interactions between students and teachers, reflects desires to transform immigrants into acceptable subjects. I argue that this politics is narcissistic; teachers' concern for the welfare of their Muslim students is blurred by anxiety about a changing Denmark and a narrow vision of how life should be lived. It reveals more about the concerned than about the subjects of concern. As Sander Gilman explains, stereotypes are protection from anxieties about the unsettledness of our worlds: "We need stereotypes to structure the world. We need crude representations of difference to localize our anxiety, to prove to ourselves that what we fear does not lie within" (1985: 240). Technologies of concern reflect the deep unsettling tensions within the modern nation-state in an era of globalization and migration. They provoke and draw on collective emotions of fear, care, and nostalgia, desires to restore an idealized vision of the nation untainted by immigration. Policymakers in the United States and across Europe exploit fears to garner votes and popularity by prominently featuring images of Muslims and immigrants associated with illegality, criminality, and sexual deviance (Maira 2009; Rana 2011) and producing dystopic images of immigrant takeover, of "counter-worlds" where majorities might suddenly become minorities in their own land. They use these images to justify policies that protect the imagined communities of nations by controlling public signs of Islam such as the wearing of *hijab*, the construction of mosques, and the elimination of religious and cultural accommodations within schools and other public institutions. This racialized politics seeks to purify the social body, to protect "our" way of life from theirs. It produces a constellation of practices, discourses, and representations—"figured worlds" of meaning—that determine how Muslims are positioned in Western liberal societies (on "figured worlds," see Holland et al. 1998). Yet, acknowledging these desires to restore white liberal national imaginaries challenges idealized images of inclusive nation-states.

My analysis explores the epistemologies of civic nationalism, the stories nations tell themselves about their inherently inclusive nature, reproducing notions of benevolent Western nations that represent a joining of diverse peoples around the liberal principles of equality, democracy, and freedom. These narratives conceal the racializing logic of liberal nations, the ways that they are imagined in relation to particular national histories, religious traditions, values, and ways of being. Talal Asad describes the dilemma this presents when it comes to the representation of Muslims in liberal nation-states: "The ideology of political representation in liberal democracies makes it difficult if not impossible to represent Muslims as Muslims. Why? Because in theory the citizens who constitute a democratic state belong to a class that is defined only by what is common to all members and its members only" (2003: 173). Western liberal notions of individualism, democracy, and freedom are ultimately narcissistic; they claim to be universal and neutral but in actuality they are national and particular. They offer up a vision of a civic nationalism and a liberal future that one can believe in, forwarding a selective vision of nationalism compatible with liberal politics.

Implications for the Anthropology of Policy

In this book, I advance the anthropology of policy as a methodology for examining how policies produce stereotyped notions of Muslim identities, and in addition, how they inspire processes of figuring identities as individual actors take up the stereotypes reproduced in policies in their everyday interactions. Tracing the rationality of policies across various sites, I have examined taken-for-granted understandings of who Muslim immigrants are and the types of interventions that they require to become acceptable subjects of the nation. Danish integration policies position their work in terms of fighting discrimination against women, describing the "gender barriers" facing Muslim women, and proposing measures that move women out of ethnic communities by exposing them to Danish values. In the school where I conducted my fieldwork, I witnessed how a teacher, Lena, took up this assimilation work in a class in which she coercively questioned a fourteen-year-old Muslim student about her choice of marriage partner. In addition, I documented the ways that another teacher in the school, Birgitte, instructed these students in a Danish-as-a-second-language class to engage in premarital sex as a way of conforming to Danish values. Woven through teachers' narratives about Muslim girls is an assumption that Muslim girls need to be liberated from immigrant communities and their families. Teachers' work echoed the figures and logic of integration policies and focused on transforming oppressed Muslim girls into free-thinking liberal subjects who adopted Danish liberal modes of thinking and behaving.

The rhetoric of education and immigration policies is often couched in the universalized language of promoting equality and democracy for all, forwarding goals that appear to be incontrovertible. Governments in Europe and the United States have enacted policies in the name of lofty goals such as providing poor students of color in cities high-quality instruction, and improving math and science curricula to increase national competitiveness and expand students' opportunities in the labor market. The anthropology of policy provides a lens for examining how educational policies respond to political and media discourses of concern, yet remain divorced from what really works on the ground in schools and how policies are experienced by various communities. It provides insight into the everyday workings of policies in schools and the ways that they privilege particular forms of knowledge and subjectivities while penalizing others. The growing body of research in the anthropology of policy and critical policy analysis examining the so-called unintended consequences of policy demonstrates that presumably well-intentioned policies born out of concern for particular populations can actually contribute to their educational exclusion (Dumas, 2011; Jaffe-Walter, 2008; Menken 2008).

My analysis does not suggest that policies operate in a top-down fashion, clearly delineating particular forms of action. Rather, I consider how particular technologies are adapted, adopted, and resisted within schools, how they interact with individual actor's histories as well as local discourses. In her work on the anthropology of policy, Gritt Nielsen explores how policies are "peopled." She explains: "The challenge . . . is to explore the connections between larger programmes or rationalities and locally negotiated practices without ending up either with an idealized production of general political rationalities . . . or with descriptions of myriads of complex local practices with no connection to larger structures and policy processes in society" (2011: 69). I recognize that teachers are not simplistically enacting policies. It is not as if Birgitte, the Danish teacher at Engby school, is responding to a policy directive to encourage premarital sex among Muslim girls. She is instead taking up her own interpretation of the urgent call set out by integration policies to educate Muslim girls about Danish gender roles. Rather than thinking about the particular actions that policies produce, it may be more useful to think about how policies create space for the expression of particular ways of thinking, feeling, and engaging. Although policy doesn't call for particular forms of instruction related to premarital sex, it does mandate that all schools have Danish-as-a-second-language classes focused on language and the cultivation of Danish ways of thinking and being. Thus, policies can consolidate understandings of Muslim "others" within the figured worlds of schools and society and inspire figuring and coercive assimilation.

The anthropology of policy also offers a window into the affective dimensions of policies and the forms of knowledge that policies produce. How do policies stir up and exploit feelings of anger, nostalgia, and care, only to be taken up and embodied by different actors differently within the spaces of schools? For example, in Chapter 3, I document Lena's desire to support her Muslim students to have a good life, access to jobs and education; "we try and try and try" she says. Her narratives also reflect her frustration with the intransigence of immigrants who refuse to conform to Danish values. These perspectives reveal that educational policies can give rise to anxieties about the changing nation and provoke expressions of "sympathy" for ethnic minority students.

Examining the affective dimensions of policies allows one to recognize that policies can incite people to take up the work of nation building by engaging in everyday acts of defending national borders. For example, a Moroccan immigrant living in a suburb of Paris explained that fining a Muslim woman for wearing *hijab* in public spaces is far less painful than the racist treatment by ordinary citizens since the passage of the law banning full-face veils in public spaces. She described being "spat at, honked at from cars and also beaten . . . assaulted" while carrying her daughter in her arms (Erlanger and Camus 2012). Anthropology provides a lens for examining how the "truths" of policy reverberate through communities, inspiring figuring and everyday acts of violence. It also allows one to hear what official policy seeks to silence and recognize that the intense attention to intervention in young people's lives can be shifted to exploring how societies might foster the recognition and equitable participation of immigrant students and their communities.

Implications for Policymakers

In recent years there has been a shift in Europe toward integration policies that emphasize "active" citizenship. European governments have positioned themselves as "supporting" immigrants to integrate themselves (Rose 1999) in order to take advantage of the offerings of European societies at the same time that these same governments enact more restrictive and coercive policies that limit immigrant rights. Joppke describes this as a shift away from a rights-based notion of liberalism that values increased rights, antidiscrimination laws, and relaxed citizenship requirements toward a "liberalism of power and disciplining" (2007: 15). Indeed, in Europe today there is a consensus that nations have reached their limit, that multiculturalism has failed, and that it is time to draw a line, or, as David Cameron says, to assert a more "muscular liberalism" (BBC News, 2011), limiting the spread of immigrants and more vigorously regulating their activities and identities.

In Gavan Titley's (2014) words, a "pig whistle politics" is sweeping Europe as politicians politicize the accommodations made for Muslim citizens. In summer 2013, leaders of the Danish People's Party publicly denounced hospitals and kindergartens that stopped serving pork meatballs, or *frikadeller*. They equated the ban on pork with discrimination against Danish values. The party complained of the problem of politicians not speaking up for the Danish community oppressed by the Muslim minority and pressured the Social Democratic prime minister, Helle Thorning-Schmidt, to make a statement about the centrality of pork meatballs to Denmark's national identity. She declared, "We have to stick with the way we eat and what we do in Denmark. There should be room for *frikadeller*" (Weaver 2013). Reacting to the anti-immigrant upswell in Europe, even centrist politicians are moving toward an anti-immigrant position. Increasingly, this kind of hard-line stance is translating into political capital and votes for politicians. On May 25, 2014, Morten Messerschmidt, a leader of the Dansk Folkeparti who was charged with hate speech in his call for a "Danish Future" as part of his 2001 campaign against Muslims, was elected to the European Parliament, receiving the largest number of individual votes for any candidate in the history of the parliament. Clearly, exploiting national concern has its political advantages.

Nationalist integration policies that view Muslim communities through the lens of concern obscure a genuine recognition of the experiences and needs of these communities. As I have argued, concern involves a complex array of emotions, all of which arise from a fear that tends to blind individuals to one another. Martha Nussbaum calls for an increased awareness of this type of chauvinism: "We have to watch out for interference that may come from our tendency to sympathize above all with people who belong to our own group—whether that is defined in terms of kinship, or race, or nationality. We need to ask what our particular blind spots are and then to address those" (2012: 147–48). I would add that it is important to explore the ways policymaking exploits fear, promising to offer protection and to restore all that is familiar. But what are the ways that in practice this fear polarizes and divides, preventing individuals and communities from seeing and understanding one another?

There is much social scientific research that provides insight into policies that might encourage the engagement and equitable participation of immigrants in host societies. Despite assumptions that the road to integration requires the dispersal of immigrant enclaves and the erosion of immigrants' religious values, research suggests that immigrants access important resources and labor market ties through their relationships in such communities. Anna Damm (2012) reveals the flawed logic of "de-ghettoization" policies to move immigrants out of immigrant enclaves. She finds that when the Danish government enacted residential quotas that forced new refugees into predominantly Danish communities, these new residents were not able to access jobs or information from their ethnic Danish neighbors. In contrast, refugees who lived in communities with large numbers of immigrants were able to find jobs through ethnic networks. Rather than blindly pressing toward assimilation, policymakers should encourage civic engagement by expanding opportunities for authentic participation in education and the labor market.

Numerous other examples reveal that policies claiming to encourage integration actually limit both Muslim immigrants' mobility within communities and their access to the labor market. For example, M'hammed Henniche, secretary general of the private Union of Muslim Associations of Seine-Saint-Denis, France, explains that as a result of the ban on full-face veils many Muslim women choose to "limit their moves and stay in their own neighborhood." A French business man of Algerian origin adds "the law was meant to protect women but it has imprisoned them instead" (Erlanger and Camus 2012). This dynamic is also evident in the experiences of Muslim women who are unable to find jobs in government and in childcare institutions because of bans on *hijab* in particular professions. In addition to instances of "official" labor market exclusion, there are well-documented instances of "unofficial" exclusion of women who wear *hijab*, like Sara, my participant, who was unable to secure a position as an administrative assistant.

Relationships and contacts within immigrant enclaves are instrumental in helping immigrant youth negotiate their identities in new host countries. Social scientific literature also points out that religion can promote the incorporation of immigrants in new host societies by providing a "psychological ballast helping to ameliorate the traumas of early settlement and frequent encounter with discrimination" (Foner and Alba 2008: 362). Policymakers need to be aware that immigrants' connections with religious and community organizations can encourage participation in the broader society.

Viewing Muslim immigration through the lens of anxiety and "moral panic" precludes an understanding of the essential social capital and community knowledge that is transmitted and shared within immigrant networks. Furthermore, policies that paint associations with religious and ethnic organizations as antithetical to the goals of the state ignore research showing that civic engagement in one sphere is likely to yield engagement in others. In his research in France, John Bowen critiques the belief that religious and ethnic affiliations threaten engagement with the nation.

> When French commentators denounce Muslims for forming their own socioreligious worlds, and thus practicing "communalism," they fail to acknowledge that citizens can draw religious and moral inspiration from their associative lives in order to better enter into broader social and political activities. That Catholics, Protestants, and Jews, and others have done so does not arouse great concern today; these activities have become part of the taken-for-granted backdrop to French social life. That Muslims do so is new, and it worries those in France who fear that French Muslims will place their global religious allegiances above their French Republican ones. In a deeper historical context, this fear is not novel. Catholics and Jews, in particular, have felt such accusations, and not only in France. These accusations move us from considering forms of sociability to considering anxieties generated about the norms and values expressed by some French Muslims. (2011: 188)

Clearly, it is time to abandon the intense preoccupation with intervention in the lives of Muslims and the regulation of Muslim bodies and consider how Western liberal societies might better meet the needs of their Muslim residents and citizens. Rather than positioning immigrants as threatening Western liberal societies, it is essential to see the contributions they have made to the growth and development of those societies. Indeed, the wealth of Western liberal societies has been built upon the hard work of migrant laborers over the centuries. While nationalist integration policies try to defend ethno-national visions of citizenship, the realities of globalization and migration demand a recognition of the complex contributions and experiences of migrant workers and the ways their lives are tied to broader economic and political forces.

Political discourse in Europe assumes that cultural conflict is inevitable, but I would argue that it is not. Like my participants who struggled to find jobs in Denmark, most Muslims citizens want to be a part of the societies in which they live (Bowen 2011: 180). They don't pursue strategies of self-segregation, but in some cases, faced with discrimination and a lack of access to resources in the broader society, they seek refuge in immigrant enclaves. Inglehart and Norris have found that the "cultural divide" between European Muslims and non-Muslims is not as great as is reflected in the media. In fact, Muslim minorities' values and gender roles are typically closer to those of their host societies than those of their countries of origin (Inglehart and Norris 2009: 18). Rather than seeing religious and cultural affiliations as barriers to be overcome, it is critical to consider the ways that cultural accommodations can support increased engagement and participation. This is not to deny the complexity of negotiating religious differences within secular schools and other public institutions. Clearly the historical treatment of issues such as prayer in school and the teaching of evolution and creationism suggest that navigating religion in schools is an area for deep work and analysis. This can begin with the recognition that some religious practices are politicized and thought to be fundamentally incompatible with liberal schooling while others are taken for granted, such as preparation for Christian confirmation, a time-honored part of the curriculum in putatively "secular" Danish schools.

Implications for Education

An educational anthropology of policy reveals that policies that claim to foster the integration of immigrants can lead to everyday processes of exclusion in schools. The Muslim youth discussed in this book described the ways that processes of figuring translate to the misrecognition of their identities. They described experiences of being "always watched" but never really understood. As Aliyah explained, "No one really asks us how we feel." Charles Taylor defines misrecognition as a "form of oppression, imprisoning someone in a false, distorted, reduced mode of being. Beyond simply lack of respect, it can inflict a grievous wound, saddling people with crippling self-hatred. Due recognition is not just a courtesy but a vital human need" (Taylor 1992: 25–26). While youth reveal their strength and resilience as they creatively devise ways of minimizing the impact of misrepresentation, it is important not to romanticize their self-authorings, to dismiss the material costs of figuring.

I argue that the more students experience scrutiny and misrecognition in school, the more likely they are to withdraw from interactions with teachers and peers who might potentially offer critical social capital to help them to navigate life in host countries. Echoing the findings of research reported in the preceding section, educational scholars have documented the psychological and strategic value of immigrant youths' ties to teachers and native-born youth as well as the importance of connections to their families and ethnic communities (Stanton-Salazar 1997; Suárez-Orozco et al. 2008). The stories of the Muslim participants in my project challenge nationalist paradigms about what it means to integrate "into" a society. They reveal that culture and traditions are central to one's identity; integration is not a simple process of shedding one identity to take on another. A narrow understanding of "integration" silences the multiple, contradictory notions of self that immigrant youth experience when they are living simultaneously in multiple worlds.

Social science research has documented that stereotyping and assimilative practices influence immigrant students' engagement in schools (Steele 1997; Valenzuela 1999). To address this issue, it is not enough to be concerned or to care for students. It is critical to interrogate the ways that certain modes of caring implicitly position immigrant students as outsiders who lack the qualities for belonging. Aysa, the Turkish teacher at Engby School, argues that it is important to develop practices that foster the recognition of immigrant students' complex experiences and lives. To do this, she points out, there needs to be a dramatic shift in how Muslim students are understood in school. Teachers need to adapt to the growing complexity of a globalizing world, to see through, as she puts it, a "wall" of difference:

It's a wall to have another background, it's a wall and they can't get through and it's easier to talk negative about something you don't know anything about. The teachers who work in this school because there are a lot of students with another background, we have to change ourselves. If we say yes to work here, we have to change ourselves, we cannot say this is my work, I teach, that is not enough.

However, transforming education for Muslim and immigrant youth is not only a matter of changing teacher's views, it is also a question of challenging public and media discourses that position Muslim youth as lacking and requiring state intervention. In Chapter 6, I have explored school communities that are transnational imaginaries where teachers resist deficit-oriented policies and discourses and encourage immigrant youth to express their various selves within the spaces of schools. These environments provide students with the social capital and knowledge to navigate schooling and careers in host countries. They create safe spaces where students experience belonging and access to tools to critique and reframe nationalist and exclusionary discourses. There is much to be learned from these school communities that are focused on visions of "care" that recognize the diasporic nature of immigrant lives.

Historically within Danish schools, there has been an understanding that talking about race or racialization in schools is taboo as it is expected to produce racial polarization and incite divisions between groups. Danish educational philosophies center on promoting a "color-blind" approach to education, developing social equality through the creation of a common cultural community in schools in which all students are treated the same. However, the ethnographic scenes in this book reveal that messages about racial, ethnic, and religious difference are constantly being broadcast through the spaces in schools. I argue that fostering the equitable participation of immigrant youth in schools requires more open dialogue about racial exclusion in order to develop what Fine, Weis, and Powell describe as "structures and practices that enable young people to work with—not around or in spite of—race, ethnicity, and power-based differences . . . [as occurs] when young people are invited to discuss, voice, critique and review the very notions of race that feel so fixed, so hierarchical, so damaging, yet so accepted in the broader society" (1997: 251). Creating opportunities for critical dialogue in classrooms fosters mutual understanding among students and provides immigrant youth with tools to strategically dodge the corrosive effects of processes of figuring.

Transforming education for a globalizing world requires moving beyond the notion that immigrants should be turned into ideal liberal subjects. Instead, policy should confront the fact that national constructions of racial difference and figurings are tied to global constellations of race, labor, and capital. For example, we need to ask whether immigrants who are conceived of as "uninvited guests" in Western liberal nations are actually populations of peoples displaced by colonial regimes or seeking to fill jobs in host countries created by economic demand. We also need to investigate the ways that migrant labor underpins the affluence of Western liberal nations. Through critical dialogues about the constructions of racial difference produced within figured worlds it is possible to challenge the processes of figuring that take place in schools, to produce alternative ways of "seeing" and "hearing" immigrant youth.

On Imagining Modes of Care That Foster Recognition

Scholars have called for policies that move away from "thick" ethno-national notions of citizenship in Denmark and elsewhere all across Europe. While nationalist Danish policies seek to maintain culturally bounded conceptions of nation and citizen, the realities of globalization and migration require new understandings of what it means to belong. Jenkins argues for an expansion of what it means to be Danish:

Not axiomatically Christian, less prescriptive, and accommodating of visible differences. In other words, 'being Danish' must gradually become something else. Alongside this, a more relaxed approach and less authoritarian official notion of integration—and indeed a more relaxed approach and less authoritarian approach to Danishness and Danish culture—is necessary. The everyday realities of multi-ethnic Denmark cannot be micro-managed by the state, within the school system or elsewhere. (2011: 305)

Creating more responsive policies is not just a matter of being more open to expanded notions of citizenship. The nationalist position is so deeply ingrained that it is difficult to discern how notions of Muslims as Others are a naturalized part of the grammar of Western liberal societies. Bhikhu Parekh suggests that any imaginings of nation and nationalisms are deeply suspect. He argues that images of the nation "cannot avoid offering a homogenized, reified, and ideologically biased abridgment of a rich, complex, and fluid way of life, and setting up false contrasts and impregnable walls between political communities. . . . Even well-intentioned liberals and socialists cannot theorize political life in that language without succumbing to its corrupting and pernicious logic" (1999: 324). As such, it is critical to imagine more a participatory political discourse that seeks out the involvement of and yields power to organizations and associations that promote and incorporate the voices of immigrant and Muslim groups.

However, it is important to point out that the politics of representation is thorny. In recent years, immigrants have been invited to participate in the Danish government in tokenistic ways while groups who challenge nationalist positions are silenced. In 2002, the Danish Ministry of Refugees, Immigration, and Integration Affairs launched an initiative, "Mere velfærd og mindre bureaukrati—sanering af råd, nævn og centre" (More Welfare and Less Bureaucracy—Cleaning up Councils, Boards and Centers), that closed down 140 councils, boards, and centers, many of which were responsible for supporting immigrant rights (e.g., the Guest Workers Council) and documenting human rights violations (the Advisory Center on Racial Discrimination and the Board of Ethnic Equality). To encourage more equitable participation of immigrants and Muslims in society, it is necessary that they have substantive representation in the political arena. It is only through more participatory forms of discourse and policymaking that nations will move beyond positions of national anxiety and sympathy. It is critical to understand the ways immigrants can tap into community knowledge and to position immigrants as having agency to address structural inequalities as opposed to requiring intervention. There are examples across the globe of participatory reforms, like those in Porto Alegre, Brazil, that engage communities to transform local conditions and imagine more demo-cratic policymaking and schooling.[1]

In conclusion, it is also important to add that there are many lessons to be learned from the positive forms of care and concern extended within Danish societies. Danish society is deeply committed to creating social structures and social welfare policies that address the needs of all members of society across the life-cycle. This is evident in, for example, Denmark's support for universal health care, publicly funded preschool and university education, unemploy-ment support, and eldercare. In many ways Danish society and Danish schools offer the ideal conditions for more equitable education for immigrant youth with a commitment to both the emotional and the academic needs of stu-dents, a lack of academic tracking or leveling, and equitable funding formulas for schools. In some ways the road to educational equity for immigrant youth looks much shorter in Denmark than it does in countries, like the United States, with more deeply entrenched political and economic inequalities. Despite my critique of current nationalist integration strategies in Denmark and how they produce narcissistic modes of care and concern, I believe it is possible to move beyond forms of concern that erect and defend rigid borders, to modes of care that foster recognition and the participation of all citizens.

Notes

Introduction

1. The names of my informants and respondents are pseudonyms.

2. A pseudonym.

3. The first phase of research was conducted in 2007–2008 with follow-up data collection trips in 2009, 2011, and 2014.

4. See Fine et al. 2007 for a discussion of how schools serving large numbers of students who are not native-language speakers are penalized under accountability policies that evaluate schools based on standardized test scores. While Danish schools have historically been opposed to standardized testing and more oriented toward constructivist experiential modes of education, there has recently been a shift toward adopting the kinds of testing and accountability regimes used in the United States.

5. The Mohammad cartoon crisis began after the Danish newspaper *Jyllands-Posten* published twelve cartoons on September 30, 2005, depicting the Prophet Mohammed. The newspaper described the cartoons as opening up a debate about freedom of speech. The publication led Muslim groups to protest in Denmark and in several Muslim countries.

Chapter 1

1. According to the 1790 Naturalization Act, Native Americans could not seek citizenship because they were not "white." The first Native Americans to be granted citizenship were the five "civilized" tribes, those that adopted European culture. Citizenship was granted to all Native Americans in 1924 upon the passage of the Indian Citizenship Act (Spring 1990: 167–168).

2. Founded in Dresden Germany in 2014, Pegida, or Patriotic Europeans Against the Islamization of the West, is a political organization calling for more restrictive immigration rules.

3. Danish demographic categories make a distinction between those with a Western background, from Norway, Germany, Bosnia and Herzegovina, the United Kingdom, Poland, Iceland, countries in the European Union, non-EU Nordic countries, the United States, Switzerland, Canada, Australia, and New Zealand, and those with a non-Western background, from Turkey, Iraq, Somalia, Pakistan, Iran, Thailand, and others. While the

United States is considered a Western country, people from Puerto Rico are categorized as from a non-Western country.

4. The following subjects are mandated for all students (in all grades unless otherwise noted): Danish, English (3–9), Christian studies in all grades except for the year in which religious confirmation takes place, history (3–9), social studies (8–9), physical education, music (1–6), visual arts (1–5), design, wood and metalwork (1–5), math, natural sciences (1–6), geography (7–9), biology (7–9), physics/chemistry (7–9), plus several optional subjects (French, photography, extra physical education, cooking) (Danish Ministry of Education 2010).

5. In some cases, the *folkeskole* offers an optional tenth grade that allows students to gain additional skills in preparation for upper secondary education. In 2008, 712,100 students attended 1,605 *folkeskolen* in Denmark, with 85 percent attending their local *folkeskole* and 15 percent attending private schools that include religious schools (Christian, Jewish, and Islamic) as well as international schools, Waldorf schools, and Montessori schools. Private schools, or *friskoler*, receive partial funding from the government. In 2008 the average class size in *folkeskolen* was 19.6, with a student:teacher ratio of 10:1. Two-thirds of all teachers in the *folkeskolen* are women, and two-thirds of principals are male. (Danish Ministry of Education 2008)

6. While this teacher's voice reflected the dominant position, there were also examples of teachers who thought that students should have a celebration for the Muslim holiday of Eid within the school.

Chapter 2

1. There are exceptions, such as the introduction of dual citizenship and some liberalization of permanent residence policies (Mouritsen and Jensen 2014: 8).

2. Responding to public criticism, the Starthelp policy was eliminated in 2011 (Mouritsen and Jensen 2014).

3. "The Integration Contract and the Declaration on Integration and Active Citizenship are, likewise, only required for refugees and reunified family members. The kind and extent of integration requirements depends, then, on the migrant category an immigrant belongs to. However, generally speaking, no general integration policies focusing only on some nationalities exist, as all nationalities are supposed to be treated equally" (Mouritsen and Jensen 2014: 11).

4. Kjærsgaard is the founder of the Dansk Folkeparti and a proponent of nativist policies in Denmark and across Europe.

5. Christian Horst has described the immigrant home visits law as "part of the general political movement of law enforcements limiting immigration and ethnic minorities' possibilities to cultivate their heritage at will" (email message to author, September 15, 2013).

6. Native-language instruction is an extra-curricular course offered to students who attend a *folkeskole*. It is not offered at all to students attending gymnasium (academic high school).

7. Khawaja (2104) documents how Muslim immigrants negotiate stereotyping gazes in their everyday life in Danish society.

8. While Mathias reproduced these deficit views in interviews, it is important to add that an immigrant student cited Mathias as a very supportive teacher who helped him to be successful.

Chapter 3

1. As mentioned earlier, Engby School is conscious of its public image as a "black" school, i.e., a school with a large population of immigrant students. In Denmark, it is considered important for schools to maintain an immigrant population of 25 percent or less; in 2009, 45 percent of the population of Engby School came from immigrant families.

2. Danish as a second language was introduced as a school subject in 1995 when the first guidelines were sent out. However, there are no formal requirements as to number of lessons nor competence assessment criteria (Anne Holmen, personal communication).

3. In 1969 Denmark became the first country to legalize pornography. Premarital sex for teenagers is seen as natural and acceptable. A large percentage of Danish couples live together without being married and Denmark was the first country in the world to recognize same-sex partnerships.

Chapter 4

1. In eliciting the maps I read the following prompt and supplied blank paper and markers.

Identities: Everybody has different selves they carry around in the same body—you may be a daughter, cousin, student, writer, athlete, friend . . .

· What are the different identities that define who you are?

· Draw a picture that describes your many selves and the messages that you receive in different spaces. This can include any place, such as: home, school, community, nation, or in your/your parent's native country.

2. International Baccalaureate programs define international education in terms of "developing citizens of the world in relation to culture, language, and learning to live together," "fostering students' recognition and development of universal human values," and "building and reinforcing students' sense of identity and cultural awareness." (International Baccalaureate 2012)

Chapter 5

1. *Perker* is a racialized slur.

2. In her book *Muslim American Women on Campus*, Shabana Mir analyzes the complex ways that Muslim American women negotiated their identities in U.S. universities, where they were subjected to surveillance and scrutiny by their peers. In turn, she notes that her participants tried to fit in with their peers by, for example, developing identities

that allowed them to negotiate the alcohol culture of U.S. universities and to move be-tween categories of being Muslim and American (2014).

Chapter 6

1. The literature on immigration and education reveals that mobilizing students' identities within the curriculum increases the engagement of immigrant students while also providing a richer synthesis of topics at hand (Sepúlveda 2011).

2. In the quotation, the interpolation "[2001,]" is in the original. Le Pen was the president of the right-wing Front National in France (FN). The FN has an anti-immigrant platform calling for restricting non-European immigration and protecting French values.

Conclusion

1. A participatory budget process was implemented in 1989 in Porto Alegre, a community that was on the verge of bankruptcy. Through consultation and debate, local residents are mobilized to decide on taxes and public expenditures. Millions of residents participate actively in the process, attending meetings, regional conventions, and specific thematic assemblies. This has led to a dramatic improvement in the living conditions of local residents, doubling the percentage who have access to the public water supply and increasing access to sanitary sewers and public schooling. Based on Porto Alegre's success, this model has been adopted by seventy other cities across Brazil. (Souza 2001)

References

Abu El-Haj, Thea Renda. 2010. "'The Beauty of America': Nationalism, Education, and the War on Terror." *Harvard Educational Review* 80(2): 242–75.

———. 2015. *Unsettled Belonging: Educating Palestinian American Youth After 9/11*. Chicago: University of Chicago Press.

Abu-Lughod, Lila. 2002. "Do Muslim Women Really Need Saving? Anthropological Reflections on Cultural Relativism and Its Others." *American Anthropologist* 104(3): 783–90.

Adelman, Larry. 2003. *Race: The Power of an Illusion*. PBS television series. Los Angeles: California Newsreel. www.pbs.org/race/005_MeMyRaceAndI/005_01-transcripts-04.htm.

Agar, Michael H. 1986. *Speaking of Ethnography*. Newbury Park, CA: Sage.

Amnesty International. 2012. *Choice and Prejudice: Discrimination against Muslims in Europe*. London: Amnesty International. www.amnesty.nl/sites/default/files/public/religious_discrm_muslims_report.pdf (accessed February 6, 2013).

Anderson, Benedict. 2006. *Imagined Communities: Reflections on the Origin and Spread of Nationalism*. Revised ed. London: Verso.

Anderson, Sally. 1996. *Chronic Proximity and the Management of Difference: A Study of the Danish School Practice of Klasse*. Copenhagen: Københavns universitet, Institut for antropologi.

Andreassen, Rikke. 2012. "Gender as a Tool in Danish Debates about Muslims." Pp. 143–60 in *Islam in Denmark: The Challenge of Diversity*, edited by Jørgen S. Nielsen. Plymouth, UK: Lexington Books.

Anti-Defamation League. 2014. "Anti-Muslim Bigotry: ADL's Role in Fighting Anti-Muslim Bigotry." www.adl.org/civil-rights/discrimination/c/anti-muslim-bigotry.html (accessed March 23, 2015).

Appadurai, Arjun. 1996. *Modernity at Large: Cultural Dimensions of Globalization*. Minneapolis: University of Minnesota Press.

———. 2006. *Fear of Small Numbers: An Essay on the Geography of Anger*. Durham, NC: Duke University Press.

Asad, Talal. 2003. *Formations of the Secular: Christianity, Islam, Modernity*. Stanford, CA: Stanford University Press.

———. 2006. "Trying to Understand French Secularism." Pp. 494–526 in *Political Theolo-*

gies: Public Religions in a Post-Secular World, edited by Hent de Vries and Lawrence Sullivan. New York: Fordham University Press.

———. 2009. "Reflections on the Origins of Human Rights." Lecture presented at the Law, Religion and Values program, Berkley Center for Religion, Peace & World Affairs, September 28. Georgetown University, Washington DC.

Augoustinos, Martha, and Danielle Every. 2007. "The Language of 'Race' and Prejudice: A Discourse of Denial, Reason, and Liberal-Practical Politics." *Journal of Language and Social Psychology* 26(2): 123–41.

Bakhtin, Mikhail. 1981. *The Dialogic Imagination: Four Essays*. Austin: University of Texas Press.

Balibar, Etienne. 1991. "Racism and Nationalism." Pp. 37–67 in Etienne Balibar and Immanuel Wallerstein, *Race, Nation, Class: Ambiguous Identities*. London: Verso.

Ball, Stephen J. 2006. *Education Policy and Social Class*. New York: Routledge.

Barreto, Manuela, and Naomi Ellemers. 2002. "The Impact of Respect Versus Neglect of Self-Identities on Identification and Group Loyalty." *Personality and Social Psychology Bulletin* 28(5): 629–39.

Bartlett, Lesley, and Ofelia García. 2011. *Additive Schooling in Subtractive Times: Bilingual Education and Dominican Immigrant Youth in the Heights*. Nashville, TN: Vanderbilt University Press.

Baumann, Gerd. 2004. "Introduction: Nation-state, Schools, and Civil Enculturation." Pp. 1–18 in *Civil Enculturation: Nation-State, School and Ethnic Difference in the Netherlands, Britain, Germany and France*, edited by Werner Shiffauer, Gerd Baumann, Riva Kastoryano, and Steven Vertovec. Oxford: Berghahn Books.

Bayoumi, Moustafa. 2008. *How Does It Feel to Be a Problem? Being Young and Arab in America*. London: Penguin Books.

BBC News. 2011. "State Multiculturalism Has Failed, Says David Cameron." *BBC News*, February 5. www.bbc.co.uk/news/uk-politics-12371994 (accessed June 24, 2012).

———. 2013. "French Veil Law: Muslim Woman's Challenge in Strasbourg." *BBC News*, November 27. www.bbc.com/news/world-europe-25118160 (accessed June 24, 2014).

Behrent, Michael C. 2013. "Foucault and Technology." *History and Technology* 29(1): 54–104.

Benei, Véronique. 2008. *Schooling Passions?: Nation, History, and Language in Contemporary Western India*. Stanford, CA: Stanford University Press.

Berry, John W. 2008. "Globalisation and Acculturation." *International Journal of Intercultural Relations* 32(4): 328–36.

Bhabha, Homi. 2005. "Race, Time and the Revision of Modernity." Pp. 291–322 in *Nation and Narration*, edited by Homi K. Bhabha. London: Routledge.

Bhatia, Sunil. 2002. "Acculturation, Dialogical Voices and the Construction of the Diasporic Self." *Theory & Psychology* 12(1): 55–77.

Billig, Michael. 1995. *Banal Nationalism*. Thousand Oaks, CA: Sage.

Bonilla-Silva, Eduardo. 2003. "'New Racism,' Color-Blind Racism, and the Future of Whiteness in America." Pp. 271–84 in *White Out: The Continuing Significance of Racism*, edited by Asley W. Doane and Eduardo Bonilla-Silva. New York: Routledge.

Bowen, John R. 2007. *Why the French Don't Like Headscarves: Islam, the State, and Public Space*. Princeton, NJ: Princeton University Press.

———. 2011. *Can Islam Be French? Pluralism and Pragmatism in a Secularist State*. Princeton, NJ: Princeton University Press.

Brown, Wendy. 2006. *Regulating Aversion: Tolerance in the Age of Identity and Empire*. Princeton, NJ: Princeton University Press.

Bunzl, Matti. 2005. "Between Anti-Semitism and Islamophobia: Some Thoughts on the New Europe." *American Ethnologist* 32(4): 499–508.

Burchell, Graham. 1993. "Liberal Government and Techniques of the Self." *Economy and Society* 22(3): 267–82.

Buskbjerg, Maja, and Najhee Jackson. 2009. "How Is Integration Possible in Denmark?" *Humanity in Action*. www.humanityinaction.org/knowledgebase/54-how-is-integration-possible-in-denmark (accessed May 1, 2015).

Calhoun, Craig. 1993. "Nationalism and Ethnicity." *Annual Review of Sociology* 19: 211–39.

Callahan, Rebecca, Lindsey Wilkinson, and Chandra Muller. 2008. "School Context and the Effect of ESL Placement on Mexican-Origin Adolescents' Achievement." *Social Science Quarterly* 89(1): 177–98.

Castells, Manuel. 2004. *The Power of Identity*. Vol. 2 of *The Information Age: Economy, Society, and Culture*. Malden, MA: Wiley Blackwell.

CERD [Committee on the Elimination of Racial Discrimination]. 2006. *Consideration of Reports Submitted by States Parties under Article 9 of the Convention: Concluding Observations of the Committee on the Elimination of Racial Discrimination: Denmark*. CERD/C/DEN/CO/17. New York: CERD, United Nations.

———. 2010. *Report of the Documentary and Advisory Centre on Racial Discrimination, Denmark (DACoRD)*. Copenhagen.

Chavez, Leo. 2013. *The Latino Threat: Constructing Immigrants, Citizens, and the Nation*. Stanford, CA: Stanford University Press.

Clifford, James. 1988 "Introduction: Partial Truths." Pp. 1–17 in *The Predicament of Culture: Twentieth Century Ethnography, Literature, and Art*. Cambridge, MA: Harvard University Press.

———. 1994. "Diasporas." *Cultural Anthropology* 9(3): 302–38.

Coleman, David, and Eskil Wadensjö. 1999. *Immigration to Denmark: International and National Perspectives*. Aarhus: Aarhus Universitetsforlag.

Comaroff, John L. 1998. "Reflections on the Colonial State, in South Africa and Elsewhere: Factions, Fragments, Facts and Fictions." *Social Identities* 4(3): 321–61.

Copenhagen Post. 2012. "Bilingual Students Better Mixed." *Copenhagen Post Online*, November 19. http://cphpost.dk/news14/national-news14/bilingual-students-better-mixed.html (accessed January 28, 2014).

Cruikshank, Barbara. 1993. "The Will to Empower—Technologies of Citizenship and the

War on Poverty." *Socialist Review*, 23(4): 29–55. http://scholarworks.umass.edu/polsci_ faculty_pubs/8/ (accessed June 24, 2014).

Cross, William E. 2012. "The Enactment of Race and Other Social Identities during Everyday Transactions." Pp. 192–215 in *New Perspectives on Racial Identity Development: Integrating Emerging Frameworks*, edited by Charmaine L. Wijeyesinghe and Bailey W. Jackson. New York: New York University Press.

Dabach, Dafney B. 2015. "My student was apprehended by immigration": A civics teacher's breach of silence in a mixed-citizenship classroom. *Harvard Educational Review* 85(3): 383–412.

Damm, Anna Piil. 2012. *Neighborhood Quality and Labor Market Outcomes: Evidence from Quasi-Random Neighborhood Assignment of Immigrants*. Institut d'Economia de Barcelona. www.ieb.ub.edu/phocadownload/documentostrabajo/Doc2012-22.pdf (accessed May 9, 2014).

Danish Ministry of Education. n.d. "Overview of the Danish Education System." www.eng .uvm.dk/Uddannelse/Education%20system.aspx (accessed December 6, 2011).

———. 2008. "The Folkeskole." Official translation. http://eng.uvm.dk/~/media/UVM/ Filer/English/Fact%20sheets/080101_fact_sheet_the_folkeskole.pdf (accessed December 5, 2010).

———. 2003. *The Folkeskole Consolidation Act*. http://pub.uvm.dk/2003/consolidation.html

Dominus, Susan 2015. "The National Front's Post–Charlie Hebdo Moment." *New York Times*, February 18. www.nytimes.com/2015/02/22/magazine/the-national-fronts-post-charlie -hebdo-moment.html (accessed April 21, 2015).

Douglas, Mary. 2013. *Purity and Danger: An Analysis of Concepts of Pollution and Taboo*. New York: Routledge.

Dreyfus, Hubert, and Paul Rabinow. 1982. *Michel Foucault: Beyond Structuralism and Hermeneutics*. Chicago: University of Chicago Press.

Dumas, Michael J. 2011. "A Cultural Political Economy of School Desegregation in Seattle." *Teachers College Record* 113(4): 703–34.

Duyvendak, Jan Willem. 2011. *The Politics of Home: Belonging and Nostalgia in Western Europe and the United States*. Houndmills, Basingstoke, Hampshire: Palgrave Macmillan.

Dyrness, Andrea. 2014. "Talking about Race in American . . . in Europe." *Migrant Crossings*. http://migrantcrossings.blogspot.com/2014/05/talking-about-race-in-americain -europe.html (accessed July 9, 2015).

Erlanger, Steven, and Elvire Camus. 2012. "In a Ban, a Measure of European Tolerance." *New York Times*, September 2.

Ersbøll, Eva, and Laura Graveson. 2010. *Integration and Naturalisation Tests: The New Way to European Citizenship: Country Report Denmark*. Nijmegen, Netherlands: Centre for Migration Law, Radboud University.

Ferguson, Ann Arnett. 2001. *Bad Boys: Public Schools in the Making of Black Masculinity*. Ann Arbor: University of Michigan Press.

Fine, Michelle, Reva Jaffe-Walter, Pedro Pedraza, Valerie Futch, and Brett Stoudt. 2007.

"Swimming: On Oxygen, Resistance, and Possibility for Immigrant Youth under Siege." *Anthropology & Education Quarterly* 38(1): 76–96.

Fine, Michelle, Brett Stoudt, and Valerie Futch. 2005. *The Internationals Network for Public Schools: A Quantitative and Qualitative Cohort Analysis of Graduation and Dropout Rates.* Teaching and Learning in a Transcultural Academic Environment. New York: Graduate Center, City University of New York. www.internationalsnps.org/pdfs/Fine Report.pdf (accessed April 17, 2006).

Fine, Michelle, Lois Weis, and Linda C. Powell. 1997. "Communities of Difference: A Critical Look at Desegregated Spaces Created for and by Youth." *Harvard Educational Review* 67(2): 247–85.

Foner, Nancy, and Richard Alba. 2008. "Immigrant Religion in the US and Western Europe: Bridge or Barrier to Inclusion?" *International Migration Review* 42(2): 360–92.

Foucault, Michel. 1977. *Discipline and Punish: The Birth of the Prison.* New York: Random House.

———. 2008. *Psychiatric Power: Lectures at the Collège de France, 1973–1974.* New York: Picador.

Francis, David. 2015. "Obama Slaps Europe for Failing to Integrate Muslims." *Foreign Policy.* https://foreignpolicy.com/2015/01/16/obama-slaps-europe-for-failing-to-integrate -muslims/ (accessed May 5, 2015).

Fraser, Nancy. 1995. "Politics, Culture, and the Public Sphere: Toward a Postmodern Conception." Pp. 287–312 in *Social Postmodernism: Beyond Identity Politics,* edited by Linda Nicholson and Steven Seidman. Cambridge: Cambridge University Press.

Fraser, Nancy, and Axel Honneth. 2003. "Introduction: Redistribution or Recognition?" Pp. 1–6 in *Redistribution or Recognition? A Political-Philosophical Exchange.* London: Verso.

Gani, Aisha 2015. "Danish Election: PM Concedes Defeat and Resigns." *Guardian.* www .theguardian.com/world/live/2015/jun/18/denmark-general-election-2015-results-live (accessed September 15, 2015).

García, Ofelia, Nelson Flores, and Heather Homonoff Woodley. 2012. "Transgressing Monolingualism and Bilingual Dualities: Translanguaging Pedagogies." Pp. 45–75 in Androula Yiakoumetti (ed.), *Harnessing Linguistic Variation to Improve Education.* Bern: Peter Lang.

García, Ofelia, and Claire E. Sylvan. 2011. "Pedagogies and Practices in Multilingual Classrooms: Singularities in Pluralities." *Modern Language Journal* 95(3): 385–400.

Gellner, Ernest. 2008. *Nations and Nationalism.* Ithaca, NY: Cornell University Press.

Ghosh, Flora, and Søren Juul. 2008. "Lower Benefits to the Refugees in Denmark: Missing Recognition?" *Social Work & Society* 6(1): 88–105. www.socwork.net/sws/article/ view/94/383.

Gilliam, Laura. 2007. *De umulige børn og det ordentlige menneske. Et studie af identitet, ballade ogmuslimske fællesskaber blandt etniske minoritetsbørn i en dansk folkeskole* (The impossible children and the proper person: A study of identity, making trouble and Muslim communities in a Danish comprehensive school). Copenhagen: Danmarks Pædagogiske Universitets Forlag.

Gilliam, Laura, and Eva Gulløv. 2014. "Making Children 'Social': Civilising Institutions in the Danish Welfare State." *Human Figurations* 3(1). http://hdl.handle.net/2027/spo .11217607.0003.103 (assessed January 23, 2015).

Gilman, Sander L. 1985. *Difference and Pathology: Stereotypes of Sexuality, Race, and Madness*. Ithaca, NY: Cornell University Press.

Gilroy, Paul. 1998. "Race Ends Here." *Ethnic and Racial Studies* 21(5): 838–47.

Gitz-Johansen, Thomas. 2006 *Den multikulturelle skole: integration og sortering*. Roskilde Universitetsforlag, Roskilde. (dissertation) please change year to 2006.

Goldberg, David Theo. 2002. *The Racial State*. Indianapolis: Blackwell.

Grant Thornton. 2012. *Women in Senior Management: Still Not Enough*. Grant Thornton International Business Report. www.internationalbusinessreport.com/files/ibr2012%20-%20 women%20in%20senior%20management%20master.pdf (accessed March 24, 2012).

Guan, Shu-Sha A., Patricia M. Greenfield, and Marjorie F. Orellana. 2014. "Translating into Understanding: Language Brokering and Prosocial Development in Emerging Adults from Immigrant Families." *Journal of Adolescent Research* 29(3): 331–55.

Gunaratnam, Yasmin. 2003. *Researching "Race" and Ethnicity: Methods, Knowledge and Power*. Thousand Oaks, CA: Sage.

Hall, Kathleen D. 2004. "The Ethnography of Imagined Communities: The Cultural Production of Sikh Ethnicity in Britain." *Annals of the American Academy of Political and Social Science* 595(1): 108–21.

Hall, Stuart. 1997. "The Centrality of Culture: Notes on the Cultural Regulations of Our Time." Pp. 208–38 in *Media and Cultural Regulation*, edited by Kenneth Thompson. London: Sage.

———. 2001. "The Spectacle of the Other." Pp. 324–44 in *Discourse Theory and Practice: A Reader*, edited by Margaret Wetherell, Stephanie Taylor, and Simeon J. Yates. Thousand Oaks, CA: Sage.

———. 2002. "The West and the Rest: Discourse and Power." Pp. 56–64 in *Development: A Cultural Studies Reader*, edited by J. H. Susanne Schech and Jane Haggis. Oxford: Blackwell.

Hedetoft, Ulf. 2006. "More Than Kin and Less Than Kind: The Danish Politics of Ethnic Consensus and the Pluricultural Challenge." Pp. 398–430 in *National Identity and the Varieties of Capitalism: The Danish Experience*, edited by John L. Campbell, John A. Hall, and Ove K. Pedersen. Montreal: McGill-Queens University Press.

Henry, Frances, and Carol Tator. 2002. *Discourses of Domination?: Racial Bias in the Canadian English-Language Press*. Toronto: University of Toronto Press.

Hervik, Peter. 2004. "The Danish Cultural World of Unbridgeable Differences." *Ethnos* 69(2): 247–67.

Higgins, Andrew. 2015. "After Attacks, Denmark Hesitates to Blame Islam." *New York Times*, February 19. www.nytimes.com/2015/02/20/world/europe/after-attacks-denmark-hes itates-to-blame-islam.html (accessed May 1, 2015).

Hjarnø, Jan, and Torben Jensen. 1997. *Diskrimineringen af unge med indvandrerbaggrund ved jobsøgning*. Migration Papers No. 21, Danish Centre for Migration and Ethnic Studies. Esbjerg: South Jutland University Press.

Hoffman, Eva. 1998. *Lost in Translation: A Life in a New Language*. New York: Random House.

Holehouse, Matthew. 2015. "David Cameron: US Terror 'Expert' Steve Emerson Is a 'Complete Idiot.'" *Telegraph*, January 12. www.telegraph.co.uk/news/uknews/terrorism-in-the-uk /11340399/David-Cameron-US-terror-expert-Steve-Emerson-is-a-complete-idiot.html (accessed April 27, 2015).

Holland, Dorothy, William Lachicotte Jr., Debra Skinner, and Carole Cane. 1998. *Identity and Agency in Cultural Worlds*. Cambridge, MA: Harvard University Press.

Horst, Christian. 2010. "Om brug, misbrug og ikke-brug af forskning i den samfundsvidenskabelige dialog om modersmålsundervisningen." Pp. 9–53 in *Tungen lige i Munden: aktuel forskning i dansk som andetsprog*, edited by Juni Söderberg Arnfast and Martha Sif Karrebæk. Copenhagen: Københavns Universitet, Det Humanistiske Fakultet.

Huggler, Justin. 2015. "Angela Merkel Joins Muslim Rally against German Anti-Islamisation Protests." *Telegraph*, January 13. www.telegraph.co.uk/news/worldnews/europe/ger many/angela-merkel/11343088/Angela-Merkel-joins-Muslim-rally-against-German -anti-Islamisation-protests.html (accessed April 9, 2015).

Huntington, Samuel P. 1996. *The Clash of Civilizations and the Remaking of World Order*. New Delhi: Penguin Books.

Ignatieff, Michael. 1995. *Blood and Belonging: Journeys into the New Nationalism*. London: Macmillan.

Inglehart, Ronald, and Pippa Norris. 2009. "Muslim Integration into Western Cultures: Between Origins and Destinations." Faculty Research Working Paper Series RWP09-007, John F. Kennedy School of Government, Harvard University. http://dash.harvard.edu/ handle/1/4481625 (accessed June 16, 2014).

International Baccalaureate. 2012. How Do You Define International Education? (blog). http://blogs.ibo.org/blog/2012/06/06/international-education/

Jaffe-Walter, Reva. 2008. "Negotiating Mandates and Memory: Inside a Small Schools Network for Immigrant Youth." *Teachers College Record* 110(9): 2040–66.

———. 2013. "'Who Would They Talk about If We Weren't Here?': Muslim Youth, Liberal Schooling, and the Politics of Concern." *Harvard Educational Review* 83(4): 613–35.

Jaffe-Walter, Reva, and Stacey J. Lee. 2011. "'To Trust in My Root and to Take That to Go Forward': Supporting College Access for Immigrant Youth in the Global City." *Anthropology & Education Quarterly* 42(3): 281–96.

Jenkins, Richard. 2011. *Being Danish: Paradoxes of Identity in Everyday Life*. Copenhagen: Museum Tusculanum Press.

Jensen, Tina, Garbi Schmidt, Mette Torslev, Kathrine Vitus, and Kristina Weibel. 2010. *Analysis of Integration Policies and Public State-Endorsed Institution at National and Regional Levels in Denmark*. Copenhagen: Danish Centre for Social Research.

Joppke, Christian. 2007. "Beyond National Models: Civic Integration Policies for Immigrants in Western Europe." *West European Politics* 30(1): 1–22.

Josselson, Ruthellen. 2007. "The Ethical Attitude in Narrative Research." Pp. 537–66 in *The Handbook of Narrative Inquiry*, edited by D. Jean Clandinin. Thousand Oaks, CA: Sage.

Kern, Soeren. 2011. "Europe: 'You Are Entering a Sharia Controlled Zone': Hezbollah Pitches Tent in Denmark." www.gatestoneinstitute.org/2530/denmark-sharia-hezbollah (accessed February 6, 2013)

Khawaja, Iram. 2014. "Gazes: The Visibility, Embodiment and Negotiation of Muslimness." Unpublished manuscript.

Korsgaard, Ove. 2006. "The Danish Way to Establish the Nation in the Hearts of the People." Pp. 133–58 in *National Identity and the Varieties of Capitalism: The Danish Experience*, edited by John L. Campbell, John A. Hall, and Ove K. Pedersen. Montreal: McGill-Queens University Press.

Kymlicka, Will. 1995. "Misunderstanding Nationalism." *Dissent* 42(1): 130–37.

Ladson-Billings, Gloria. 1995. "But That's Just Good Teaching! The Case for Culturally Relevant Pedagogy." *Theory into Practice* 34(3): 159–65.

LaFromboise, Teresa, Hardin L. K. Coleman, and Jennifer Gerton. 1998. "Psychological Impact of Biculturalism: Evidence and Theory." Pp. 123–58 in *Readings in Ethnic Psychology*, edited by Pamela Balls Organista, Kevin M. Chun, and Geraldo Marín. New York: Routledge.

Lee, Stacey J. 2005. *Up Against Whiteness: Race, School, and Immigrant Youth*. New York: Teachers College Press, Columbia University.

Lewis, Amanda. 2003. *Race in the Schoolyard: Negotiating the Color Line in Classrooms and Communities*. New Brunswick, NJ: Rutgers University Press.

Lichtenberg, Judith. 1999. "How Liberal Can Nationalism Be?" Pp. 167–88 in *Theorizing Nationalism*, edited by Ronald Beiner. Albany: State University of New York Press.

Lopez, Nancy. 2003. *Hopeful Girls, Troubled Boys: Race and Gender Disparity in Urban Education*. New York: Routledge.

Lowe, Lisa. 1996. *Immigrant Acts: On Asian American Cultural Politics*. Durham, NC: Duke University Press.

Maira, Sunaina Marr. 2009. *Missing: Youth, Citizenship, and Empire after 9/11*. Durham, NC: Duke University Press Books.

Malsbary, Christine B. 2014. "'It's Not Just Learning English, It's Learning Other Cultures': Belonging, Power and Possibility in an Immigrant Contact Zone." *International Journal of Qualitative Studies in Education* 27(10): 1312–36 .

Mamdani, Mahmood. 2005. *Good Muslim, Bad Muslim: America, the Cold War, and the Roots of Terror*. New York: Doubleday.

Mannitz, Sabine. 2004. "The Place of Religion in Four Civil Cultures." Pp. 242–303 in *Civil Enculturation: Nation-State, School and Ethnic Difference in the Netherlands, Britain, Germany and France*, edited by Werner Shiffauer, Gerd Baumann, Riva Kastoryano, and Steven Vertovec. Oxford: Berghahn Books.

Matar, Nabil. 1999. *Turks, Moors, and Englishmen in the Age of Discovery*. New York: Columbia University Press.

McCarthy, Maureen. 2006. "Fatima and Saret." Pp. 11–17 in *Blue Cat Reader: engelsk for niende*, edited by Aase Brick-Hansen, Wendy A. Scott, and Lars Skovhus. Copenhagen: Gyldendal.

Melamed, Jodi. 2006. "The Spirit of Neoliberalism: From Racial Liberalism to Neoliberal Multiculturalism." *Social Text* 24(4): 1–24.

Menken, Kate. 2008. *English Learners Left Behind: Standardized Testing as Language Policy*. Clevedon, UK: Multilingual Matters.

Ministry of Children, Equality, Integration and Social Affairs. 2015. *§§ 11 and 12LBK nr 167 Bekendtgørelse af lov om dag-, fritids- og klubtilbud m.v. til børn og unge* (Law on day-care facilities). Copenhagen. www.retsinformation.dk/forms/r0710.aspx?id=168340.

Ministry of Gender Equality. 2005. *Beskæftigelse, deltagelse og lige muligheder til alle—regeringens handlingsplan for at nedbryde kønsbestemte barrierer til uddannelse, arbejde og foreningslivet blandt kvinder og mænd med anden etnisk baggrund end dansk* (Employment, participation and equal opportunities for everyone—government action to break down gender barriers to education, work, and community life of women and men with ethnic backgrounds other than Danish). Copenhagen.

Ministry of Justice. 2013. *Order of the Aliens Act (Immigration Act), Consolidated Act No 863 of 25.06.2013*. www.nyidanmark.dk/NR/rdonlyres/2A42ECC8-1CF5-4A8A-89AC-8D3D75EF3 E17/0/aliens_consolidation_act_863_250613.pdf.

Ministry of Social Affairs and Integration. 2006. *Danish Integration Contract*. Copenhagen.

———. 2013. *Integration in Denmark*. Copenhagen.

Mir, Shabana. 2014. *Muslim American Women on Campus: Undergraduate Social Life and Identity*. Chapel Hill: University of North Carolina Press.

Modood, Tariq. 1997. "Introduction: The Politics of Multiculturalism in the New Europe." Pp. 1–26 in *The Politics of Multiculturalism in the New Europe: Racism, Identity and Community*, edited by Tariq Modood and Pnina Werbner. New York: Palgrave Macmillan.

Mouritsen, Per, and Christine Hovmark Jensen. 2014. *Integration Policy in Denmark*. INTERACT RR 2014/06, Robert Schuman Centre for Advanced Studies. San Domenico di Fiesole, Italy: European University Institute. http://cadmus.eui.eu/handle/1814/32020 (accessed April 20, 2015).

MRII [Ministry of Refugees, Immigration, and Integration Affairs]. 2002. *Citizen in Denmark: A Manual for New Members of Danish Society*. Copenhagen. www.nyidanmark .dk/NR/rdonlyres/DCE16534-CED4-48D3-80B8-F3D56A0B40D7/0/medborger_i_dan mark_engelsk.pdf (accessed January 25, 2014).

———. 2003. *Visions and Strategies for Better Integration*. Copenhagen.

———. 2005. *A New Chance for Everyone: The Danish Government's Integration Plan*. English summary. Copenhagen.

———. 2006. *Aliens (Consolidation) Act No. 945*. Copenhagen.

New York City Department of Education. 2009. *New York City School Progress Report*. New York.

Nielsen, Gritt B. 2011. "Peopling Policy: On Conflicting Subjectivities of Fee-Paying Students." Pp. 68–85 in *Policy Worlds: Anthropology and the Analysis of Contemporary Power*, edited by Cris Shore and Susan Wright. Oxford: Berghahn Books.

NPR [National Public Radio]. 2015. "After Students Went to Wage Jihad, Teacher Highlights Youth Radicalization." NPR.org. www.npr.org/2015/03/21/394500965/after-students-went-to-wage-jihad-teacher-highlights-youth-radicalization (accessed April 20, 2015).

Nussbaum, Martha C. 2012. *The New Religious Intolerance: Overcoming the Politics of Fear in an Anxious Age*. Cambridge, MA: Belknap Press of Harvard University Press.

Ogbu, John U. 1987. "Variability in Minority School Performance: A Problem in Search of an Explanation." *Anthropology & Education Quarterly* 18(4): 312–34.

Omi, Michael, and Howard Winant. 1994. *Racial Formation in the United States?: From the 1960s to the 1980s*. 2nd ed. New York: Routledge & Kegan Paul.

Ong, Aiwa. 1996. "Cultural Citizenship as Subject-Making: Immigrants Negotiate Racial and Cultural Boundaries in the United States." *Current Anthropology* 37(5): 737–54.

Orellana, Marjorie Faulstich. In Press. *Immigrant Youth in Transcultural Spaces: Language, Literacy and Love*. New York: Routledge.

Østergård, Uffe. 2006. "Denmark: A Big Small State—The Peasant Roots of Danish Modernity." Pp. 53–98 in *National Identity and the Varieties of Capitalism: The Danish Experience*, edited by John L. Campbell, John A. Hall, and Ove K. Pedersen. Montreal: McGill-Queens University Press.

Parekh, Bhikhu. 1999. "The Incoherence of Nationalism." Pp. 295–325 in *Theorizing Nationalism*, edited by Ronald Beiner. Albany: State University of New York Press.

Pelvey, Laurent. 2000. "The Republic Explained to My Friends." France Républicaine. www.france-republicaine.fr/french-republic.php (accessed February 16, 2014).

Pew Research Center. 2014."A Fragile Rebound for EU Image on Eve of European Parliament Elections" English Summary. http://www.pewglobal.org/files/2014/05/2014-05-12_Pew-Global-Attitudes-European-Union.pdf (accessed October 20, 2015).

Planas, Roque. 2013. "Arizona's Law Banning Mexican-American Studies Curriculum Is Constitutional, Judge Rules." *Huffington Post*, March 14. www.huffingtonpost.com/2013/03/11/arizona-mexican-american-studies-curriculum-constitutional_n_2851034.html (accessed September 15, 2015).

Puwar, Nirmal. 2004. *Space Invaders: Race, Gender and Bodies Out of Place*. New York: Berg.

Rana, Junaid. 2011. *Terrifying Muslims: Race and Labor in the South Asian Diaspora*. Durham, NC: Duke University Press.

Rasmussen, Lars. 2010. "Opening Speech in the Parliament." Danish: www.stm.dk/_p_13260.html; English: www.stm.dk/_p_13265.html (accessed March 6, 2012).

Razack, Sherene. 2008. *Casting Out: The Eviction of Muslims from Western Law and Politics*. Toronto: University of Toronto Press.

Ríos-Rojas, Anne. 2011. "Beyond Delinquent Citizenships: Immigrant Youth's (Re)Visions of

Citizenship and Belonging in a Globalized World." *Harvard Educational Review* 81(1): 64–95.

Rose, Flemming. 2006. "Munammeds Ansigt." *Jyllands-Posten*, January 6.

Rose, Nikolas. 1999. *Powers of Freedom: Reframing Political Thought*. Cambridge: Cambridge University Press.

Said, Edward. 1993. *Culture and Imperialism*. New York: Alfred Knopf.

———. 2000. *Out of Place: A Memoir*. New York: Vintage.

Sassen, Saskia. 1999. *Guests and Aliens*. New York: New Press.

———. 2006. *Cities in a World Economy*. 3rd ed. Thousand Oaks, CA: Pine Forge Press.

Sepúlveda, Enrique, III. 2011. "Toward a Pedagogy of Acompañamiento: Mexican Migrant Youth Writing from the Underside of Modernity." *Harvard Educational Review* 81(3): 550–73.

Shapiro, Ari. 2015. "Story of Missing Schoolgirls Captivates Britain." NPR.org. www.npr.org /2015/02/24/388796121/story-of-missing-schoolgirls-captivates-britain (accessed April 21, 2015).

Sheth, Falguni A. 2009. *Toward a Political Philosophy of Race*. Albany, NY: SUNY Press.

Shore, Cris, and Susan Wright. 1997. *Anthropology of Policy: Critical Perspectives on Governance and Power*. London: Routledge.

———. 2011. "Conceptualizing Policy: Technologies of Governance and the Politics of Visibility." Pp. 1–26 in *Policy Worlds: Anthropology and the Analysis of Contemporary Power*, edited by Cris Shore, Susan Wright, and Davide Però. New York: Berghahn Books.

Silverstein, Paul A. 2005. "Immigration Racialization and the New Savage Slot: Race, Migration, and Immigration in the New Europe." *Annual Review of Anthropology* 34: 363–84.

Sirin, Selcuk R., and Michelle Fine. 2008. *Muslim American Youth: Understanding Hyphenated Identities through Multiple Methods*. New York: New York University Press.

Smith, Robert C. 2006. *Mexican New York: Transnational Lives of New Immigrants*. Berkeley: University of California Press.

Solorzano, Daniel, Miguel Ceja, and Tara Yosso. 2000. "Critical Race Theory, Racial Microaggressions, and Campus Racial Climate: The Experiences of African American College Students." *Journal of Negro Education* 69(1/2): 60–73.

Southern Poverty Law Center. 2012. "FBI: Dramatic Spike in Hate Crimes Targeting Muslims." Southern Poverty Law Center. www.splcenter.org/get-informed/intelligence-re port/browse-all-issues/2012/spring/fbi-dramatic-spike-in-hate-crimes-targetin (accessed February 16, 2013).

Souza, Celina. 2001 Participatory Budgeting in Brazilian Cities: Limits and Possibilities in Building Democratic Institutions. *Environment and Urbanization* 13(1): 159–84.

Spring, Joel H. 1990. *The American School, 1642–1990: Varieties of Historical Interpretation of the Foundations and Development of American Education*. 2nd ed. New York: Longman.

Stanners, Peter. 2012. "How Pia's Influence Spread Across Europe." *Copenhagen Post Online*, August 16. http://cphpost.dk/news14/international-news14/how-pias-influence -spread-across-europe.html (accessed March 3, 2013).

Stanton-Salazar, Ricardo D. 1997. "Social Capital Framework for Understanding the Social-
    ization of Racial Minority Children and Youths." *Harvard Educational Review* 67(1): 1–41.
Statistics Denmark. 2015a. "Immigrants and Their Descendants." www.dst.dk/en/Statistik/
    emner/indvandrere-og-efterkommere.
———. 2015b. *Statistical Yearbook, 2015.* www.dst.dk/en/Statistik/Publikationer/VisPub
    ?cid=20195 (accessed July 2015).
Steele, Claude M. 1997. "A Threat in the Air: How Stereotypes Shape Intellectual Identity
    and Performance." *American Psychologist* 52(6): 613–29.
Storhaug, Hege, and Human Rights Service. 2004. *Human Visas: A Report from the Front
    Lines of Europe's Integration Crisis.* Translated from the Norwegian by Bruce Bawer.
    Oslo: Kolofon.
Suárez-Orozco, Carola, and Marcelo M. Suárez-Orozco. 2001. *Children of Immigration.*
    Cambridge, MA: Harvard University Press.
Suárez-Orozco, Carola, Marcelo M. Suárez-Orozco, and Irina Todorova. 2008. *Learning a
    New Land: Immigrant Students in American Society.* Cambridge, MA: Harvard Univer-
    sity Press.
Suárez-Orozco, Carola, and Desirée Baolian Qin. 2006. "Gendered Perspectives in Psychol-
    ogy: Immigrant Origin Youth." *International Migration Review* 40(1): 165–98.
Suárez-Orozco, Marcelo M., and Desirée Baolian Qin-Hilliard, eds. 2004. *Globalization:
    Culture and Education in the New Millennium.* Berkeley: University of California Press.
Sutton, Margaret, and Bradley A. U. Levinson. 2001. *Policy as Practice: Toward a Compara-
    tive Sociocultural Analysis of Educational Policy.* Westport, CT: Ablex.
Taylor, Charles. 1992. *Multiculturalism and the Politics of Recognition.* Princeton, NJ: Prince-
    ton University Press.
Thorup, Mette-Line. 2007. "Falske jomfruer." *Information,* September 27.
Timm, Lene. 2008. *Danmark ondt i modersmålet.* Copenhagen: Dokumentations- og Råd-
    givningscentret om Racediskrimination.
Titley, Gavan. 2014. "Pork Is the Latest Front in Europe's Culture Wars." *Guardian,* April 14,
    sec. Comment Is Free. www.theguardian.com/commentisfree/2014/apr/15/le-pen-pig
    -whistle-politics (accessed January 16, 2015).
Tuck, Eve, and K. Wayne Yang. 2012. "Decolonization Is Not a Metaphor." *Decolonization:
    Indigeneity, Education & Society* 1(1): 1–40.
Valdes, Guadalupe. 1996. *Con Respeto: Bridging the Distances between Culturally Diverse
    Families and Schools.* New York: Teachers College Press.
Valencia, Richard R., ed. 2010. *The Evolution of Deficit Thinking: Educational Thought and
    Practice.* New York: Routledge.
Valenzuela, Angela. 1999. *Subtractive Schooling: US-Mexican Youth and the Politics of Car-
    ing.* Albany: State University of New York Press.
Van Laar, Colette. 2011. "Motivation for Education and Work in Young Muslim Women: The
    Importance of Value for Ingroup Domains." Public lecture, Lecture Series Program in
    Social Personality Psychology, January 17, New York.

Van Laar, Colette, Belle Derks, and Naomi Ellemers. 2013. "Motivation for Education and Work in Young Muslim Women: The Importance of Value for Ingroup Domains." *Basic and Applied Social Psychology* 35(1): 64–74.

Villegas, Ana María, and Tamara Lucas. 2002. *Educating Culturally Responsive Teachers: A Coherent Approach.* Albany: State University of New York Press.

Wallerstein, Immanuel. 1991. "The Construction of Peoplehood: Racism, Nationalism, Ethnicity." Pp. 71–85 in *Race, Nation, Class: Ambiguous Identities*, edited by Etienne Balibar and Immanuel Maurice Wallerstein. London: Verso.

Waters, Mary C. 1997. "Immigrant Families at Risk: Factors That Undermine." Pp. 65–84 in *Immigration and the Family: Research and Policy on US Immigrants*, edited by Alan Booth. Mahway, NJ: Lawrence Erlbaum.

Weaver, Ray. 2013. "Helle on Halal: We Shouldn't Lose Sight of Our Own Culture." *Copenhagen Post Online*, August 12. http://cphpost.dk/news14/national-news14/helle-on-halal-we-shouldnt-lose-sight-of-our-own-culture.html (accessed June 25, 2014).

Winant, Howard. 2006. "Race and Racism: Towards a Global Future." *Ethnic and Racial Studies* 29(5): 986–1003.

Wood, Josh. 2013. "Palestinian Refugees Flee Syria to Find Poor Conditions in Lebanese Camps." *New York Times*, May 29, sec. World/Middle East. www.nytimes.com/2013/05/30/world/middleeast/palestinian-refugees-flee-syria-to-find-poor-conditions-in-lebanese-camps.html (accessed June 24, 2013).

Wortham, Stanton. 2008. "Shifting Identities in the Classroom." Pp. 205–28 in *Identity Trouble: Critical Discourse and Contested Identities*, edited by Carmen Rosa Caldas-Coulthhard and Rick Iedema. New York: Palgrave Macmillan.

Yack, Bernard. 1996. "The Myth of the Civic Nation." *Critical Review* 10(2): 193–211.

Yuval-Davis, Nira. 1999. "The 'Multi-Layered Citizen.'" *International Feminist Journal of Politics* 1(1): 119–36.

Zaal, Mayida, Tahani Salah, and Michelle Fine. 2007. "The Weight of the Hyphen: Freedom, Fusion and Responsibility Embodied by Young Muslim-American Women during a Time of Surveillance." *Applied Development Science* 11(3): 164–77.

Zhou, Min, and Carl L. Bankston III. 1994. "Social Capital and the Adaptation of the Second Generation: The Case of Vietnamese Youth in New Orleans." *International Migration Review* 28(4): 821–45.

Zine, Jasmin. 2001. "Muslim Youth in Canadian Schools: Education and the Politics of Religious Identity." *Anthropology & Education Quarterly* 32(4): 399–423.

Index

Note: Page references followed by *f* refer to figures.

Messerschmidt, Morten, 180

methods of study, 7–13; analysis of media and
policy documents, 12; focal participants,
11–12; interviews, 9; observations, 8–9;
positionality, 9–11, 77–78; terms used in,
12–13

Ministry of Gender Equality (Denmark), 53, 62

Mir, Shabana, 191–192n2

misrecognition, 99, 183, 185–187

Mohammed cartoon crisis of 2005, 13, 100–101,
189n5

mother-tongue instruction, 38, 65–66, 86, 125,
129, 190n6 (Ch. 2)

Mouritsen, Per, 50, 56

multiculturalism: avoidance of, in Denmark, 13,
59–60; in Europe, 28, 42, 179; in integration,
12–13; in international schools, 157

multiple identities: 161–165; blended identities,
135–140, 136f, 137f, 152–154; Danishness as
biologically determined, 16, 136–137, 139–
143; figured identities and, 138; integration
paradigms and, 131–132; "New Dane"
label, 149–150; parallel versus conflictual,
135–136; responses to, 106, 141; transnational
imaginaries, 121–128, 168–172, 184. See also
identity negotiation

Munch, Peter, 30–31

"Muslim" as race category, 25–28. See also Islam

Muslim identity, 113–114, 128–129, 135–136, 136f

Muslim immigrants: accommodations for,
179–180; benefits of enclaves of, 180–181;
concealing identities by, 98–99; in Denmark
versus United States, 136–138; on eating
pork, 39–40, 47, 93, 129, 140, 180; everyday
encounters (see everyday encounters);
expectations of, 16, 54; far-right on, 48f,
49–50, 52, 175, 179–180, 190n4 (Ch. 2); hijab
wearing (see hijab); holiday celebrations,
156, 162, 190n6 (Ch. 1); in immigrant ghettos,
67–69, 69f, 84–85, 180–181; integration of
(see integration); national imaginaries and,
19–20, 22–25, 28–29, 34; neo-nationalism
and, 32–33; as Other, 25, 47, 55–56, 80–81,
186; political benefits from fear of, 52–53, 176;
profiling of, 138; public anxieties from (see
public anxieties about immigrants); reliance
on family, 142, 149; state violence against,
42–43. See also Islamophobia; Muslim men
and boys; Muslim women and girls

Muslim men and boys: in Engby houses, 68–69,
69f; everyday microaggressions against,
138–139; figured identities of, 57–58, 63,
80–81, 133–134, 153–154, 165; identity
negotiation in, 135–145, 136f, 137f, 153–154;
job discrimination against, 62–63; school
experiences of, 145–147; in special education
classes, 145, 156

Muslim women and girls: arrogance in concern
for, 101–103; as false virgins, 86–88, 87f;
female genital mutilation and, 60–61,
83–84, 99; figured identities of, 57–61,
80–85, 90, 145, 153; in German schools, 90;
"playing Danish," 160–165; sexual behavior
recommendations for, 85–89, 114, 129, 191n3;
in United States schools, 90–91; as visible
reminders of changes, 51. See also forced
marriage; hijab; liberalization of Muslim
girls

Muslim youth, meaning of term, 12

narratives of concern, 3

nationalism: cultural solidarity and, 18, 20–21,
29–31, 179–180; ethnic versus civic, 19–21,
22, 51, 176–177; fictive ethnicity in, 21–24,
25, 51; globalization and, 13, 17–18, 186;
Muslim signs and symbols and, 17, 23–25, 28;
national imaginaries, 19–20, 22–25, 28–29,
34; neo-nationalism in Denmark, 32–33; in
schools, 33–37, 65–67, 85; technologies of
concern and, 180; transnational imaginaries,
168–172, 184

Native Americans, as Other, 19, 22, 26–27, 189n1
(Ch. 1)

native country visits. See home country visits

native-language instruction, 38, 65–66, 86, 125,
129, 190n6 (Ch. 2)

neoliberalism, 6–7, 11

A New Chance for Everyone, 57, 62–63, 67

"New Dane" label, 149–150

Nielsen, Gritt, 178

9/11 events: anti-Muslim discourses after, 17,
27–28, 52; everyday encounters after,
137–138, 137f, 159; violence after, 4–5

niqab, 23–24. See also hijab

Norris, Pippa, 182

Nussbaum, Martha, 5, 17, 180

Obama, Barack, 29

Anthropology of Policy

Cris Shore and Susan Wright, editors

SERIES DESCRIPTION:

The Anthropology of Policy series promotes innovative methodological and theoretical approaches to the study of policy. The series challenges the assumption that policy is a top-down, linear and rational process, and a field of study primarily for policy professionals. Books in the series analyze the contradictory nature and effects of policy, including the intricate ways in which people engage with policy, the meanings it holds for different local, regional, national, and internationally-based actors and the complex relationships and social worlds that it produces.

Fragile Elite: The Dilemmas of China's Top University Students
Susanne Bregnbæk
2016

Navigating Austerity: Currents of Debt Along a South Asian River
Laura Bear
2015

Drugs, Thugs, and Diplomats: U.S. Policymaking in Colombia
Winifred Tate
2015